MUSIC TO MY EARS

MUSIC TO MY EARS

The *Billboard* Essays

**PROFILES OF
POPULAR MUSIC
IN THE '90S**

TIMOTHY WHITE

HENRY HOLT AND COMPANY   NEW YORK

Henry Holt and Company, Inc.
Publishers since 1866
115 West 18th Street
New York, New York 10011

Henry Holt® is a registered
trademark of Henry Holt and Company, Inc.

Published in Canada by Fitzhenry & Whiteside Ltd.,
195 Allstate Parkway, Markham, Ontario L3R 4T8.

Library of Congress Cataloging-in-Publication Data
White, Timothy.
    Music to my ears: the Billboard essays: profiles of
popular music in the '90s / Timothy White.
          p.   cm.
    1. Popular music—1991–2000—History and criticism.
I. Billboard (Cincinnati, Ohio: 1963)   II. Title.
ML3470.W53   1996   96-9181
781.64—dc20   CIP
                                               MN

ISBN 0-8050-3975-9

Henry Holt books are available for special
promotions and premiums. For details contact:
Director, Special Markets.

First Edition—1996

Designed by Paula R. Szafranski

Printed in the United States of America
All first editions are printed on acid-free paper. ∞

10   9   8   7   6   5   4   3   2   1

The author dedicates this book to
Howard Lander, whose support was as
integral as words and music

CONTENTS

FOREWORD

IT WAS IN THE MARCH 28, 1992, ISSUE THAT *BILLBOARD*'S readers first found Timothy White's "Music to My Ears" column. From that moment on these award-winning essays would be distinguished by their highly skilled writing style and Timothy White's unique approach to examining the record business. Drawing upon his more than two decades of experience writing for and editing such trailblazing magazines as *Crawdaddy, Rolling Stone,* and *Musician,* or authoring *Catch a Fire: The Life of Bob Marley, Rock Lives: Profiles and Interviews,* and *The Nearest Faraway Place: Brian Wilson, the Beach Boys, and the Southern California Experience,* Timothy White invited the public to truly experience the music with his rhythmic prose and by carefully tailoring his work to reflect the artistic spirit of each subject.

In contrast to traditional reviews or critiques, "Music to My Ears" used in-depth interviews and fresh research while focusing exclusively on superior records at the pre-release stage (often as many as three months before commercial availability) and frequently nominating unsung talents for industry support. It is critical to understand that the columns collected in this book were written for *Billboard*'s trade readership before the future happened. And because "Music to My Ears" also functions as a media advisory in the realms of rock, classical, blues, world music, jazz, rap, R&B, alternative, reggae, calypso, Latin music, and other genres, readers of this book will realize that a wealth of ideas, insights, and talking points found in the consumer press were originally borrowed from these columns.

In publishing "Music to My Ears," *Billboard* signaled our more music-intensive approach to our trade coverage, using this regular editorial feature as the linchpin for our passionate metamorphosis as we neared our one hundredth birthday. First published in Cincinnati on November 1, 1894, by the son of a local poster printer, *Billboard* has ascended over the decades to our unrivaled position as the worldwide bible of the record and home entertainment industries. With readers in more than 110 countries, *Billboard* has enjoyed a growth that has paralleled the global explosion of the music business itself.

The record industry saw its fortunes climb continually throughout the fifties and sixties. Rebounding from the overheated effects of the seventies disco craze, the eighties were marked by the industrialization of popular music at the hands of multinational conglomerates, which believed there truly was gold in this artistically driven field. The emerging six behemoths carved the music world into their own fiefdoms: BMG, EMI, MCA, Polygram, Sony, and WEA. *Billboard* chronicled every buyout, merger, and takeover, and the accompanying executive shuffles soon caught the attention of the mainstream business and consumer press.

The industry also found itself in the midst of a technological boom in CD formats, digital cable, and on-line computer networks that promised to alter traditional hardware and conventional distribution channels well into the next century. Retailers, already besieged with an over-crowded marketplace, shrinking bottom lines, and the growing presence of conglomerate-owned discount record clubs, now faced an electronic demon that they believed could threaten their very existence. With few exceptions, retail was dominated by publicly held or highly leveraged companies accountable to stockholders or financial institutions more interested in rates of return than in pop harmonies.

Coincidentally, *Billboard* was deep in our own revolutionary process to modernize our chart methodology by adopting Soundscan piece-count technology and Broadcast Data System's computer-monitored airplay in the late eighties and early nineties in order to remove any possible hype from our weekly charts. Having served as the industry standard bearer since the introduction of the most popular sheet music tabulation in the early 1900s, the *Billboard* charts saw wider dissemination via television, radio, and newspapers, and thus became crucial to artists' careers.

Such was the world I inherited upon becoming *Billboard*'s chief executive in 1990. It quickly became apparent to me that *Billboard* needed to reach back to its show business roots, not only to flourish but also to remind this multibillion-dollar industry that the process all began with a song. Regardless of how it was financed or what distribution channels it relied on, music required gifted individuals who could compose, arrange, sing, play, produce, market, and promote. Each link in the chain ultimately required a passion. Therefore, it was vital that *Billboard*'s editorial team be guided by a passionate writer-journalist-editor who could connect emotionally with the artistic lifeblood of the business.

In Timothy White, I found the skills, experience, and vision that would enable *Billboard* to broaden our role and deliver on our most important mandate—helping the music business do better business. For the next twelve months, Timothy and I worked in countless meetings to deliver our message of change. Our only disagreement was the creation of the editor's column. Without a forum representing the personal perspective of the editor in chief, I feared *Billboard* would seem soulless in the nineties.

The trouble was, Timothy did not want to produce a column filled with anecdotes on industry events, milestones, and trends. He felt uncomfortable with that kind of writing, believing that his opinions on such workaday trade subjects were inconsequential. The debate raged on until *I* threatened to author a publisher's column. Timothy acquiesced.

Waiting anxiously at home for his first draft, which he wrote in New Orleans during the annual convention of the National Association of Recording Merchandisers (NARM), I was unprepared for what Timothy delivered. I expected some insights from the just-completed meetings. Instead Timothy used the Crescent City as the background for his thoughts on Bruce Springsteen's latest releases: the *Human Touch* and *Lucky Town* albums. His impassioned essay was some of the finest short-form writing I had ever read. It was truly music to my ears.

Over time, the most rewarding aspect of the columns was their effect on the trade (and eventually the general public) as a forecast of both critical and commercial success. The column even became the basis for an in-house promotional campaign, "Music to *Your* Ears, Too!"

Many of the essays in this book served as the earliest documentation of the nineties' most important releases. The first profile ever published of lo-fi Chicago alternative rocker Liz Phair appeared in "Music to My Ears" prior to the release of her debut album, *Exile in Guysville.* Thus, months before *MTV News* dared to ask Phair about losing her virginity, "Music to My Ears" had already posed that question with regard to her intimate coming-of-age songwriting themes. Timothy's column with Mariah Carey contained the first substantive details of her difficult upbringing, and transformed her previously unsympathetic public image. Similar in impact was Timothy's unprecedented interview with Madonna concerning the poignant role that memories of her late mother played in her music.

Then there was the pre-release column on Elmore James *(Elmore James: King of the Slide Guitar—The Fire/Fury/Enjoy Recordings)* became one of the most acclaimed blues recordings of the year, winning a coveted W. C. Handy Award from the Memphis, Tennessee–based Blues Foundation.

Eric Clapton gave his only pre-release American print interview for his landmark *From the Cradle* blues album to "Music to My Ears," revealing the untold story of the romantic heartache behind a project that went on to become one of the best-selling blues records in history, as well as the first number-one release on the Top Blues Albums chart Timothy instituted in *Billboard* in 1995.

The column foretold the fresh commercial peaks of established artists like Sting *(Ten Summoners Tales)* and Billy Joel *(River of Dreams)*; and acclaimed new artists such as PJ Harvey, Alanis Morissette, Jack Logan, Rage Against The Machine, Paula Cole, Belly, Joan Osborne, Dar Williams, Tracy Bonham, and the solo Aimee Mann were first featured in "Music to My Ears." And records initially covered in "Music to My Ears" have annually garnered numerous Grammy nominations and wins, whether by new sensations like Morissette, established stars like Sting, veteran artists like Joni Mitchell and Ray Charles, or underappreciated performers like Flaco Jiménez.

In 1993, the American Society of Composers, Authors, and Publishers honored Timothy's "Music to My Ears" column with the ASCAP-Deems Taylor Award for excellence, one of the most prestigious honors in the nation for music journalism. It was the first time a *Billboard* writer had ever achieved such recognition, and by doing so Timothy joined a remarkable list of honorees that includes Gunther Schuller, Ned Rorem, Duke Ellington, Ralph Gleason, Aaron Copland, Gary Giddins, Dan Morgenstern, Leonard Feather, Albert Murray, Maynard Solomon, Nancy Reich, Samuel Charters, Judith Vander, Robert Greenfield, and other distinguished music journalists of this century.

On those frequent occasions when Timothy complains to me of the difficulty of selecting, researching, and capturing the essence of his subjects, it always brings a smile to my face because it fortifies my stock answer when *Billboard* readers question why there are only twenty to twenty-five columns a year from him. With thousands of releases, only a handful are truly music to his ears.

> Howard Lander
> President and Publisher
> *Billboard*

INTRODUCTION

His Master's Voice:
A Matter of Trust

FOR SOME IT MEANT THE DEATH OF MEMORY, FOR OTHERS it signaled the rebirth of wonder, but for all it took a marked adjustment to accept the richly nuanced sound of something that wasn't really there.

Since most familiar physical traces were absent, and yet the aural evidence was overwhelming, the process of perceiving disembodied recorded noises, talk, and music became a matter of trust. Thomas Edison coined the term "phonograph" to describe the device he successfully demonstrated to his Menlo Park, New Jersey, lab assistants in December 1877, but when his helpers first heard the crusty sound of their curmudgeonly master uttering a children's nursery rhyme, they exclaimed that the diaphragm-and-needle contraption had "spoke!" Edison sought to market what he saw as a useful office appliance under the banner of the Edison Speaking Phonograph Company, but people were uneasy with the spooky machine.

A year onward, when Edison unveiled his speaking phonograph in the offices of *Scientific American,* the scholarly journal's employees were astounded by its ingenuity but disoriented by the ghostly aura of its operation. "No matter how familiar a person may be with the modern machinery, or how clear in his mind the principles underlying this strange device may be," the magazine stated, "it is impossible to listen to this mechanical speech without experiencing the idea that his senses are deceiving him."

A century later, this book is a collection of contextual critiques of various recording artists' output during the heyday (1992–1996) of the compact disc. Virtually all of these interviews-cum-assessments appeared in *Billboard* before the albums in question ever reached consumers. Since each installment of the "Music to My Ears" column was a pre-release judgment offered prior to the onrush of marketing campaigns, convenient categorizations via radio formats, or the safety nets of commercial consequences and popular consensus, the aim was to provide the music industry and the consumer media with an advance understanding of the musicians' personal intent and socioartistic subtext.

Many of the albums were debut works, appraised at an interregnum when careers were about to be launched. I'd obtained an advance copy of PJ Harvey's first album during a trip to *Billboard*'s London bureau, and my convictions about the act and its leader coalesced some time before Polly Harvey performed or issued music in America. The Liz Phair record arrived in the mail almost two months in advance of release, a characterless clear plastic cassette heralding the work of an obscure new performer whose performances had only recently progressed from her bedroom to slightly more public settings.

At the point at which I spoke with her, Annie Lennox was nervous about the viability of her solo voyage as a singer-songwriter; Pam Tillis hadn't gained acceptance as a rising country music star; Jann Arden was little known outside her native Canada; Rage Against The Machine and the Goo Goo Dolls were hitless bands with great new songs but grimly precarious prospects, and Alanis Morissette's *Jagged Little Pill* was five weeks away from purchasability.

I was familiar with Michael Nyman's film scores when I heard a pre-release tape of the soundtrack to the Jane Campion film *The Piano*, but I hadn't yet seen that movie; nonetheless, Nyman's work seemed so fully realized I did a column on the music well ahead of the debut of the motion picture or its companion recording, feeling the latter would do well regardless of the fate of the former. The interview with Cab Calloway was his last in-depth talk prior to his death in November 1994 at the age of eighty-six, the column seeing print just as a wealth of Calloway's most influential recordings were being readied for deservedly well received reissue. And so forth.

A goodly number of the records reported on in "Music to My Ears" would later represent commercial high points for the musicians involved, but others in this anthology symbolized artistic peaks rather than sales pinnacles. Still, my enthusiasm for each album featured herein is undiminished—unless otherwise indicated—and I commend them to the reader's attention.

Just as important, I also celebrate the mystery that once surrounded all these then untested records and their creation, because the uncertain circumstances of my initial encounters with them seemed to amplify the powerful mystique recorded sound has possessed since its inception. Indeed, we might all take care, perhaps, not to become too comfortable with the incongruities of this unique entertainment medium, lest we lose awareness of its eerie mood of expansive intimacy.

Alexander Graham Bell had also been active at the time of Thomas Edison in researching the transmission and reception of sound, particularly speech, and Bell patented versions of his telephone in 1876 and 1877. Bell would also develop a "Graphophone" a decade later that utilized wax cylinders—rather than Edison's fragile tinfoil surfaces—to replay recordings.

German immigrant Emile Berliner, who had become prosperous by improving the transmission fidelity of Bell's telephone, decided to do as much for Edison's phonograph. Building on the 1877 theories of scientist Charles Cros that a flat glass disc would be superior to any recording cylinder, Berliner obtained a patent in 1887 for the grooved zinc-coated platters and hand-driven playing mechanism that became the basis of the Berliner Gramophone Company in 1895. When Berliner associate Eldridge Johnson conceived a spring motor to facilitate continuous turntable speed, the contemporary record player was born.

By May 1889, Edison's North American Phonograph Company was supplying commercial wax-cylinder musical recordings for coin-operated "phonograph parlors" in San Francisco. To feed demand for the public novelty, the Columbia Phonograph Company (founded in January 1889) issued its inaugural record catalog in October 1890, with product choices consisting of assorted martial pieces by John Philip Sousa's U.S. Marine Band. As the father of modern march fanfare and author of such stirring standards as "Semper Fidelis" (1888), Sousa was one of the foremost popular musical figures of the age. The nickel purchase of an earful of Sousa's marches could be deemed a patriotic gesture, thus making the otherworldly and vaguely Faustian phonograph more accessible to discomfited consumers. Like Edison, who had exhibited his phonograph at the Paris

Exposition of 1889, Berliner ached to interest both European businessmen and the general overseas populace in the potential of his machine, so he sent foreign-rights agent William Barry Owen to London to seek investors during the year of Queen Victoria's Diamond Jubilee (1897). After numerous demurrals, Owen was able in May 1898 to secure financial support to establish humble London-based recording facilities for The Gramophone Company (as it was called in England) at 31 Maiden Lane, just off the Strand. Beloved British music hall artists (Bert Shepard, Ada Reeve, Dan Leno, Vesta Tilley) who frequented the adjacent Rule's Restaurant were tapped to record their most crowd-pleasing numbers for The Gramophone Company's fledgling catalog, and the discs were pressed by Berliner's brother in a German factory in their native Hanover.

The recorded outpourings of these earthy music hall artists proved yet another proletarian enticement for the awe-inspiring but still off-putting invention, the spectral qualities of which had moved British gothic-romance writer Abraham "Bram" Stoker to include the Edison phonograph as a plot device in his macabre 1897 novel of vampirism, *Dracula*. Indeed, the Victorian stage performers who recorded their repertoire were sufficiently ill at ease with the procedure that they often had to be relaxed with cases of stout stockpiled for the occasion.

Back in America, the advent of ragtime music as pioneered by composer-pianist Scott Joplin lent another common touch to the marketing of the phonograph, with such artists as banjo player Vess Ossman removing the lingering air of alchemy from the device.

Whether by aesthetic choice or industrial design, today's compact disc and its noiseless player remain streamlined, laser-era adaptations of the flat disc and Gramophone conceived in the late 1800s by Berliner and friendly competitor Johnson, who combined forces in October 1901 as the Victor Talking Machine Company. That company's marketing symbol became the painting by British artist Francis Barraud of his brother's dog, Nipper, listening to a Type-B Victor Gramophone. Originally purchased by William Barry Owen and later filed by Berliner as U.S. trademark number 34,890 on July 10, 1900, the image would be immortalized under the slogan by which Barraud offhandedly dubbed his finished work: "His Master's Voice."

The simple premise of Barraud's original artwork (executed with Edison's phonograph but redone on the same canvas to tout Berliner's Gramophone) was that a loyal dog would naturally be deceived into believing the machine's lifelike emanations were the in-the-flesh discourse of his owner. There already were ample anecdotal indications that this quaint miscomprehension was commonplace, and shop-window passersby spying the bemused white mongrel with the charcoal ears knew instantly the clever point being conveyed.

Meanwhile, the hardware and other physical embodiments of recorded sound were undergoing myriad alterations. With only the freshly conceived telephone as a precedent, there were neither obvious rules governing the appearance of such apparatus nor abstract guidelines for what the listener was supposed to imagine when in the presence of such potent aural replication.

Unlike the manufacturers of Singer's sewing machine, who strove to overcome late-nineteenth-century distaste at the horrors of factory life in order to spread the machine's appeal beyond the rapidly satisfied industrial quarter, phonograph makers had to conquer something far more chimerical than rueful class consciousness or the displacement of a servant-seamstress. Still, phonograph/Gramophone promotions paralleled the elevating spiel accorded Singer's highly decorative 1858 "New Family" model ("The great importance of the sewing machine is in its influence upon the home; in the countless hours it has added to women's leisure for rest and refinement") by offering the phonograph as a prime purveyor of that newly attainable family refinement.

The Industrial Revolution had given rise to unprecedented production and tradecraft outside the confines of the home. The indignities of factory management and regimentation (even at the white-collar level of bookkeeping and invoicing departments) had conspired to transform the Victorian household into a bourgeois palace of refuge and enforced fantasy—a veritable lair of illusion in which theatrical decor and rococo accoutrements deliberately dispelled all vestiges of the outside world. As indicated by the moral confusion and errant mysticism (theosophy, Neoplatonism, seances) that pervaded the heavily escapist leisure hours of this oppressive era, the ideal home had to become everything the dirty, dangerous, dehumanizing workplace was not, even in defiance of reality.

If a home-model sewing machine could be poised atop vine-entwined wrought-iron legs and adorned with gilt-edged pastoral scenes, then a phonograph could be portrayed with similarly suggestive dashes of social drama and romantic charm. Gramophone designers settled on a cozy cross between the horn shapes prevalent in the modern orchestra, the look of the voguish Acousticon "ear trumpet" hearing aid, and ornate belle epoque/art nouveau or austere English arts and crafts cabinetry of the period.

Seeking music that might appeal to every possible taste, talent-scouting technicians such as The Gramophone Company's Fred Gaisberg traveled across Europe and Asia with acoustic field recording equipment, cutting zinc masters of every form of folk music and bistro entertainment imaginable. Serious opera stars were loathe to involve themselves with such gadgetry, but just when phonograph records seemed in peril of becoming an exponent of all things rustic, exotic, and vulgar, legendary Italian tenor Enrico Caruso was signed in 1902 by the Victor company, which soon issued his renditions of "Vesti la Giubba" from *I Pagliacci* and other great arias on the prestigious Red Seal label. In 1907, a recording by Caruso of his signature *Pagliacci* solo became the first classical disc to reach the million-selling mark.

With high culture now in the grip of the Gramophone ethos, advertisements for Victrola consoles beckoned purchasers to perceive recorded music as the magical materialization in their living rooms of grand opera's greatest stars. Victrola brochures of 1907 asked buyers, "WILL YOU OPEN YOUR DOOR TO ALL THE MUSIC OF ALL THE WORLD?"; the full-color illustrations depicted a young couple in their study, as miniature classical composers and characters from opera held forth from perches on their furniture. A similar ad for Victor's costly Victrola XVI floor model suggested, "After dinner, introduce your guests to the world's greatest artists," with full-size performers from the casts of *La Bohème*, *Aïda*, and *Madama Butterfly* greeting a ballroom's worth of party-goers over demitasse. Even ads for Victor's small forty-dollar Victor III table model asserted, "A home without a Victor is a stage without a play."

In 1916, Columbia was calling its own phonograph a "Grafonola," and its rotogravure ads showed four smart young specimens of the beau monde in formal dinner dress, singing along with one of the company's two-sided 78 rpm "double discs" (first sold in 1908) in a den with medieval wall hangings. The group appeared to prefer the conviviality of the animated one-hundred-ten-dollar Columbia Grafonola to the fine grand piano peeking out of the lower left corner of the illustration; their backs are turned to the open instrument as if it had been puttered with and then abandoned.

Come 1917, both Columbia and Victor were emphasizing the ability of their machines to supplant a dance orchestra at the most elegant and stylish affairs. In their magazine promotions, revelers were shown engaged in fashionable steps (fox-trot, hesitation waltz, tango) executed to dance recordings "superintended" by the likes of the chic ballroom team of Vernon and Irene Castle.

Recorded music was now a sensation, fueling both festive domestic entertaining and the frenzied national dance crazes it had embraced to help make its presence palatable. As the Victor-Columbia-Edison patent monopoly began expiring circa 1917, eager new labels (OKeh, Pathé, Vocalion, Brunswick, Emerson) sprang up or entered the American market, proffering boogie, rural blues, and other so-called race music, in addition to gospel, church, and spiritual songs, minstrel acts, urban and backwoods comedians, Cajun vocal and instrumental groups, cowboy crooners, and "hillbilly" mountain music, much of it ferreted out by mobile recording teams. Listeners forgot their qualms and queries about the medium itself as they grew intoxicated with the joys of regional, topical, and idiomatic self-recognition. The talking machine not only spoke to them but spoke for them, and it defeated the distances between provincial custom and popular critique.

Thanks to the phonograph, sales of sheet music soared into the multibillions, and song publishers regarded it as an indispensible tool. As *Billboard* noted in an editorial in its September 15, 1917, issue, "To say that the phonograph has revolutionized the music publishing field sounds like a mighty statement, but, as a matter of fact, its truth is almost self-evident. The phonograph performs an important double function. It takes songs which have earned their share of popularity on the regular sheet music market and repopularlizes them in a field far more far-reaching and profitable. It also takes songs which would never experience spirited counter sales and popularizes them over the instrument. . . . The phonograph—the greatest of all musical carriers—covers too broad a field to be monopolized by any one interest. It belongs to all of us and we intend to treat it as a sacred trust."

Vaudeville leapt to an explosive peak in 1918, with twenty-five thousand entertainers scuffing the footlights in four thousand theaters, and all of them hustled to have their tunes and routines preserved on discs. In 1921, production of records exceeded one million units (a quadruple increase over the 1914 totals). A sharp dip in sales during the Great Depression was offset by the advent of the jukebox and its ambient influence on the pop agora. The appetite for recorded music in public places had reached ravenous proportions by the early thirties, and for two decades the pages of *Billboard* had carried ads for the coin-operated phonographs popular at carnivals and fairs, in addition to select disc ads from the publishers of ascendant recording artists. *Billboard* was also printing notices from firms whose heavy-duty public address phonographs were essential equipment for everything from amusement parks to municipal pools. As Western Electric proclaimed in a full-page ad from April 1932, "Now the same music can be heard in your dance pavilion, your merry-go-round, your swimming pool—wherever you want it."

No longer an atmospheric curiosity, recorded music had become a solid commodity, its technological marvels a foregone conclusion, its fixed moments on vinyl the principal object of fascination. Recorded music had harnessed time and space, transforming a given performance into an article valuable unto itself. Now one could *own* such things, reusing them to mock time, instill moods, restart the awkward tenor of an emotional interlude. The clock's cold output of alternately tedious or fleeting information could now be halted, redirected, stalled, or intensified. (Indeed, this is how records themselves were actually made, particularly after the inception of taping technologies.)

The equally new media of film, photography, and wireless radio had a strictness to their functional essences that entranced the beholder but still compressed time and culture into orderly contexts. Recorded music triggered the sensation of total freedom while respecting all the scientific and procedural logic of the other dawning visual or audio diversions. Record purchasers understood but quickly disregarded the fact that recorded music was itself a kind of illusion, sounding spontaneous but having been willingly—if not meticulously—submitted to limited conditions in order to be effectively reexperienced by the buyer.

Music is an amorphous enhancement, as well as a tangible entity, firing the imagination with arguably the fewest sensory restrictions of any art form. In the case of recorded music, no actual contact with the artist and the process of creation or expression is necessary for complete and almost unconditional enjoyment. The average listener rarely if ever hears—or seeks to hear—the recorded music played in its incipient developmental environment. Why journey to a certain distant studio or control room to play a favorite album? The notion is itself a hollow and silly distraction, for the greater the transporting sweep of the recorded work, the more marginal its original source and even its composer can often seem.

Recorded music also allows the tactile satisfaction of "playing" it, adjusting the volume, tempering the essential mix and the compression, varying the tone and duration of the doses, allowing its changeable inner meaning to comingle with its transient outward setting. To the true audiophile, recorded music does not grow old; it exists only in the eternal present.

In its stunning variety, enveloping power, and capacity for metamorphosing the psychic purview, modern recorded music—especially as played on the most hermetic headphone hardware—could be considered the phantasmal ideal the Victorians sought when they redecorated their domestic spaces to achieve seamless disassociation from everyday life.

A century ago, when music of any kind was far less convenient or prevalent, a summer visit to a public park, for instance, occasioned the possibility of communion with a wide range of fellow citizens as a brass band rang out from an open-air orchestra stand. In the sparkle and serenity of such an afternoon or evening, the spell of a Sousa-like instrumental ensemble could inspire shared excitement, palpable uplift, and the unifying social ease that made all sorts of kindly human encounters possible. It was a special magnet for people's democratic instincts.

Playing music remains the closest humanity has come to confirming the existence of sorcery. Across history, no one has yet been able to completely explain how or why music affects us so profoundly, prompting many of the deepest private feelings that a public gesture can possibly generate.

Like memory, recorded music is, to my ears, a treasure. Its considerable pleasures are owed in part to the maturation of the science of recording as well as to the skillful concord achieved between the artist, the technician, and the once-incredulous audience. Nonetheless, all music happens first in the heart. As we learn to assimilate the enhanced CD, CD-ROM, and future sound carriers, we will be likewise challenged to recall and preserve the impulse that moved us to covet an edifying force like music in the first place: the desire to celebrate the unfolding uniqueness of others—those we wish to know, those we need to understand, and, above all, those we long to trust.

TIMOTHY WHITE

IF WE SHOULD FALL BEHIND: SPRINGSTEEN'S SECULAR HYMNS

AS WITH THE BEST OF AMERICAN POPULAR MUSIC, THE thrust of New Orleans' earthy style of expression has always occupied a special place between sensualism, sacrilege, and simple common need. These are the things that inspired seminal Crescent City musicians as diverse as flamboyant nineteenth-century composer Louis Moreau Gottschalk, cathouse jazz pianist Jelly Roll Morton, and the late Professor Longhair, whose oeuvre was rooted in folk idioms. These enduring folkloric elements may also have been the magnet that recently drew Bruce Springsteen to the Crescent City to shoot the music video for the eponymous single off his *Human Touch* album. Directed by Meiert Avis, the video is most notable for the recurring imagery of the lone headlamp

Bruce Springsteen

on the cab of the ancient trolley that courses through the clip, a sad searchlight complementing the pilgrim tone of the song.

After viewing the video on my hotel TV during last week's NARM convention in New Orleans, I took a battered Walkman and two advance cassettes of Springsteen's forthcoming *Human Touch* and *Lucky Town* records along with me on a long twilight walk through New Orleans' old French Quarter. There were revelries in progress for the Feast of St. Joseph, and Bruce's music suited the heady, haunted surroundings. In his own way, Springsteen shares the bittersweet brio of Gottschalk and Longhair, and Bruce's finest moments show the same purity of purpose: to link honest impressions of the present with the meaningful folklore of our hybrid heritage.

"Human Touch" kicked in on the tapedeck as I passed the derelict municipal building that served as Jim Garrison's office headquarters in the controversial film *JFK*. Locals say the dingy edifice may soon be restored as a new courthouse; observers think "Human Touch" sounds like a track that could have been left off the earlier *Tunnel of Love* album—in either case, it seems that something distinctive and imposing is at least being put to good use. But I wouldn't judge either New Orleans or the *Human Touch* album on the evidence of any single artifact.

As a song, "Human Touch" is the new beginning that *Tunnel of Love* couldn't contain, because the crises in Springsteen's romantic life hadn't yet been resolved; some might perceive both the *Human Touch* and *Lucky Town* albums as the songwriter's meditations on his second marriage. More accurately, they seem the absorbing spiritual and artistic saga of his second chance at self-fulfillment. If you agree that *The River* (1980) revealed Springsteen waking up to the depth of his public talent, and that *Tunnel of Love* (1987) disclosed Bruce waking up to the depth of his private myth, then the stark truth-telling of his two new albums may rouse his audience to a new awareness of the singer's impact on us.

However, the title track of *Human Touch* is more a prelude than an epitomization of the remarkably varied fourteen-song collection. The record really begins with "Soul Driver," whose taut, percussive tread describes a man stumbling out of a carny-like sphere, wondering if sincerity can survive in our tawdry buy-and-sell society. On the wry, remote "57 Channels (and Nothin' On)," Springsteen discovers via satellite dish that the whole planet craves the chance to make the same mistakes America has. Thus, Bruce reasons, any new information about who we are must be sought within ourselves—assuming we still retain the requisite humility for the task.

The rest of *Human Touch* is a probing quest—sometimes grievous, sometimes glorious—and well seasoned with utterly singular potential hits like "Cross My Heart," "Gloria's Eyes," "Man's Job," and the robustly happy "Real Man"—a romp unlike anything Springsteen has ever written. Along the way, the songwriter sheds his skin right down to the sinew on such soliloquies as "I Wish I Were Blind" and "All or Nothin' at All."

The music is crisp and rich, spare but ingeniously picturesque. Luminous electric guitar lines are often employed in place of vocal narrative, and guest vocalists swell behind the singer like organ or piano; a muted trumpet rises to supplant rhythm guitar or bass, and drums pepper the melody like horns. The lyrics evoke superstitions and lost souls, catfish and cottonwoods, black rivers and inky skies. Sex arrives as a snake bite and/or a bed of roses—"With every wish there comes a curse."

The Robert Johnsonesque dangers of the devil's bargain are expressed more directly on the *Lucky Town* album, an intimate diary of proverbs and allegories in which Springsteen plays all the instruments except for Gary Mallabar's drums. The title track and "Leap of Faith" display the same bright chart promise of *Human Touch*'s highlights, but the most beguiling songs may be the secular hymns about Bruce's wedding vows with Patti Scialfa ("If I Should Fall Behind") and the birth of his son, Evan ("Living Proof").

Like Springsteen, we are all groping through a time in which religion's moral force has fallen away, with little to replace it. Entertainment is heartening because it celebrates the human scale that our government currently lacks or conceals; there is extraindustry fascination with the record charts because they are one mirror in which we can still glimpse our collective will, lending an air of control and logic to a landscape that sometimes appears on the brink of chaos. At its high end, rock'n'roll can periodically bridge the spiritual chasms of this cynical era—especially when the music espouses values that carry a ring of emotional candor. Like Gottschalk, Morton, Longhair, Johnson, or any other correspondent/ composer who found poetry in the wonder of ordinary truths, Springsteen understands the anchoring role that folklore plays in the soul of a nation.

When institutions crumble and the commonwealth is imperiled, the enduring touchstones for a people are its folkways: those things created, transmitted, and ennobled by the human touch. As universal as speech, as individual as jargon, folk beliefs are the tools we devise when machines fail us, the fables we tell to chase our modern fears, the rhymes and recipes we concoct to remind ourselves how an average person might nurture his neighbor.

The greatest exponents of American popular music have always been gifted appreciators—seeing charity and courage in small moments where most observers saw little or none.

Human Touch and *Lucky Town* help remind us why, after World War II, the bold hybrid of rock'n'roll was spontaneously conceived: to make a common sound, bigger than the Bomb, that said the spirit of the individual will always matter most.

IMMIGRANT SONG
FADES IN GOVT. DIN

MUCH OF THE FINEST POPULAR MUSIC HEARD YEARLY IN this country must pass through customs to reach American ears, whether it arrives as a master tape from a studio in Budapest, Hungary; as a field recording from the foothills of the Rif Mountains of Morocco; via portable DAT equipment from a patio in Port Antonio, Jamaica; or carried in the imaginations of artists visiting from Haiti or South Africa.

Among the standout album releases of the last several months have been Hungarian singer Márta Sebestyén's exquisite *Apocrypha* (Hannibal/Rykodisc); the deeply spiritual Haitian dance contours of Boukman Eksperyans's *Vodou Adjae* (Mango) and Rara Machine's *Break the Chain* (Shanachie); South African reggae star Lucky Dube's visionary *House of Exile* (Shanachie); Jamaican mento at its most buoyant on the Jolly Boys' *Beer Joint + Tailoring* (First Warning/BMG); and the spellbinding Moroccan trance cadences of the Master Musicians of Jajouka Featuring Bachir Attar, whose pan pipes and *tebel* drums tilt the firmament on *Apocalypse Across the Sky* (Axiom/Island).

While it is relatively easy for exceptional foreign recordings of this variety to enter this land,

Márta Sebestyén

alien composers seeking to perform their works in this country can find the process rather problematic.

Happily, protests here and abroad from music and arts groups recently resulted in the amendment of provisions in the Bush administration's new immigration statutes, eliminating an absurd annual cap of twenty-five thousand foreigner-performer work visas (encompassing orchestras, sports teams, etc.), as well as provisions requiring a ninety-day wait and prohibiting entrance to a musical group that hadn't been together for a year. However, the Bush administration reportedly acquiesced to AFL-CIO lobbyists and assorted others by insisting on a compromise rule requiring that visa applications undergo a screening consultation by the American Federation of Musicians, which felt Bush's former, much decried regulations had protected U.S. workers.

Since it's unlikely many American union musicians could fill in for members of Boukman Eksperyans or the Masters of Jajouka the way they'd sub for a Mexican top-forty lounge band or a traveling symphony's nonfeatured woodwinds, the AFM's decisive role as adviser-arbiter in any such supposed issues is dicey at best. This regulation also paves the way for possible government involvement in judging the artistic merit of foreign performing artists—a bad business in a pluralistic nation predicated on multicultural liberties. The Land of the Free does *not* need protectionism in the arts. Period.

Moreover, as noted by visa regulations expert Bob Tulipan, whose Traffic Control Group coordinates international visa petitioning for touring popular, classical, and ethnic folk musicians, "In the case of entertainers, most other countries generally don't grant work visas based on a review of professional or artistic worth or any comparable criteria, and they *don't* impose a complex list of rules and regulations like the U.S. does. They simply issue foreign entry permits for artists based on having a reputable employer who wants to sponsor them for specific work dates. Essentially, if that employer commits to hiring a foreign entertainer during a certain calendar period, they file a local application specifying the job order and their need for the artist—and that's that. In many countries such as England, once the local application has been approved, you can just pick up your visa at the airport after you land."

In contrast, we put foreign performers through a veritable obstacle course of intricate scrutinies for the privilege of appearing here—including demands they submit substantial dossiers of native and global press clippings, critical reviews, chart listings, and letters from specialists in the field attesting to their abilities.

Adding untimely injury to recent insult, it was revealed in last week's issue of *Billboard* that, with the newly modified visa laws due to take effect in a matter of days, the U.S. Immigration and Naturalization Service had not even taken the necessary administrative steps to render those new rules operable—including the printing of revised forms. This negligence shows a contemptuous disregard for the concerns of the international creative community. Any chaos—encompassing the potential loss of millions in revenues to unionized support staff in the nation's top venues—that could result from major tour cancellations due to the simple unattainability of the most basic bureaucratic paperwork would be a debacle for the global touring industry. And the apparent need to cobble together a makeshift interim procedure is a diplomatic and political disgrace.

But that's not the most shameful part of this strange saga. One of the most fundamental responsibilities of America's federal bureaucracy is ensuring that the rest of the world is able to participate in our unique democratic social laboratory. If Washington cannot handle this job efficiently, then it is failing at one of the most pivotal tasks of the republic.

To be an American is not simply to belong to a nationality but also to devote oneself to a surpassing social experiment, an experiment fueled by the belief that we are all one of a kind, yet united in our humanity—and that we are all bound here by a desire to learn from each other.

In music, as in all other pursuits, America is the sum of its diverse, difficult, and audacious pan-cultural past. And our government is not a private supercorporation authorized to spin its own exclusionary racist web. Whenever any agency acting for America dares—by design or damned ineptitude—to ration access to other cultures and their artistic fruits, it denies this country a vital facet of its future.

There seems to be no verifiable explanation beyond veiled racism for the almost wholesale expulsion of Haitian refugees from U.S. territory; and beyond blatant foot-dragging incompetence, no good excuse has yet surfaced for the shoddy INS implementation of the national will as expressed in the newly modified O- and P-performer–category visa regulations.

Meantime, the world music albums cited above are recommended for their passion and craft—and also for their implicit faith in the American doctrine that an independent people are always eager to listen to the free expressions of others. U.S. record consumers comprise one of the largest markets in the world, and the staggering sweep of their musical tastes reflects the openness of our society as well as its ethnic multiplicity.

Let's strive to keep this country's official policies both caring and welcoming toward the global music pulse. As an industry of music lovers within a nation of freedom lovers, we have a responsibility to make certain this system fulfills our most rudimentary cultural expectations, as well as our highest democratic ideals.

ANNIE LENNOX
CASTS A SOLO SPELL

LAST WEEK, ALL OF LONDON SEEMED IN THRALL TO A bittersweet Scottish lament. The elegiac ballad could have been linked to the losers in the British general elections—most appropriately, the United Kingdom's defeated Scottish separatists.

But this lament was both more personal and universal in nature, and prefigured a rebirth rather than a wake. Entitled "Why," it was the affecting farewell for Aberdeen-born ex-Eurythmic Annie Lennox to a stretch of semiretirement begun in February 1990. And as the first single from *Diva* (Arista/BMG), Lennox's debut solo album, "Why" also confirmed the long-rumored mutual decision to dissolve the collaboration with composer Dave Stewart that had made the Eurythmics one of the most successful acts of the last decade.

Arriving in the midst of an international album-sales sweepstakes between Def Leppard and Bruce Springsteen, Lennox's *Diva* album became the U.K.'s best-seller by a comfortable margin in its initial week of release, ac-

Annie Lennox

cording to Britain's major retailers. A spokesperson for the 310-store Our Price chain (the nation's largest) commented, "*Diva* entered the [chain's] sales chart at No. 1. It is anticipated it will maintain this position over Easter."

Chatting in London following that first week's outpouring of commercial support, Lennox's reaction to the public's response was one of grateful exuberance.

"To be honest, after being away so long, I wasn't sure who might be waiting for my new music," she confessed in her bubbly Aberdeen burr. "So I feel like a cat with nine lives!"

Indeed, during the course of her former career with cohort Dave Stewart, first as part of the Tourists (who notched a number-four U.K. hit in 1979 with a crackling cover of Dusty Springfield's "I Only Want to Be with You") and then in the Eurythmics (whose slew of global smashes commenced in 1983 with "Sweet Dreams [Are Made of This]"), Lennox has concocted enough starkly contrasting personas to rival David Bowie or Madonna. But whether embodying a New Romantic mannequin in a tangerine flattop, a gender-bent Elvis impersonator at the Grammys, or a reflective diva dressing for a Venice masque, the crux of Lennox's appeal has remained her eerie voice: a throaty, dexterous instrument that throbs with pathos.

Indeed, no matter how exotic Lennox's stage pose has become, her vocals have never felt performed. Rather, they've been potent for their gut vulnerability. It's this curious combination of visual artifice and complete emotional authenticity that has made Lennox a singularly compelling artist.

Annie Lennox calls "Why" a "deep dialog with myself," and that admission may offer clues to its power. As anyone who has seen the "Why" video can attest, the climactic final verse—"a denouncement of things applied to me"—is rendered by Lennox with a trembling resolve that veers near tears.

Perhaps it's because the single arrived at a point when both Britain and America are grappling with a cynical electoral process, but the final anguished verse of "Why" ("Do you know how I feel? 'Cause I don't think you know what I feel . . . You *don't* know what I feel") seems a metaphor for the mistrustful social mood.

"For me," said Lennox, "the most important thing is to be willing to *try* to reach others, to want the challenge of representing my sensibilities as truly as possible to people, both stylistically and representationally. You must think to yourself as you write songs that 'the buck stops here.' "

It's this urgent sense of creative candor, coupled with the unique hot-house environment of the British music scene, that may have helped "Why" and the rest of *Diva* (with its stunning eight-selection companion home video) engender such a startlingly tangible word-of-mouth campaign. This observer overheard fans discussing "Why" in a Kings Road café, watched cabbies and clerks turn it up whenever it was broadcast, and saw strangers on Oxford Street openly sharing the stirred feelings the song sparked as it oozed from an HMV record shop.

"When I sit down to write," Lennox explained, "I always try to think of all the great songwriters who've moved me, so their inspiring songs walk before me and stimulate me for my process. I suppose I'm working to reconstruct my own intimate reflections, though it may well be cloaked in symbology—but for me the ultimate goal of songwriting is far beyond that. What you really want to do," she said, "is send shivers up people's spines, to create a jolt of recognition so that people want to hear a song again because it makes personal sense to *them*."

For Lennox, her own primary experience with this sort of ecumenical synapse occurred in the Scotland of her childhood when listening to certain wistful bagpipe airs. Herself the daughter of a bagpiper-boilermaker, Lennox recently told Scottish BBC television how close she still feels to the all-embracing lamentations of the pipes, particularly those pealing out the ancient *piobaireachd* (pi-broch) forms, which somehow convey a transcendent poignancy.

While determined as an adolescent to leave Scotland, she has since come to appreciate its profound influence on her. And after a difficult life encompassing a lonely childhood spent in a two-room tenement, one failed marriage, and a professional passage marked by much psychic suffering, Lennox has found substantial recent happiness (she wed filmmaker Uri Fruchtman in 1988 and they have a daughter, Lola, born in December 1990). It may be the strength of that new home life that permitted her to pour so much of her distilled past into *Diva*, molding the record into an astoundingly powerful document of one artist's attempts at communion with her audience.

Certain albums galvanize a moment in time and then forever own it. Whether contemplating the emotional wreckage of her passage ("Walking on Broken Glass") or evoking the professional failure that might have been ("Legend in My Living Room"), Lennox generates an aural beauty and a conversational flow seldom achieved in contemporary rock.

"I use the word *diva* ironically," said Lennox, "because I'm singing about how people respond to the act of performing and also how *I* respond to it."

Near the end of the fifteen-odd months it took to make *Diva*, producer Stephen Lipson heard Lennox humming "Keep Young and Beautiful," a 1934 hit from the film musical *Roman Scandals*.

"Stephen asked me what the tune was—he loved it. I wanted to lift the mood after the somber fire of my final song, 'The Gift.' It was strictly an afterthought, a postcoital moment; it's a liqueur [on the CD version of the record] after the ten-course meal I tried to present with *Diva*.

"Actually," Lennox concluded, wryly emphasizing her sensuous Scottish brogue, "the lyrics are so sexist, charming, and bizarre, they seemed a perfect way to break the spell of my own songs!"

NATIVE-AMERICAN SONG, THEN AND NOW

HISTORY IS MEMORY HEWN BY POLITICS. CULTURE IS POETRY carved by experience. Somewhere between the two lies the simple human truth.

"This year America is glorifying its five hundredth anniversary of the 1492 Columbus voyage, and since you can't celebrate Columbus without acknowledging the American Indian, this country's indigenous people will once again come into view," says John Trudell, a Santee Sioux whose new spoken-word album *AKA Graffiti Man* (Rykodisc) offers his own eloquent perspective on his ancestry's untold story. "We always have the potential to see the plain facts, but my experience in life has taught me that no one does anything unless it serves their own self-interests. I don't mean that cynically, I mean it *clinically.*"

In Native-American culture, five hundred years is a mere finger snap in time. As Peter Nabokov writes in *Native American Testimony: A Chronicle of Indian-White Relations from Prophecy to the Present, 1492–1992* (Viking): "Before the coming of the white man, bronze-skinned men and

John Trudell

women from northern Asia had been exploring and settling the Americas for anywhere from ten to fifty thousand years." Thus, it was actually this migratory race (who by A.D. 1250 had already built cities larger than London and tribal mounds bigger than the Great Pyramid of Cheops) that discovered America.

At the close of the fifteenth century, a forlorn Columbus made landfall in the Bahamas, believing he'd found a new passage to India. The indigenous people befriended Columbus, and he responded by taking twenty-five Indians back to Spain as slaves. Columbus financed all of his subsequent explorations of the Americas by trafficking in Indian slaves, and his son Diego made the first formal petition (to King Charles V of Spain in 1519) to commence the African slave trade.

Native Americans still wonder why a society would honor cunning explorers like Columbus, yet ignore the highly skilled Indian guides, mapmakers, and diplomats (Hernando Cortez requiring the Aztec woman Malinche, the Lewis and Clark expedition dependent on the great female Shoshone scout Sacajawea, etc.) who trustingly escorted each of them across the Americas.

Similarly, the Wampanoag tribe saved the lives of the former city-dwelling pilgrims by teaching them to hunt and plant in the New World—and the pilgrims repaid them with bondage. Yet, as Jack Weatherford notes in his new book, *Native Roots—How the Indians Enriched America* (Crown): "In the four hundred years since the European settlers began coming to North America, they have not found a single American plant suitable for domestication that the Indians had not already cultivated." Even our Founding Fathers' concepts for governing the wilderness settlements were shaped by the Iroquois Confederacy Great Law instituted in the fifteenth century by the legendary Hiawatha and Deganawidah.

"If people in this country really want to know how to help the Indian people, they must learn to help themselves," says Trudell in his taut, nasal drawl, "because the wheel has turned to where all the things we've suffered are now becoming the norm of the average citizen: the lack of representation, the political deception, the ethnic and class discrimination, the loss of jobs and health and property."

Expounding on these themes, *AKA Graffiti Man* is the sound of an edgy orator ("probably the most charismatic speaker I've ever heard," says Bonnie Raitt) seeking to merge his social activism and traditional tribal music with what he terms "modern electric song."

Trudell was born and raised on the Santee Sioux Reservation on the border of northeastern Nebraska and South Dakota. Following four years of Vietnam-era navy duty, during which Trudell was deeply affected by the racism directed at his fellow minority troops as well as the Asian adversaries, he found himself drawn in the late sixties to the American Indian Movement. Trudell's key role in AIM's Indian rights campaigns is recounted in Peter Matthiessen's newly republished best-seller *In the Spirit of Crazy Horse,* which should be required reading in high school social studies classes.

Trudell's segue from social activism into performance art occurred circa 1979 while he was appearing with Jackson Browne and Bonnie Raitt at various environmental and Indian benefits. With his musician friends' encouragement, Trudell channeled his speech-making verve into verse, and ultimately set his spoken stanzas to tribal tempos.

"I started out with just indigenous drums," Trudell recalls, "but once I met the Kiowa guitarist Jesse Ed Davis in 1985, his incredible leads gave me the compulsion to rock the words."

Billboard's Hot 100 has seen the periodic appearance of Native-American rock'n'roll, with Redbone scoring a hit in the early seventies with "Come And Get Your Love" and Buffy Sainte-Marie reaching the top forty with "Mister Can't You See." However, Trudell's hybrid *AKA Graffiti Man* experiments (most intriguing on the title track, "What He'd Done," and "Beauty in a Fade") sound far more organic and heritage-based.

Indeed, Trudell's Jackson Browne–produced record seems a timely counterpart to another recent Rykodisc release, *Honor the Earth Powwow: Songs of the Great Lakes Indians,* produced on location at Wisconsin and Minnesota reservations by the Grateful Dead's Mickey Hart. The tremolo chants and rhythmic invocations preserved on *Powwow*'s nighttime sessions are transporting in their timelessness, and their keen unity of ancestral song, story, and spirituality also reveal a custodial philosophy toward the physical world.

Historians tend to characterize this continent's timberlands as having been "wild" when Columbus beheld them. But as the book *Native Roots* documents, North America's Indian peoples had over the course of millennia conceived an intricate array of forestry practices—like selective firings of woods to remove undergrowth, aid soil fertility, and direct the grazing of animal life—whose sheer scope and parklike efficiency stagger the modern imagination. By the 1870s, though, white lumber companies had left the Midwest's settled forests so ravaged and debris-cluttered that a new word—*firestorm*—was coined to describe the dozens of cata-strophic blazes their negligence had precipitated. (The fires ceased after many Indian forestry practices were restored.)

"There's a character in the old Sioux folk songs and stories called Iktome the Spider," says Trudell. "Iktome always thinks he knows what's best, but he inevitably goes about things the wrong way, con-suming more than he should, not listening to owls and other fellow crea-tures who warn of danger. So everyone suffers the consequences.

"The Sioux used the Iktome character to teach moral lessons and learn from their mistakes," adds Trudell. "My music and all Indian music just tries to offer the same food for thought. We believe we're *all* here to learn—and to avoid turning out like Iktome."

LINDSEY BUCKINGHAM ROCKS THE *CRADLE*

"THEMEWISE, THE NEW RECORD TOUCHES ON THE IRONY of a forty-two-year-old man beginning a rebirth," says Lindsey Buckingham with a chuckle, alluding to his new album, *Out of the Cradle,* which takes its name from poet Walt Whitman's 1874 memoir of childhood, *Out of the Cradle, Endlessly Rocking.* "Its title has a double meaning for me, referring to my transition from my old band, and also to the child still rocking around inside of us after we become adults."

Buckingham's old band, of course, was Fleetwood Mac, from which he departed in 1987, shortly after permitting the band to plunder his solo project-in-progress to steady its foundering *Tango in the Night* album. He gave his cohorts his four best songs, among them "Big Love"—which promptly became a top-five hit. "I surrendered my own songs to the situation," he now muses, "in order to preserve our sense of family."

He then lavished his wizardry as an arranger on his cohorts' own *Tango* material. "If I had to choose my main contributing factor to the band, it wouldn't be as a guitarist, a writer, or a singer; it would be as someone who knows

Lindsey Buckingham

how to take raw material from Christine [McVie] and Stevie [Nicks] and forge that into something," Buckingham told this writer during an 1987 talk in his home studio. "That's a nice gift to have, and be able to help people with."

Five years later, still holed up in the Slope, the recording workshop in his Bel Air, California, residence, Buckingham shows the same multilateral outlook on his musical skills. "I always perceived my role in Fleetwood Mac as being the 'studied eclectic,' " he explains. "I was the band's built-in sidebar, working within the mainstream—while also delving into strange areas of experimentation in an effort to be myself. Now I have a greater confidence, and with the new record I'm just myself naturally, without taking any side trips."

Out of the Cradle ultimately reminds the listener that, for two decades, Lindsey Buckingham has been one of rock'n'roll's most original musical draftsmen. His creative confidence is apparent on the new album, a dramatically cohesive work that combines his quirky virtuosity on acoustic and electric guitar with a panoramic knack for sonic collage. While tracks like "Don't Look Down" or "This Is the Time" fall well within rock's melodic tradition, they feature eccentric constructions and sudden harmonic shifts, each surprise element enhancing their overall appeal.

As *Out of the Cradle* demonstrates, the Palo Alto–born Buckingham is both a pupil and prime inheritor of a rich California rock heritage whose atmospheric studio craft stretches from the Beach Boys through the Byrds to the 1973 *Buckingham Nicks* record (Polydor) that proved to be the stylistic foundation of Fleetwood Mac at its commercial peak. Pretty but never prissy, *Buckingham Nicks* was a tensile pastiche of folk-rock strains wholly compatible with early seventies Mac efforts like *Kiln House* and *Bare Trees*. (A perfect example of Buckingham's Fleetwood Mac–friendly approach was "Monday Morning," a song meant for *Buckingham Nicks* that he wound up giving to the Mac when he and Nicks joined in 1975.) And Lindsey's most effective arranging trait, which later helped lift the *Fleetwood Mac* and *Rumours* records into the commercial stratosphere, was an ability—"a tiny, repeating sense of event," as he terms it—to make electric music seem both warmly acoustic and utterly spontaneous.

Out of the Cradle has these same qualities in profusion, the spine of each track being the alternatingly plucked and brailing guitar lines in which Buckingham specializes. On a new song like "Soul Drifter," contrasting layers of Lindsey's multitracked vocals are interwoven with various metronomic riff sounds that constantly supplant each other before their essential sameness can be detected. The sum effect is akin to moving through a musical forest where nature has achieved an intuitive orchestration; it feels mighty eerie yet immensely satisfying.

Buckingham's background reflects the fine-tuned intensity of his art. The youngest of three competitive boys (his brother Gregg won a silver medal in swimming in the 1968 Olympics), Lindsey grew up in the cultural and social environment of a college town, with Stanford University as its centerpiece. The Buckinghams were coffee growers, his father's small Alta Coffee label in Daly City having emerged from the regional Keystone brand his grandfather founded in the twenties.

Buckingham's hobbies as a youth encompassed drums and guitar as well as participation with his siblings in the nationally recognized Santa Clara Swim Club. His pursuit of swimming trophies lapsed after an aunt died and left him a twelve-thousand-dollar inheritance, which he spent on recording equipment. Tinkering with an Ampex four-track tape deck in a back room of his dad's coffee plant, he began developing songs for a Palo Alto band called Fritz, which he joined in 1967. The group's female vocalist was one Stephanie "Stevie" Nicks. Fritz disintegrated after four modest years of Bay area gigs, although its core singing-songwriting duo of Buckingham and Nicks landed the brief Polydor recording deal that produced *Buckingham Nicks.*

"A few years ago," says Lindsey, "Stevie and I bought back the rights to the 'Buckingham Nicks' album"—whose assistant engineer was Richard Dashut, still Lindsey's best friend and co-producer. "That record has become one of the most requested albums not yet on CD, and we may put it out around the same time as a Fleetwood Mac boxed set that's planned for Christmas. Incidentally, Stevie and I have agreed to go into the studio in a week or so to contribute some new stuff to the boxed set."

Despite this fondness for former alliances, Buckingham says he's looking forward to what he believes will be a permanent solo path. "I've had enough time to get my feet back on the ground careerwise," Buckingham explains. "As rock moves further away from melody, I'd like to find new ways to bring melody back. . . . A lot of times while working alone here at my studio, I'd take 20-minute breaks and read some Whitman and the collected works of Dylan Thomas, to get a sense of how good lyrics should sound. And while my songs are not about a specific world view, they address the current lack of idealism or the inclination to act on that emotion."

Radio gets its first taste of *Out of the Cradle* when the up-tempo, feverish "Wrong" (for which a video has just been completed) is sent to album-rock stations Tuesday (19). The Warner Bros. album will be shipped to retail June 16. Buckingham says he's eager to reconnect with his public—and to perform live for it. "All the things I've done since the late eighties have been survival moves, yet they've given me a fresh optimism. I've managed to make myself happier just by concentrating on what, for me, rings true."

THEREMIN SINGS
THE BODY ELECTRIC

THERE IS AN ART TO MAKING MUSIC OUT OF THIN AIR. Standing stock-still in a packed lower Manhattan drawing room, a middle-aged woman is poised between a gilded baby grand piano and an antique black cabinet from which two thick silver antennae protrude. As the young female pianist provides sparse accompaniment, the woman bows slightly before the tall, narrow box, holding one palm over the looped volume antenna extending from its side, while the fingers of her other hand hover beside the strange device's vertical pitch antenna.

With a fluid series of sculpting motions, the woman fills the room with a floating whine resembling a phantom violin or a spectral coloratura soprano. Suddenly, the tartly pitched sound is transformed into Rachmaninoff's bittersweet "Vocalise," and for the next four minutes the small crowd is transfixed by a demonstration that is equal parts musical recital and electronic seance. Afterward, Wendy Carlos of *Switched-On Bach* synthesizer fame leads the guests in a standing ovation for both the players and the Russian physicist who made this otherworldly display possible, Leon Theremin.

Clara Rockmore, 1945, playing a theremin

Presented at the home of writer Michael O'Donoghue and *Saturday Night Live* music director Cheryl Hardwick last fall, the reception was held to welcome ninety-five-year-old Lev Sergeivitch Termen (anglicized to Leon Theremin) back to this country for the first time since 1938. Among the occasions for his return were receipt of Stanford University's prestigious Centennial Medal for his contributions to electronic music, principally his invention in 1918 of what he called the *aetherphon* or *thereminvox*—later known as the theremin.

But these honors and activities might not have happened without the efforts of filmmaker-theremin enthusiast Steven M. Martin, who has been working since 1989 with the support of noted record producer Hal Willner and Moog synthesizer creator Dr. Robert Moog to complete a documentary chronicling the saga of the theremin.

"These days," says Martin, "most music fans know the theremin because Brian Wilson featured one in 1966 on 'Good Vibrations,' and also on songs on the Beach Boys' [1968] *Wild Honey* album. More recently, Jimmy Page played one himself on Led Zeppelin's 'Whole Lotta Love,' getting those wonderful grinding and whooping passages."

But as Martin recounts, the theremin's initial and most illustrious exposure was via high culture, with the Leningrad Philharmonic debuting "A Symphonic Mystery" for theremin and orchestra in 1924. Upon reaching New York in 1927, Theremin held salon exhibitions for Toscanini and Rachmaninoff and would also appear at the Metropolitan Opera House and Carnegie Hall.

Last autumn, when addressing the audience after the Rachmaninoff piece played by his daughter Natasha, the now-stooped Professor Theremin explained in halting English that his aim in contriving a free-form instrument that could be played "without physical contact" was to force modern industrial technologies into the idealized realm of the arts.

The theremin would ultimately find its most masterful player in Russian emigré Clara Rockmore, née Reisenberg, a former violin prodigy whom Theremin met and fell in love with in the late twenties when their concertizing paths intersected in New York. And it was Martin's meeting with the semiretired Rockmore at her New York home in 1989 that inspired him to visit Leon Theremin in Moscow and undertake the ambitious documentary.

America's first mass-culture acquaintance with the theremin occurred in the score of the 1935 horror classic *The Bride of Frankenstein.* Its subsequent use during 1945 in Alfred Hitchcock's *Spellbound* and Billy Wilder's *The Lost Weekend*, and then in the 1951 sci-fi thriller *The Day the Earth Stood Still* also helped—in Martin's words—"to define the term 'eerie' for generations of film and television audiences."

"But what's of prime importance," Martin asserts, "is that the theremin was literally the first commercially manufactured electronic musical instrument. The professor licensed the patent for it to RCA in September 1929." Thus, domestic mass production of the theremin—in handsome, four-legged walnut cabinets—predated the early-thirties manufacture of the first Dobro, Rickenbacker, and Vivi-tone electric guitars.

"Moreover," says Martin, "all the electronic synthesizers used in today's popular music are derived from Theremin's invention. Robert Moog began his own career by constructing a theremin in high school from a diagram in a hobbyist magazine!

"Professor Theremin had his own sizable group of theremin students and a thriving New York laboratory until 1938, when he was kidnapped at gunpoint by Stalin's KGB and returned to Russia, where he was forced to do electronic research in prison for the Soviet war effort," he continues.

As for Martin himself, he, Hal Willner, and Moog are currently researching a soundtrack-anthology album of vintage theremin music for his nearly completed documentary, titled *Theremin: An Electronic Odyssey*. Early records of theremin music include RCA Victor's concept record *Perfume Set to Music,* as well as two post–World War II Capitol collections, *Music Out of the Moon* and *Music for Peace of Mind.* A rare gem Moog has located is a live transcription of Anis Fuleihan's *Concerto for Theremin and Orchestra*, performed in 1945 by Rockmore and the New York City Symphony under the direction of Leopold Stokowski.

"The theremin has produced some of the most haunting and penetrating sounds ever recorded," says Martin. "Imagine what it's like to act as a human capacitor, interrupting an electromagnetic field to create music!"

While the theremin's ethereal feedback can be shaped by the body electric to an almost supernatural extent, the skill required to "trim" the sounds into note patterns is considerable, since there are no keys or fretboards to indicate pitch or intonation. Moog praises Rockmore's near-balletic style for its "exacting technique and brilliant musicianship," and those eager for a dose of it should seek out her 1987 CD *The Art of the Theremin*, which preserves her uncanny facility on twelve selections ranging from Saint-Saens's "The Swan" to Tchaikovsky's "Serenade

Melancolique." Rockmore's record, which also features extensive liner notes by Moog, can be obtained from Delos International in Hollywood, California.

"Since my childhood," says Martin, "the theremin has seemed like a window to another, less pessimistic era when people still believed progress meant a better, more visionary life. When I look at the film footage of the professor and his theremin that we shot at O'Donoghue's apartment last fall, I realize that evening resembled a theremin salon just like the ones the professor held in Manhattan more than sixty years ago. Leon Theremin pioneered the concept of artist as scientist. I just want to see the creative journey of a great man come full circle."

CLAPTON AND STING CLICK ON HOT SINGLE

LIKE CREATIVITY, FRIENDSHIP IS A SUDDEN SPARK, APPRECI-ated and protected. Chance provides the opportunity; care preserves the light.

Click! Fump! Click! It was late March of this year, and Eric Clapton was hunched before a lone microphone in a control room of London's SARM Studios West, striking a metal lighter to ignite his umpteenth cigarette as he strummed his new Ramirez acoustic guitar. Time was tight, each nervous tic and probative chord progression assuming a tempoed intensity, as Eric tested various tone sequences for a movie soundtrack-in-progress.

The film score in question was *Lethal Weapon 3,* and Clapton was brainstorming with composer-arranger Michael Kamen, with whom he'd scored the first two installments of Hollywood's most successful crime-and-comedy adventure series. The release date of the movie was scarcely two months away—and creative pressure had built to the per-colation point.

"Eric kept picking out the bluesy chords of the basic 'Lethal Weapon' theme, re-examining the melody line," recalls Kamen, "and in this quick, continuous clicking motion, he'd simulta-

Eric Clapton and Sting

neously light one cigarette after another with his Zippo. *Click! Fump! Click!* It was a three-part ritual: the metal lighter case popping open, the flick of ignition, and the shutting of the case. Steve McLaughlin, a mad Scotsman who was co-producing the sessions, decided to sample the Zippo and reshuffle its sequence."

The demo segment combining Clapton's guitar, his cadent lighter, and Kamen's pliant electric piano was added to a compilation of approximately twenty musical cues for the basic screen music. Seeking input for a unifying song, Clapton and Kamen impulsively decided on April 6 to send the cues off to a pal of Eric's. "We wanted a 'buddy song,' " says Kamen, "since the unlikely friendship between Mel Gibson and Danny Glover has always been the basis of the three films' plots."

Soon the package arrived at a farmhouse in Wiltshire, England, where it was immediately opened by the laird—Sting. He'd known Clapton for several years, and their mutual fondness and musical respect had recently deepened in the aftermath of personal losses. Following the tragic death in March 1991 of his four-year-old son, Conor, Eric had found a measure of solace in *The Soul Cages* (A&M), Sting's album inspired by the passing of his parents. Sting was similarly touched by *Tears in Heaven* (Reprise), Clapton's eulogistic tribute to his child.

"There's a maturity in Eric's work that we need," says Sting, "and there's an integrity there that just gets better and better. I've always thought he was one of the greatest 'feel' players ever.

"I walked around the property, listening to the cassette of rough ideas, and I especially liked the percussive motif of the lighter sounds and the way the guitar chords moved. So I worked out a melody that would go over the theme's changes, and my pop training told me it also needed an old-fashioned bridge.

"I began to think about the film's characters and how there was a bond between them—but they'd probably be fairly reticent about expressing that bond because of the somewhat macho type of characters they were. Two days later, I came up with a key lyric phrase that said: When everything else fails, at least there's one person that will stand up for you, and 'it's probably me.'

"I carefully phrased the lyrics and wrote out melodies that I thought would be Eric Clapton–like," Sting continues, chuckling. "And Eric came back, saying, 'Well, could *you* sing it?' "

Kamen had arranged for all hands to converge on Manhattan's BMG Studios that weekend (April 11–13) in an all-out assault on the raw material, so Sting hopped a flight from London to New York, reaching the BMG facilities on Sixth Avenue at 8:30 A.M. to greet his session mates. The core rhythm infantry consisted of Sting on electric bass, Steve Gadd on drums, and Don Alias on additional percussion. Clapton improvised on both electric and acoustic axes. His pensive leads were subtly tinted by Kamen's keyboard interpolations, while David Sanborn wove a wistful sax break over Sting's aptly bashful vocal. The Greater New York Alumni Orchestra was enlisted to lend some string nuances.

Recording stretched into Sunday, its stressful logistics redoubled by the presence of *Lethal Weapon* director Richard Donner, who shot the proceedings for a companion music video.

"As a rule," says Sting, "songwriting is painful to me; it's a tabula rasa in which I have to deal with who I am and what I think. But in this case, the naturalness of both the song and the video came from us having to get on with the job!"

Kamen concurs. "Even though it was very high pressure, ideas for the track came together fast because friendship and coincidence constantly worked in its favor. Sting's lyrics set the tone: They express a classic sentiment, and the music's mood is evocative of a simpler time.

"It's funny about the effectiveness of the Zippo lighter, too," adds Kamen, "because—by another pure coincidence—throughout the movie the Mel Gibson character is trying to give up smoking."

Moreover, it was exactly sixty summers ago, during a muggy 1932 evening in the depths of the depression, that a former machinery salesman named George Blaisdell stepped out on the terrace of the Pennhill Country Club in Bradford, Pennsylvania, and encountered a tuxedoed friend firing up his cigarette with a bulky twenty-five-cent Austrian lighter. "You're all dressed up," Blaisdell chided his chum. "Why don't you get a lighter that looks decent?!" "Well," the friend demurred, "it works."

On impulse, Blaisdell obtained U.S. distribution rights for the Austrian lighter and redesigned its cumbersome brass casing as a slender brushed-chrome unit that fit in the palm of one's hand. Blaisdell adapted his product's trade name from the "zipper" term coined by B. F. Goodrich in 1923 for its rubber boots' "hookless fasteners." To this day, the patented (number 3,032,695) Zippo carries an unrestricted lifetime guarantee, the company fixing and returning any lighter free in order to satisfy its slogan: "It works."

The Zippo has since become the stuff of fable, the vest-pocket presence of its sturdy case saving the lives of GIs in World War II by deflecting bullets. Ever-dependable Zippos have kindled the rescue fires of mountain climbers and shipwreck survivors, received gratis repairs after being mangled by golf fairway gang mowers, and been recovered from the bellies of fish. And now, during one of the most refined and rhythmically adroit efforts on record by either Sting or Eric Clapton, a Zippo sets the tempo for "It's Probably Me."

"I'm really pleased," says Sting of the new single, which was released June 9 on CD and cassette by A&M Records, with the film soundtrack being issued by Reprise. "Everyone and everything helped, including the Zippo that runs through the whole track. And the song fulfilled exactly what was required of it. The rest is up to chance, but as far as I'm concerned: It works."

HARRISON LIVE: HERE COMES THE FUN

TO PARAPHRASE A CERTAIN CELEBRATED LIVERPOOL SONG-
writer: Had he come another day, it might not have been like this. But
George Harrison's return to concert touring after a seventeen-year hiatus
has proven well worth the wait, as demonstrated by the forthcoming
George Harrison/Live in Japan (Dark Horse/Warner Bros.), a true listening event and an indispensable document from one of rock's most
reluctant superstars.

His long absence from the road allows one to approach Harrison's considerable body of work from a fresh perspective. It has also given him the
freedom to rethink his repertoire.

"Even my older songs are new for me, because I've never performed
them!" says Harrison, relaxed and reminiscing at his Friar Park estate in
Henley-on-Thames outside London. "With the exception of my *Dark Horse*
tour in 1974 and a
couple of shows like
the [1971] Bangla-
desh benefit, where I
would always have
to do 'Here Comes
the Sun,' most of my
songs I've never done
before in concert."

Recorded with
Eric Clapton and his
seasoned road band

George Harrison and Eric Clapton

over the course of a dozen Osaka and Tokyo dates from December 1 to December 17, 1991, the two-CD, nineteen-track *Live in Japan* collection brims with material spanning Harrison's Beatles-era classics ("Taxman," "Piggies"), numerous early solo hits ("My Sweet Lord," "What Is Life," "Give Me Love [Give Me Peace on Earth]"), and later chart successes ("All Those Years Ago," "Got My Mind Set on You").

The decision to resume his performing career was a difficult one for Harrison. "The idea of touring was so distant to me," says George, "and if you don't ever do something, it becomes a mystery. I mean, how many years can you think about doing it?" Eventually, however, Clapton convinced him by "very generously" offering to back him up.

Thus committed, Harrison compiled thirty-odd songs as possibilities for Clapton's band, and cassette copies were presented to the support troops. Rehearsal time was booked at rural Bray Studios in Windsor, England, and the musicians gathered there on November 4, 1991.

"Before we ever went to rehearsal," says Harrison, "I decided 'I Want to Tell You' would make a good opener. And 'If I Needed Someone' was one that the Beatles actually did in Japan at the Budokan in 1966. And of course Eric played on 'Devil's Radio,' 'Cloud Nine,' and 'While My Guitar Gently Weeps,' so they were perfect ones to do live."

Yet the Harrison canon is not a quick study. "My songs aren't that simple to play," Harrison admits almost sheepishly. "They've got a lot of chords and a lot of little parts which are very integral. 'All Those Years Ago' has all the synth sounds, the slide parts, the counter-melodies, and the 'shoo-bop shoo-ba' in the backing. Unless you get them rehearsed, you're just fooling yourself," he says with a laugh, "and you might as well do 'Roll over Beethoven'!" (Ultimately, Harrison employed that very tune as an unbridled finale.)

Meantime, requests had been mounting from various associates for access to the closed-door practice sessions. "I didn't want people coming and going all the time," says Harrison, "so I said, 'OK, on the last day, November 24, we'll invite all our friends.' And so we had this audience of some TV actors, musician friends like Jim Capaldi and Steve Winwood, and family, *and* the osteopath's wife, and so forth. After that, nothing could be as difficult!"

Once the crack ensemble hit Japan, it swiftly eclipsed his fondest hopes. Consequently, *George Harrison/Live in Japan* is that rarest of contemporary artifacts—a bona fide concert transcription whose content often surpasses the originals. The vibrant ambient sound by engineer John Harris was achieved without any postproduction sweetening beyond an impeccable mix, and the track-to-track flow benefits from the tight pacing of the actual program. And, whether swapping arpeggios with George or taking flight alone, Clapton's fret-fraying filigrees represent a new peak in his guitar oratory.

The passion on display is scintillating rather than solemn, with Harrison slipping a George Bush swipe into "Taxman" and a "Hey Jude" refrain into "Isn't It a Pity," and peppering the rest of the proceedings with witty asides. "Although we didn't want to do the songs exactly like the record," says George, "we wanted to do them in the *spirit* of the records. Even 'Something': I think that's much better than the studio record, and it gives me goose bumps—chicken skin—every time the solos come and Eric follows me!"

As Harrison himself replays *Live in Japan* at home, the now-preserved experience continues to trigger a stream of memories.

"They all say that 'Something' was inspired by Patti [Boyd Harrison, later remarried to Clapton] but it wasn't really," George confides with an impish chortle. "She was my wife at the time, but when I wrote that I had Ray Charles in my head. I always imagined Ray singing it, and eventually he did record it. There was a period of time when that became a Muzak tune; you'd hear it in elevators, and I started feeling a bit embarrassed, but now I'm back into it and so happy to have written it.

"Sinatra was doing it for years," he notes slyly, "so now I always think of Frank Sinatra when I'm doing it. In fact, I've got that in the live version: 'Stick around *Jack*, it may show.' "

Another thing that shows is the renewed vigor of Harrison's vocals since he resolved to quit smoking last June.

"I'm singing much better than I ever sang on those old records," he states bluntly. "One of the reasons to do the tour was I needed to get out of the rut of being a smoker. I knew if I was ever to sing again live, I had to stop. I did breathing exercises to catch up."

While George ponders the logistics of a possible late-September "touring lark in the States, England, Europe, and eventually Australia" with Clapton's outfit, he's writing songs for his next studio effort, producing some tracks for veteran English rocker Joe ("It Only Took a Minute") Brown, and relishing the comprehensive reissue of his entire Apple/Capitol and Dark Horse/Warner Bros. solo catalogs; "Wonderwall

Music"—the inaugural (November 1, 1968) solo Beatle record—is due in stores Tuesday (30).

As for *George Harrison/Live in Japan,* it will be released July 14, with a five-track sampler shipping to radio this week. And will George be performing in your town? Well, as the man himself has put it: "Carve your number on my wall and maybe you will get a call from me."

"Although I'm older now than I've ever been," he quips, "I've got more energy and I feel much better than I've felt for twenty-five years. It's funny how life goes, isn't it?"

RAP ROOTS: THE STORY OF BRER SOUL

THE CRAFTSMAN EARNS HIS KEEP THROUGH HIS EXPERTISE, but the artist invents his job. Aside from being an acclaimed novelist, playwright, and film and TV director, Melvin Van Peebles is a recording artist who pioneered the metered musical monologues now referred to as rap. Before seminal Jamaican DJ King Stitt, dub artist U Roy, the Last Poets, and Gil Scott-Heron helped draw the map for the rappers who would follow, Melvin Van Peebles laid the foundation of the modern rap ethos on September 26, 1968, with the release of *Brer Soul* (A&M).

Recorded during a series of live sessions in a Manhattan studio just off Forty-second Street, *Brer Soul* consisted of nine narrative vignettes of the urban African-American experience, or "tunes from blackness," as Van Peebles came to call them.

"When I was growing up in the streets of Chicago, a brer was a bro, a homeboy," recalls Van Peebles. "The idea of doing a record employing the Brer Soul character arose back in 1967, when I returned to this country after living for several years in Holland

Melvin Van Peebles

and France. From abroad I knew the ferment of the civil rights movement, but I was struck when I got back here that almost none of the black
popular or protest music mirrored the black experience per se."

A graduate of Ohio Wesleyan and a former navigator-bombardier in
the Strategic Air Command, Van Peebles had been invited to France by
the Cinémathèque due to several distinguished film shorts he'd done in
San Francisco. While in France, Van Peebles published five well received
but modest-selling novels and toiled intermittently as a busker.

"Eventually, after qualifying for a French Director's card," recalls Van
Peebles, "I made my first feature film, a French-language movie called *La
Permission* [*Story of a Three Day Pass*], a love story about an American
soldier and a French girl. Because of that picture, I came back here as a
French delegate to the San Francisco Film Festival. My film became the
critic's choice at the festival, but they didn't know I was an American, let
alone black, and that created a furor, because there were no black direc-
tors in the States."

There were also no black rappers in America at the time—and it was
Van Peebles's rhythmic spoken-word muse, a guiding spirit pursued on
the boulevards and back alleys of Europe, that the rising young filmmaker suddenly itched to reinvoke.

"In my head I've always put music to every tale I've written, and vice
versa, and since nobody in this country was letting folks like me do what
they wanted anyhow, it was all the same creative battle. People'd say,
'How can you call these *songs?!*' And I'd just say my famous phrase, 'Kiss
my black ass!' and then press onward."

Realizing that most of the music industry establishment—from publishing to A&R—would have great difficulty grasping his notion of taping
a gritty spoken-language session backed by a live band, Van Peebles
decided to approach A&M Records, which at the time had few black
artists on its roster.

"I went to A&M because I was smart," says Van Peebles, grinning
sagely. "Any of the other companies I would have gone to would have
assumed, since they had a number of black artists, that they were *nig-
gerologists*. But A&M knew something that's invaluable with white
people; they knew what they *didn't* know! Jerry Moss was the guy I dealt
with, and he was very visionary, very laid back. He and [Herb] Alpert let
me do what I wanted to do."

Which was to "meticulously" rehearse his melodic soliloquies with a
funky, jazz-edged Manhattan combo. Van Peebles's songs had titles like

"You Can Get Up Before Noon Without Being a Square," "Tenth and Greenwich (Women's House of Detention)," "Catch That on the Corner," and "Lilly Done the Zampoughi Everytime I Pulled Her Coattail."

"We got together in a downtown hall to woodshed," says Van Peebles. "And I said, 'I don't want you to play the music, I want you to play the *words!*' "

And what words they were, delivered with quaking fury and dramatic bounce. Each piece lent esprit and episodic form to an array of inner-city witnesses. A badly rattled Romeo calls to his Juliet from the sidewalk below her jail-cell window ("Make some kind of sign so I know it's you, 'cause you so far away"); and a lover eulogizes the woman he killed in a jealous rage ("Towering above me like some African Queen, 'cept for the flypaper in the ceiling").

"In each song, I wanted to describe a part of life rarely seen," says Van Peebles, so he invested each persona with a deep-background dignity that made it impossible to take the predicaments lightly. " 'Lilly' was taken from a girl I knew who was always *so* quiet, 'til one day we wind up in the Gramercy Hotel doing the funky monkey, and she leaps up in the middle of the bed and starts dancing! 'Tenth and Greenwich' came from my experiences as a broke young guy sleeping on a park bench across from the Women's House of Detention."

Van Peebles hasn't been broke for quite a spell, having done handsomely in the stock market. And his many acclaimed Broadway plays (*Ain't Supposed to Die a Natural Death, Don't Play Us Cheap*), films (*Watermelon Man, Sweet Sweetback's Baadasssss Song*), television productions (*Sophisticated Gents* and the Emmy-winning CBS anticensorship special *The Day They Came to Arrest the Book*) have left him comfortably fulfilled. He also plans the reissue of most of his eight inimitable albums.

The slim, sinewy Van Peebles remains the same outspoken, effervescent wag he was back in 1967, bursting with ideas and playful self-deprecation. And now with his thirteenth novel just completed (*Dirty Pictures*), Van Peebles is again turning his attention to music. A preview of new tracks recently co-produced with William "Spaceman" Patterson—among them the splenetic "No Justice, No Peace (The White Man Ain't No Fool)," the tender "Blinded by Your Stuff," and richly pulsative rearrangements of "Lilly Done the Zampoughi" and "My Love Belongs to You"—reveal him to be a wily innovator just a step ahead of Arrested Development.

"My latest stuff is what you would probably call post–hip-hop or alternative rap," Van Peebles allows. "Now that people have gotten into the habit of listening closely to cute things like Kris Kross or the hard edges of an Ice-T, I figure I can make it as simple or complex as I please. But modern rap's subject matter has gotten too formalized, and I mean to cover the whole spectrum of life—not just nookie and confrontational politics. I'm still a storyteller in the ancient tradition, and anytime somebody says I can't try something, I just smile and say, 'Kiss my—' Well," he smirks, "I think you know what I tell 'em."

ELMORE JAMES: THE
SLIDE IS CRYING

ELMORE JAMES'S BLUES WERE THE OUTBURSTS OF A TORTURED soul making the best of life's big surprises. Nearly thirty years since his death in 1963, his music remains the adroit soundtrack to acute reversals and sudden victimizations.

Hearing James's panicky renditions of "One Way Out" and "Baby Please Set a Date," it's easy to picture the anguish of a traveler at the cross-roads of a hopeless quest, or the vacuum of a love nest ruined by the rattle of a husband's key in the lock. And nobody could depict *and* inhabit such tableaux with the raw intensity of James, his startled vocals and full-octave slide guitar fused in a passion fierce enough to strip the paint off Heaven's gate.

As evidence, Capricorn Records is planning to release on August 11 *Elmore James: King of the Slide Guitar—The Fire/Fury/Enjoy Recordings*, a fifty-song boxed anthology of sides cut in Chicago, New York, and New Orleans for Bobby Robinson's Fire, Fury, and Enjoy labels from 1959 onward. These Robinson-produced

Elmore James

sessions have a seasoned heat absent in James's earlier Meteor Records work, and also contain his biggest R&B chart successes of the sixties: "The Sky Is Crying" (later covered by Stevie Ray Vaughan) and "It Hurts Me Too."

If Elmore James couldn't even sing a lullaby without screaming, he might have had just cause. Born out of wedlock on January 27, 1918, in Richland, Mississippi, young Elmore seized on the blues line as the outlet of last resort. He escaped the suffocating Jim Crow drudgery of the Delta farming communities by shadowing the circuit of Robert Johnson and the second Sonny Boy Williamson (aka Alec "Rice" Miller), whom he met in 1937. Within months, James was playing alongside Johnson and Williamson in local haunts like the Harlem Tavern.

"Robert Johnson influenced him a lot," says Robinson. "And Elmore told me he used to go for Saturday night 'frolics' in rural Mississippi, where the girls *swooned* over Robert Johnson!"

James has been justly praised as a popularizer of the Robert Johnson legacy, since his recording debut was a 1951 rehearsal take of "Dust My Broom"—a familiar part of Johnson's repertoire—that was issued by the tiny Trumpet label. Johnson's version had not featured slide guitar, however, and Johnson himself may not have been the author of "I Believe I'll Dust My Broom," since versions of that song had been recorded previous to Johnson's 1936 Texas session by such artists as James "Kokomo" Arnold (under the title "Sagefield Woman Blues") and by Carl Rafferty (as "Mr. Carl's Blues").

Moreover, Elmore James's hard-driving slide tonality and radiant bottleneck force on his own classic songs ("Look on Yonder Wall," "Shake Your Money Maker," "Talk to Me Baby," "It Hurts Me Too," "The Sky Is Crying") were far too distinctive to be seen just as Johnson-derived. Those whose playing was shaped by James's piercing inflections include fellow Mississippians B. B. King and Jimmy Reed, as well as electric blues modernists Freddie King, Jimi Hendrix, Johnny Winter, and Capricorn Records' own Duane Allman.

Little "Elmo's" first instrument had been a "one-strand," a wire taken from the binding of a broom that he would either lay across the opening of a lard can or nail to the wall of a shack and stretch until taut. Sliding a bottle or can along its length would alter the pitch when plucked and, in the case of the "wall strand," the entire house would serve as a resonator.

This basic form of open tuning led to James's habit of favoring an open E setting, and by the time James got his first conventional guitar, his slide attack had grown almost brutal. With the subsequent boost from electric amplification, his ricocheting riffs raised a commotion in Delta juke joints, on a decade's worth of Deep South radio broadcasts, and, eventually, in the hippest blues dives (the Tuxedo Lounge, Sylvio's, Tay May Club) on the south side of postwar Chicago.

Slim and handsome, James would take the stages attired in a smart worsted suit, crisp white shirt, and charcoal tie. The spotlight bouncing off the thick, clear lenses of his trademark hornrim glasses only enhanced his mystique, and women found the boyish James an alluring figure. Although he was said to have been married three times, the personal life of this committed loner was one whose finer emotions were writ mostly in the lower case, since the blues man tended to view romantic love as little more than betrayal minus the bus fare home.

Although taciturn around strangers, James sang in a convulsive snarl that skirted the edges of hysteria. "He was laid back when not performing," says Robinson, "but he had a sly humor—practical jokes—especially after he'd had a couple of drinks of House of Lords, his brand of scotch."

The veteran songwriter–label chief still laughs when recounting a mischievous public "touch" James put on him. "He was playing in Chicago at this club one night," says Robinson, "and it was a radio broadcast. As I came through the door, he stopped—this was being broadcast over the radio—and said, 'Hold everything! My boss just walked in!' Then he said, 'You don't believe this is my boss?' Everybody was saying, 'Naaah!' And he said, 'Boss, *give me fifty dollars.*'"

Robinson's Fire and Fury labels boasted number-one R&B hits (Wilbert Harrison's "Kansas City" and Buster Brown's "Fannie Mae") in 1959, the year Robinson chanced to encounter James in a small Chicago cocktail lounge. He signed James on the spot and then partied with him and his band at James's rooming house all through the next rain-drenched day.

"I said, 'Gee, it sure is raining out!'" recalls Robinson. "Elmore said, 'Yeah, looks like the sky is crying.' It kind of hit me, and I said, 'Just strike up a lonesome, rainy-day chord,' and I started to write." Recorded that same evening in a local demo studio, "The Sky Is Crying" was a comeback record for James, reaching number fifteen in 1960 on *Billboard*'s R&B chart.

Included between assorted tracks on *Elmore James: King of the Slide Guitar* are snatches of studio gab and backwoods tall talk from James about the Mississippi he left behind. Like the sob of the one-strand on which Elmore James found his calling, there is a timeless immediacy to each exchange.

"Elmore was in Chicago when he died," recalls Robinson. "He was working in a nightclub, and the band had come around to pick him up. Elmore was inside getting dressed, and the guys were saying, 'Come on, Elmore, we're running late!'

"He said, 'OK, I'll be right there,' and he sat on the side of the bed. He reached down to pull up his socks, had his third and fatal heart attack, and never stopped falling."

ROGER WATERS'S
DEATH AND REBIRTH

IT IS THE POET'S RESPONSIBILITY TO FORESEE THE FUTURE, and it is his neighbor's duty to prevent the worst of it from taking place. With *Amused to Death*, surely one of the most provocative and musically dazzling records imaginable, Roger Waters has fulfilled his part of the bargain.

It was three years before the Gulf War that Waters, the British founder and former chief composer of Pink Floyd, began work on *Amused to Death*, his third solo album, by writing "Perfect Sense," a two-part song suite envisioning a world in which live television transmissions of war and upheaval become the principal form of mass entertainment. According to the album's thesis, since there is nothing in the history of civilization that generates more profit for the power elite than war, its creators see the enterprise as a can't-miss proposition.

"The idea for the album," says Waters, "was a strangely prophetic one. I was working within the general metaphor of a gorilla watching television, the ape being a symbol for anyone who's been sitting with his mouth open in front of network and cable news for the last ten years. The record explores the

Roger Waters

idea of television as medicine: It's either healing us or killing us. The truth is it's doing *both*, healing us as a target audience but killing off our respective cultures."

If "Perfect Sense" expresses the corporate philosophy for what Waters calls "conflict programming," then it is the thundering trio of tracks that compose "What God Wants (Parts I–III)" that spells out the rationalization for this odious stroke of global hucksterism.

"What sparked the writing of 'What God Wants' was the accumulation of all the 'God-is-on-our-side' claptrap from Desert Storm," says Waters. "It just seems so crass that we're reaching the end of a millennium and yet, even with our incredible ability to exchange information between cultures, we still cling to our narrow dogmas. Thanks to television, we watched a murky missiles-and-fireworks display from the roof of a Baghdad hotel, and learned no more than we could see with our own eyes—which was deliberate. Now Bush is shopping the election-year idea of invading Iraq again—and it's all the same cheap, dishonest game show."

From the start, Waters realized that, in order for *Amused to Death* to be frightening, it had to be woven around rock'n'roll that was convincing. Listeners familiar with Waters's distinctive but uneven earlier solo offerings (*The Pros and Cons of Hitchhiking*, 1984; *Radio K.A.O.S*, 1987) will find the new album to be much closer in mood and execution to Pink Floyd's *The Dark Side of the Moon* (1973) and *The Wall* (1979), for which Waters was the guiding creative force. However, it must be stated that, from the near-tactile quality of its musical fiber to the epic scope of its theme, *Amused to Death* is a masterful rock parable that ranks with or surpasses Floyd's finest work. (Particularly since the post-Waters Floyd is a musically vapid marketing ploy; it's a pity that patrons can't whistle the packaging designs.)

Give this record your full concentration for one listening and be riveted to the point of palpable distress. Play it just once more and you will be hooked in perpetuity, its brilliant design etched in your brainpan, each lavish mise-en-scène invading your dreams. Waters's imploring vocals have never been more polymorphic, changing in shape and coloration as they rise from a hiss to a clarion call, and they traverse a narrative path that's darkly iridescent with spooky detail. No meadow footfall, flutter of a fax machine, or throttled surge in the cockpit of an F-1 bomber is overlooked in the album's lustrous auditory spectrum. Yet the foreboding noises are so nimbly merged with Patrick Leonard's sighing keyboards, the frightful beauty of Jeff Beck's lead guitar, and the chordal ring of Andy

Fairweather Low's rhythm passages that they become a single vivid scheme. It's a grim feast of sound, enthralling and unforgettable.

But the accomplishment doesn't stop there, because the human dimension of its story line is also fully explored. We get skin-close to a serenely detached young F-1 ace from Cleveland whose on-camera high-altitude bombing runs make him a mammoth video star. And, within the pitiless logic of "conflict programming," the same fate befalls a philosophy student slain in Tiananmen Square.

"In the more than five years it took to make this record, my songwriting has become more passive, more of a conduit, with less ego," says Waters. "And it now allows me to attach more directly to the individual experiences I'm writing about, like that of the imaginary girl in Tiananmen Square. It allows me to enter her mind, to give her an engineer for a father and a part-time job as a pastry chef, and it allows me to weep for her. Maybe," he adds, "I've succeeded in the last five to ten years in tearing down more of my own wall."

Aspects of *Amused to Death* were molded by the onrush of events that paralleled its assembly. Waters feels that a project he interrupted the recording to undertake likewise influenced his personal transformation—the massive charity concert, "The Wall—Berlin 1990," which he staged in the former no man's land on Potzdamer Platz as a benefit for the Memorial Fund for Disaster Relief. The spectacular show and live album raised $10 million for the care of international victims of disasters, with the concert's companion home video continuing to gather funds through sales of a half-million pieces in the United States alone.

Waters has called the World War II death of his own soldier-father "a wrenching waste." On *Amused to Death,* he openly mourns the dad he never knew in the song "Three Wishes," intoning at its dramatic crest: "I wish somebody'd help me write this song/I wish when I was young/My old man had not been gone."

Waters notes that the only enduring rogues in war television as delineated on *Amused to Death* happen to be the peacemakers—because they threaten the programming schedule. And the biggest villains on conflict TV are the victims who dare call for forgiveness and reconciliation. Nobody likes a killjoy, and hatred as hedonism—as described in the title song of *Amused to Death*—is destined to become "the greatest show on earth."

If there have been intervals of late when this forecast seems as if it may already be unfolding, then *Amused to Death,* due for release from Columbia September 1, may not reach us an instant too soon. "At the start of my record," says Waters, "an actual World War I survivor speaks about a fallen comrade he couldn't carry to safety. There's something in me that says the sentiments of that survivor are an experience common to all humanity. It's the feeling of 'Is there something more *I* could have done?' In my own life, I'd like to learn the answer to that question if I can."

PJ HARVEY: A LOVER'S MUSICAL MUSING

THE PURPOSE OF THIS COLUMN IS TO SHARE THE EXCITEMENT
of discovery. There is never any shortage of projects in the music
industry pipeline, but the focus here is on pivotal undertakings by established players, significant endeavors by emerging artists, work by unher-
alded musicians that merits closer scrutiny, or the phenomenon of
performers suddenly discovering the depth of their own potential. And
sometimes the column is simultaneously about all of these things, as in
the case of England's PJ Harvey, a band about to play its first North American dates August 11–18 after recently conquering the British independent charts with *Dry* (Indigo/Island).

The trio takes its name from singer-songwriter Polly Jean Harvey,
whose marvelously
undefinable 1991
"Dress" single on
the Too Pure label
was one of the
most impressive
U.K. indie debuts
of that year. Me-
lodic, clangorous,
meditative, and as
clinging on the
dance floor as the
garment it de-
scribed, the song

PJ Harvey

explored the practical and sensual considerations—as well as the emotional absurdities—of a young woman who might "dress to please." If the premise sounds flimsy, the execution was anything but, since Harvey has a gift for articulating the nagging insights that lend meaning and difficulty to the politics of self-esteem. As on "Sheela-Na-Gig," PJ Harvey's ingenious second single issued last February, the composer probes the principle that morality, sexuality, desire, and attachment remain secret truths, no matter how public or "exhibitionist" any facet might seem to be.

Both of the aforementioned tracks are collected on *Dry*, which has just been released in the States, and the conflicts inherent in the songs' cerebral issues and carnal urges are boldly sketched by Polly's reverberate guitar, Stephen Vaughan's libidinous bass, and the temperamental percussion of Robert Ellis. The album's conceptual axis, however, is "Oh My Lover," in which a jilted lover wrestles with arousal and rejection. The track can be perceived as heartrendingly tender or richly ironic, yet its deeply erotic spell prevails. This disquieting ambiguity is precisely the point of Harvey's songwriting, which is why she customarily declines to discuss it. She speaks out on the subject only when she sees her lyric style described (in the presumptuous praise of one British critic) as "cynical."

"No! It isn't, it *isn't*," states Harvey emphatically, as she talks in her parents' home in the tiny Dorset village of Yeovil—a temporary refuge while she composes the sequel to *Dry*.

"Honesty," she adds, "was the most important thing around the time of *Dry*: to play in an honest way *and* to record it as honestly as possible, in an approach that wasn't using a lot of effects. It's actually a selfish thing; it's for myself, and the fact that others are enjoying it as well pleases me."

As for the stark sensualism she bares in *Dry*'s content and presentation, the twenty-two-year-old former art student simply says, "This nakedness, it's the music's."

As she confides with surprising shyness, "The reason I started to do music instead of what I was doing before, which was sculpture, was because I feel that music is a better, more *physical* way to reach people. Pieces of artwork can make you think, but they don't grab you by your stomach, shake you around for three minutes, and then leave you feeling exhausted and drained."

Yet Harvey wants it both ways, jolting the passions into a fresh state of alertness and the intellect into a freer mode of intake; and she uses the work of a favorite author (William Burroughs's *Nova Express*) and visual artist (Andres Serrano's *Piss Christ*) to convey the kind of impact she aims to attain: "The stream of consciousness, where it just goes straight into your head and bypasses any process of seeing or judgment, and there are no barriers."

Raised in Yeovil by supportive "hippie-generation" parents who were local concert promoters, Harvey grew up feeling there were no immediate obstacles to her fulfillment. "Except," she chuckles, "I wanted to be a boy until I was about twelve, because Yeovil is quite a quiet village and there weren't any other girls."

Harvey took up the saxophone at ten, playing Glenn Miller standards in the school band ("I loved it"), then hurrying home to cull R&B riffs and Captain Beefheart honks from her parents' record collection. At eighteen, she switched from horn to acoustic Yamaha guitar and began appearing solo in pubs. Accepting an invitation to join the group Automatic Dlamini, she toured Europe for two years.

The travel awakened her to the world beyond Yeovil ("I'd never been to clubs") and to rock beyond the Rolling Stones ("the Pixies, Tom Waits, Nick Cave"). She formed PJ Harvey in July 1991, and the subsequent British success of *Dry* has acquainted Polly with the things she wants ("to develop more as a writer on the next two albums") and doesn't ("I lived in London for six months but I couldn't stand it. I had to come back home; I need to live far from this agitation, and not to belong to the music business.").

Her most recent ponderings of intellect vs. intimate desire have occurred via the pages of French author Roland Barthes's 1977 book *A Lover's Discourse*. Barthes was a literary scholar whose writings on semiology (the study of the signs and symbols underlying culture) centered in this case on the linguistics of love. In a manner echoed by Harvey's songwriting, Barthes explores the inner meaning of a lover's idioms and declamations. As the author relates, the goal is an unsentimental "portrait" of "someone speaking within himself, *amorously*, confronting the other (the love object), who does not speak."

As Harvey sees it, the book examines "each different aspect of being in love and"—she laughs—"the suffering that goes with it. I'm quite interested in that." And if one were to examine, along Barthes's analytical lines, a song like Harvey's "Oh My Lover," the visceral, moaning sigh ("Ohhh . . .") that begins the track would be deemed the most direct and truthful message, with the meaning of all that follows (". . . my lover, don't you know it's all right . . .") being far less certain.

The solitary representations of love giving and love taking, a stream of physical and mental sensations that defy resolution yet confirm humanity—this is the grist for the searching, momentous music of Polly Jean Harvey and band. In their first shows in venues from L.A.'s Whisky A Go-Go to Manhattan's CBGB, expect something honest, without barriers or effects, and still in the early stages of self-discovery. Yet capable of leaving the stunned listener feeling exhausted and drained.

And how, in the privacy of her head, does Polly hear the new album that PJ Harvey will commence recording this October? "As a natural move forward, taking the things that were used in *Dry* and pushing the extremities of the dynamics, the sounds, a little bit further." Out spills her secret laugh. "Also, the lyrics, I think, are a *lot* more extreme."

EROS AND ENCHANTMENT: GABRIEL'S *US*

EROS IS THE GOD OF LOVE IN ALL ITS MANIFESTATIONS, whether love ascendant or love in decline. According to Greek mythology, Eros emerged from Chaos yet personified harmony. According to Plato, Eros was "a great *daimon,*" meaning a dispenser of fate. And according to Peter Gabriel, it is the fable of Eros that underlies his forthcoming album *US* (Geffen), as well as the record's acerbic first single, "Digging in the Dirt."

US, Gabriel explains, "is primarily about relationships. Most of it is the 'us' of two people, but there are also references to the 'us' of a larger group, meaning all that isn't 'them.' "

For Gabriel, the romantic "us" in his own life would shift over the last decade from his wife of nearly twenty years, the former Jill Moore, to actress Rosanna Arquette, with both attachments ultimately culminating in painful partings.

"Coming off a divorce and the breakup of another relationship, I was trying to sort myself out in various areas," says Gabriel. "I've done about five years of group therapy, so I'm trying to peel the layers of the onion a bit.

Peter Gabriel

So I did have this feeling like I was 'digging in the dirt,' trying to expose the devils down there to the daylight.

"I think part of that process is accepting what is down there and trying to come to terms with it. Plus, I was also looking outside of myself and then recognizing bits of myself in what I was seeing. The record is a journey. Its theme became self-evident over the eighteen months I made it; I feel the music flows and works as a whole piece."

Notwithstanding Gabriel's characteristic candor, the personal emotional turmoil that catalyzed *US* ultimately gave rise to a more universal dramatic fable about emotional development.

Most of us grow up with exposure to fairy tales, particularly those in which struggle, hardship, and trust result in some degree of character building. One of the oldest such tales in the Western tradition is the myth of the handsome young god Eros and his mortal lover, Psyche. Forbidden to woo the comely Psyche (the Greek word for soul), whom envious gods have condemned to death, Eros rescues and hides her, visiting her to make love only after nightfall. When she breaks the taboo of illuminating her lover's face because her scheming sisters convince her she's sleeping with a hideous monster, Eros must leave her. After a literally hellish quest to regain him, the gods reward Psyche's devotion with immortality, and her marriage to Eros produces a child: Pleasure.

This ancient allegory was the forerunner of the Grimm Brothers' tale of "The Frog Prince" as well as "Kiss That Frog," the pivotal track on Gabriel's *US*, wherein a princess must have faith in the affections of a bewitched amphibian in order to restore him to human form. Gabriel says he concocted his droll rock bestiary after "reading this book by [child psychologist] Bruno Bettelheim called *The Uses of Enchantment*, in which he talked about different fairy stories and what they might've been used for from a psychological perspective."

As Bettelheim writes, "It is difficult to imagine a better way to convey to the child that he need not be afraid of the (to him) repugnant aspects of sex. The story of the frog—how it behaves, what occurs to the princess in relation to it, and what finally happens to both frog and girl—confirms the appropriateness of disgust when one is not ready for sex, and prepares for its desirability when the time is ripe."

The learning curve of fairy tales as celebrated in the witty/wise "Kiss That Frog" permits the child in all of us to attain a vivid prior comprehension of life's most complex maturational challenges.

"In terms of sex education, the fear and horror that actually go with young people's first sexual experiences aren't always addressed," says Gabriel. "And Bettelheim was arguing that the legend of the princess and the frog was very good, because what sat in the psyche after the story was that something that might at first seem repulsive can turn out to be very pleasant."

The concept of "creation as therapy," to use Gabriel's own phrase, has been the crux of his musical drive. Since his post-Genesis debut as a solo performer in 1977 with the first of four discrete eponymous *Peter Gabriel* albums, Peter has examined such solitary dilemmas as the loss of childhood innocence ("Solsbury Hill," 1977) and the animal rages that adult jealousy can trigger ("Shock the Monkey," 1982). By 1986's exuberant *So* album, he knew that the swirling tempo tapestries of his sound had grown as cathartic as they were compelling: "What I'm interested in doing in my music is communicating relief from psychic pain."

At the same time, Gabriel has continued to investigate the spiritual/ therapeutic role that music plays in other cultures, with the annual World of Music, Arts and Dance (WOMAD) festival he instituted in 1982 leading directly to the pantheistic psalms of his 1989 *Passion* album. "And I was trying," Gabriel assures, "to integrate what I learned from *Passion* into the songwriting on the new album—and I feel it's worked pretty well."

Which brings us to *US*, whose unsparing personal inquiry and post–world beat arranging feats find Gabriel at an instinctive new plateau. It would have been easy for Gabriel to distance himself from the vulnerability of the arresting "Loved to Be Loved," as well as the earthy rage of "Digging in the Dirt." But the artist in him recognizes that candid attempts at communion with one's audience often transcend even a determined effort at autobiography. As shown by the elemental sense of renewal in "Secret World"—maybe the most discerning song Peter Gabriel has ever wrought—the more a composer strives to share the essense of his insights, the more completely his presence will disappear into his work: "I stood in this unsheltered place/'Til I could see the face behind the face/ . . . In all the places we were hiding love/What was it we were thinking of?"

At a time when sexuality is generally discussed in terms of personal freedom, political liberation, or casual denigration, there is seldom adequate sensitivity paid to the painful fears and trials that are the necessary stages of any individual's real emotional metamorphosis. Like fairy tales, song can bring order out of inner chaos, by revealing the hidden meanings of life's lessons at a pace the listener is able to accept. Subtle and stunning, Peter Gabriel's *US* is itself a useful form of enchantment, sparking a new appreciation of the potential of Eros and the pitfalls of Psyche.

"To plug directly into emotions is a goal common to rituals all over the world," says Gabriel. "When I get most satisfied with music, it takes me to another place emotionally and *then* tickles my brain. But there's also a tradition in countries under heavy censorship where the arts can—not preach, but rather—*reflect* ideas that people feel strongly about that are considered off-limits."

"It was such a long, hard process," says Gabriel of his new album (due in stores September 22) and the profound rejuvenation it chronicles, "but getting to the end of it does feel *good.*"

LUSH LIFE: THE EVOLUTION OF A SOUND

THERE IS A BEAUTIFUL BUZZ SURROUNDING LUSH. IT BEGAN as a purring peal on the 1989 *Etheriel/Second Sight* demos that got them signed with the British 4AD label, surged to the vociferous knell of "Sweetness and Light" from their 1990 *Gala* release (4AD/Reprise), and then swelled into the august undulations of "Nothing Natural" from the second album, *Spooky,* issued in January 1992.

But the resounding clincher for the band's gorgeous megadrone arrived this summer as Lush landed the opening slot on the Lollapalooza '92 tour—a gig that allowed them to unleash the fortissimo hum of *Spooky*'s billowy "Superblast!" on unsuspecting throngs of Pearl Jam and Red Hot Chili Peppers fans. Consequently, as the "Lolla Two" alternative cavalcade edges toward its concluding September dates, Lush's more exuberantly sculpted rumble is now being supplemented by mounting murmurs of audience approval.

"It's surprisingly good, the response,"

Lush

laughs deceptively undemure Lush lead singer Miki Berenyi, an angelic vocalist whose brusque North London speaking accent is never more than a beat away from comic self-detraction. "Whatever stereotyped image you have of this sort of rock crowd—you know, 'Get your tits out!'—it hasn't been like that at all. Everyone from the record company to the booking agency painted the blackest picture possible, saying, 'You realize what you're letting yourself in for as the opening act: The place will be empty when you come on; your band has the only two women on the bill; no one will know who the hell you are; it could be really UGLY.' So anything would have been a bonus! We expected hell, and it's turned into . . . *purgatory.*"

Admittedly, everything about the group *is* at variance with the pumping bluster and perspiration-drenched pectorals of the otherwise all-male Lollapalooza lineup. Lush is led by two slim and rather striking twenty-five-year-old women: ruby-haired lead guitarist Berenyi, who carries her big Gibson electric twelve-string with an elegant swagger, and her sable-tressed songwriting partner, crowd-shy rhythm guitarist–harmony singer Emma Anderson. Drummer Chris Acland and new bassist Philip King are the photogenic, forceful rhythm section. And, while there is no posturing in the show, no attitude beyond general bonhomie and a great deal of stentorian swing, Lush's ingenuous glow has the pith and the pluck of true style.

As the story is told, Lush was formed in a chilly dorm at North London Polytechnic in 1987 by four English Literature majors (Berenyi, Acland, since-departed bassist Steve Rippon, and Meriel Barham, now with fellow 4AD artists Pale Saints). From the start, Lush was a club and indie favorite; the various EPs collected on *Gala* were produced by the likes of John Fryer of This Mortal Coil fame, Tim Friese-Green of Talk Talk, and most notably Robin Guthrie of the Cocteau Twins. Guthrie took the helm in the studio for the entire *Spooky* record, but Berenyi, who grew up singing Abba hits in her bedroom, dismisses any direct artistic correlation between Lush's boiling ballads and the Twins' spangled dirges.

"If you were a kid in England, Abba was number one constantly," says Berenyi. "And *rock* used to be a dirtier word in England than pop, where there has always been a pop underground. New Order's *Everything's Gone Green* is probably the first good record I ever bought, and I respect the ascent of the Smiths and the Cocteau Twins, whose music remained most important to them. We were a bit reticent working with Robin, thinking we'd be looked on as protégées of the Cocteau Twins, but his ideas for our songs were exactly like ours—and they're not at all 'rock' ideas."

Lush's dense, turbulent approach is too dissonant to be deemed power pop, too pretty to be an offshoot of thrash, and too grittily gossamer onstage to fall anyplace in between. Home viewers fortunate enough to have caught director Brett Turnbull's apparitional new performance video of "Superblast!" could be forgiven for supposing they were seeing the post–B-52's future of party beat. Except that Lush's appeal is more sirenlike than celebratory, with wounded, poignant incantations submerged in a portentous squall of guitar fury.

"We didn't know what our sound was when we started," insists Berenyi, the daughter of a Hungarian sportswriter and his Japanese actress wife. "It was very experimental, and it came from negative inspiration. Emma and I went to school together in Willesden Green, and we used to go see all these bands to the point where we'd think, 'They're all so fuckin' awful, even we could do that!' [Which they did, starting a combo called the Bugg.] A lot of people go, 'Oh, your harmonies, you must be trained in music.' But it was complete guesswork!

"The band does *not* get together to write a song," she cautions. "Basically, me or Emma just sit home with a Portastudio—we've graduated to Tascam eight-tracks and Roland drum machines—and record everything: the bass line, melody, backing vocal. And then everyone gets their little piece to play. We're not a jamming band; it's the drawback of not being very good musicians. So all the songs are written in the way that pop songs are written, with no real room for ad libs. But live, we really try to bring some energy to it."

The group is admired in its native England for a litany of genial self-reproofs ("Me and Emma couldn't sing for toffee," Miki is fond of stating, "so we *had* to turn the guitars up a bit!") that eclipse even the most scathing cracks from the British music press. There are few putdowns Albion's critics can level that haven't been expressed first (and more humorously) by Lush itself. But the group's disdain for rock sham belies a real desire to protect and sustain the genuine accomplishments of its sound.

For example, Berenyi resists any attempt to discuss the inception of Emma's forlorn, phantasmal "Nothing Natural" single ("Before I met you I was blind/Pills and liquid filled my mind"), saying, "I can't really elaborate because Emma will cut my head off." But when asked how she personally feels when she plays and sings it, Miki drops her caginess and gives an assessment as direct and kindly as the music itself: "Although it's about Emma not being very happy, I think it is a very romantic song. Those lyrics are *moving*."

As with the rest of Lush's resonating repertoire, "Nothing Natural," "Etheriel," "Sweetness and Light," and "Superblast!" each contains earnest sentiments that battle to escape the obstructive tumult of the modern maw.

Berenyi's private opinions demonstrate that to embrace the frailty embedded in the band's music is to be seduced into joining the fray. Lush makes you care whether genuine feeling is slowly being filtered out of the lively arts.

"Most of the stuff is accidental, a layering process, in which you find different bits that you didn't notice before," says Berenyi. "If it takes people by surprise, well," she chuckles, "it takes *us* by surprise. But we really *mean* it."

SINÉAD: THE *GIRL* IN THE WOMAN

SINÉAD O'CONNOR'S SECRET LOVE IS NO SECRET ANYMORE. "As a child," she discloses, "I adored film musicals, and it was the songs from them that made me want to be a singer. I'd go into my room and close the door and sing something like 'Secret Love' from Doris Day's movie of *Calamity Jane.* These things seemed like such excellent vehicles for sensitivity when I was younger because, like the lines of a great play, they allowed you to be yourself and speak in a universal way while also interpreting your own place in the world."

O'Connor offers these admissions and insights in reference to the impending September 22 release of *Am I Not Your Girl?* (Ensign/Chrysalis), an album containing eleven penetrating renditions of classic stage and screen tunes from the midcentury heyday of popular songwriting. "These songs show that my inner self is just the same as *your* inner self—that's what music is supposed to do. Songs are supposed to be the expression of the shared feelings of the human race."

If the manner of one's life is the banner of one's heart, then

Sinéad O'Connor

song may indeed be its natural herald, since it can convey both public ideals and latent desires in the same vulnerable breath. The fidelity of Sinéad O'Connor's music to her own experience has always been apparent, with the vehemence of both firmly in sync on her debut record, *The Lion and the Cobra* (1987), as well as its sequel, *I Do Not Want What I Haven't Got* (1990).

"The job of actors and poets and dancers and musicians is to cultivate love," says O'Connor, and on *Am I Not Your Girl?* her selection of pop perennials by composers like Rodgers and Hart ("Bewitched, Bothered and Bewildered") and Norman Gimble and Antonio Carlos Jobim ("How Insensitive") reveals a person who makes no apologies for honest sentiment. However, *Am I Not Your Girl?* excels where other artists' portfolios of period standards have stalled because of O'Connor's personal investment in each vocal turn. Her emotionally incisive reinterpretations of fare as familiar as "Love Letters" or Marilyn Monroe's sultry "I Want to Be Loved by You" yield a pathos the originals lacked.

"Ten women could have redone that Marilyn Monroe song ten different ways," says O'Connor. "It was not my intention to update or even reflect her style with the song. My mind was more on the skills of the original lyricists. Amazingly, many of these songs were written by men, and the tenderness and understanding of women in them staggers me. They allow you to be yourself and show compassion, which isn't easy these days. When you don't see yourself reflected in other people, there's not a lot to hold on to."

The empathies O'Connor hopes to engender through these engrossing tracks are exemplified by the surreal video for the album's first single, "Success Has Made a Failure of Our Home." The singer is depicted on a sleekly nightmarish dais, delivering her clement declaration as if responding to some sinister state inquisition. Her simple lament is soon transmuted into an indictment of the social atrocities of a wayward age, while actual Amnesty International slides of international torture victims are flashed upon the walls behind her.

"These songs," O'Connor asserts, "are the way pop music was before the sudden, horrible 'Machine Age' of music, which hopefully we'll all be able to kill soon. You don't write a love song by saying, 'Oooh baby, I want to sex you up.' That's just condom music. Love and romance are lost arts."

Sinéad O'Connor was born in Glenageary, Ireland, in 1966, one of five children whose suburban Dublin upbringing allowed only remote access to the great Broadway and Hollywood musicals. "On TV in Ireland, they'd show film musicals often," she recalls. "Plus, I owned sound-tracks like *Fiddler on the Roof*, and 'Don't Cry for Me Argentina' from *Evita* was an anthem for people of my generation.

"What really started me wanting to do the album," confides O'Connor, "was the Julie London record called *The Liberty Years*. When I heard her brilliant, strippy 'Why Don't You Do Right?' I just wanted to be beautiful like her, and that song made me get off my ass to do this."

Such impulses may seem a far cry from the days when O'Connor was discovered by Ensign Records' Nigel Grainge and Chris Hill while fronting a Dublin rock band called Ton Ton Macoute. While Sinéad acknowledges the skepticism of some regarding the decision to assemble *Am I Not Your Girl?* she also recalls the reluctance of her record company to accept the final tapes in early 1990 of *I Do Not Want What I Haven't Got*, certain execs feeling the finished product was excessively introspec-tive and confessional. (Upon its release that summer, the unaltered record spent six consecutive weeks at the top of the *Billboard* 200 and became one of the preeminent artistic and commercial blockbusters of the nineties.)

Just as the previous album bespoke the disarray that fame helped det-onate in her life (a split from her initial manager, a break from a serious boyfriend, and then the demands of her marriage to drummer John Reynolds—"He's still my closest friend"—that produced a son, Jake), *Am I Not Your Girl?* was influenced by fans' conflicting perceptions of her notoriety.

"The reasons I called it *Am I Not Your Girl?* are partly personal and partly public," says O'Connor. "I've found it difficult over the last years because of not being perceived as a person—basically I'm still just a young girl. I love people, and I want people to love me. That's what I'm talking about at the end of 'Success Has Made a Failure of Our Home,' when I sing, 'Am I not your girl?' several times. People are always trying to make me out to be a bad girl, and I'm trying to say that I'm not. I'm a nice girl, and I have a heart."

That singularly open heart has rarely been more observable than on "Scarlet Ribbons," a song choice that speaks volumes about the sorrows of her own broken home, the violent abuse she suffered from her mother (since deceased), and the counseling Sinéad sought in recent years through Adult Children of Alcoholics/Dysfunctional Families. During the studio performance of "Scarlet Ribbons," O'Connor is heard struggling to avoid weeping.

"My father was going through my head when I was singing 'Scarlet Ribbons,' " she says. "He used to sing that to me when I was a little girl, and I always used to be in tears after he was finished. An angel left those ribbons there; it just showed me that if you ask God for something you'll always get an answer.

"I picked all these songs because I have personal relationships with each one. Despite all my troubles growing up, I still love both my parents very deeply. So I was thinking how 'Scarlet Ribbons' has been an influence on my whole life—and therefore how much of an influence my father has been on me. By singing that song, he gave me the knowledge of God."

PAM TILLIS'S TALENT: TELLING IT LIKE IT IS

THE BEAUTY OF PAM TILLIS IS THAT SHE CAN'T ENTIRELY SEE IT.
But anyone else within squinting distance of the grandstand at last summer's Fan Fair in Nashville knew he or she was in the presence of a beguiling new brand of Southern belle when the laughing lady in tight white jeans swung her Mystic Biscuits band into a blistering version of "Cleopatra, Queen of Denial."

What is the essence of Tillis's appeal? It's not just that the ditty— written by Tillis, husband Bob DiPiero, and Jan Buckingham— is a wonderfully wisecracking sendup of every self-deluding female archetype in the country annals ("Yeah, he's probably stuck in traffic/He'll be here in a little while / Just call me Cleopatra everybody/Cause I'm the Queen of Denial"). Or the fact that the tune pitched and rolled in live performance with all the bruised bravado of a road-house arraignment. What's most persuasive about the song—and for that matter, the other nine tracks on her new record, *Home-*

Pam Tillis

ward Looking Angel (Arista)—is the drop-dead vivacity of the vibrato-rich vocalist delivering the saga.

Girlish and garrulous, but with a gutsy poise unmatched by anyone of either sex in modern country, Pam Tillis is the backporch realist nonpareil. And while she may harbor private apprehensions about her physical charms, she does not pine or fret; she just offers a good, pared-down story—frequently her own. If Pam stole every blessed heart in the fairgrounds (and she did, her set being a talked-about sensation for days afterward), it was simply because her music told the bone truth. And in a genre where all romantic missteps are customarily rendered with maximum regret, the clear-eyed directness of the Pam Tillis approach threatens to dismantle the woman-as-victim school of Nashville thought forever.

"Let's face it, women don't always act with men the way we would *ideally*," states Tillis, suddenly giggling at her own solemnity. "I have a song on the new album called 'How Gone Is Goodbye.' People're always cutting songs where the guy screwed up, and this is one about a woman who made a mistake. There's a cool guy in the song, and she took him for granted. Now, somebody who's thinking too hard may say, 'Wait a minute, Pam! Is this girl crawling back to this guy?' The answer is *no*. But to me, if you're writing honestly about real-life situations, you're making a valid statement."

Since the first time a Kentucky immigrant fiddler spun a pan-Celtic variation on "Sally Gooden," the image of women in American country music has remained rooted in the mythic male impulse toward the one thing that purportedly surpasses a "piece of pie and a little piece of puddin'"—namely, a "hug" from Sally. Despite the pioneering efforts of thirties recording artists Sarah and Maybelle Carter, Lulu Belle Wiseman, the Coon Creek Girls, Cousin Emmy, Patsy Montana, the Girls of the Golden West, and others, the stigma attached to country women who dared forsake their traditional roles within the proprieties of southern ruralism continued to prevail. That conservatism also defied the postwar breakthroughs of Kitty Wells, Molly O'Day, and Texas Ruby, and even the later ascendance of Patsy Cline, Tammy Wynette, Loretta Lynn, and Dolly Parton.

"In the recent past," Tillis adds, "I don't think there was a very strong woman's point of view in country, because women were still cutting a lot of men's songs. This is publishing heaven here in Nashville, and there were only a handful of really great women writers. But Rosanne Cash pioneered things for women country writers, and now we have alternative artists like Pam Rose and Mary Ann Kennedy. My influences were George Jones and the country-style Rolling Stones, but I stayed out of country in the sixties and seventies because it seemed like country was ashamed of itself, like it was apologetic and wanted to be pop. But now it's the last bastion of song, with melodies and lack of artifice."

Born in Plant City, Florida, but reared in Nashville, Tillis is the eldest of five children by popular country performer Mel Tillis and his wife Doris. Her first stage experience, she remembers, was a duet at age eight with her dad on the boards of the legendary Ryman Auditorium. But she feels her earliest local repute was as the foremost teenage roustabout in suburban Nashville.

"I was your basic misfit, and a professional partier," she recalls, "and I think my temperament used to be much darker. I have a homemade ego—I didn't have much self-esteem or a strong emotional center, and constantly looked outside myself for it. I think some of it was genetic. The song 'Melancholy Child' on my first Arista album [*Put Yourself in My Place*, 1991] was drawn from early childhood memories of my mom, who at sixteen to seventeen was 'a baby with a baby.'

"People might see me at a gathering and say, 'God, she's an awkward girl,' or 'She's not really a looker, is she?' But if I sang to them, I knew I could outshine any girl in the room."

After a stint as a staff writer for Tree Publishing, she obtained a recording deal with Warner Bros. Her breakthrough, however, came with her supremely assured Arista debut, *Put Yourself in My Place*, which spawned an array of hits, among them "Maybe It Was Memphis," the title track, and the number-one country smash "Don't Tell Me What to Do."

If that album was a near-perfect union of blunt autobiography and keen workmanship, *Homeward Looking Angel* (due in stores September 29) is unerring in its ability to convey the scarred spunk that made Pam the stunning artist she has become. A case in point is the song "Rough and Tumble Heart," in which she relates, "It took a few falls till it got smart/But it's still tender in the deepest part."

Is there any particular youthful trial from what Tillis calls "the lost years" that represented the crossroads in her uphill passage?

"The public tends to think of the childhoods of the offspring of famous parents as idyllic, and not conducive to what might produce a serious artist," she says quietly, "but that's not so. It was extreme trauma that probably turned me around. I've always felt uncertain about my own attractiveness, thinking my appearance was kinda flawed, but then at sixteen I was in a car crash in which my face was shattered in over thirty places from my cheeks down to my chin.

"My nose was flattened, my eye sockets were damaged, and it took five years of operations to put it all back together again. On days when the weather's odd, I still have pain, and the ongoing surgical upkeep makes me self-conscious sometimes about the angles of my album cover photos or my video shoots.

"We all have our own setbacks and struggles in life, and most of them you accept rather than get over. If listeners think there's a straightforward tone in my records, I think I know why. To me, music is regular medicine to heal hurts. 'Cause while you might look mended and great to the outside world, in your mind and heart you can still feel as if things are broken."

SHAWN COLVIN'S LONG TREK TO *FAT CITY*

FAME IS A BYPRODUCT OF FLAMBOYANCE. ESTEEM IS THE currency of accomplishment. But gratification is the gift of hearing a hero sing one's praises.

"Hey—hi! You're one of my favorite singers!!" exclaimed Bonnie Raitt, stepping behind the curtain after her 1990 Farm Aid set in the Indianapolis Hoosier Dome to find Shawn Colvin spectating in the backstage shadows.

"Oh—no, no!" squealed the spindly Colvin as Raitt embraced her, Shawn's eyes fluttering with shock and jubilance. "You're one of *my* favorite singers!!"

Colvin's admiration for Bonnie stemmed, of course, from a twenty-year body of concert and recording work that first gained national regard with Raitt's 1971 Warner Bros. debut album. But Bonnie's accolades were occasioned by Shawn's sole release at the time, a Grammy-winning 1989 convergence of folk and roll called *Steady On* (Columbia).

In the interval between the release of that album and its follow-up, *Fat City*, due October 20, Colvin has seen still more of her

Shawn Colvin

private dreams come true. She toured at Richard Thompson's invitation in 1991 as a guest star in his band and also recorded with Joni Mitchell, who sings backup on Shawn's new album, and Joni's bassist husband Larry Klein, who produced the record.

Like Raitt and Mitchell, Colvin is an artful yet seemingly effortless vocalist whose prismatic grasp of intonation is married to a serene sense of control. Like her idols, she also boasts a highly fluent guitar style. (Indeed, her measured brace of tolling chords and bongolike bastinadoes upon the face of her hollow-body acoustic magnifies her material with the eerie force of an alter ego.) And, like the songs of those who have influenced her, Shawn Colvin's brave but haunted music is the sounding board of her spirit.

"I think the way that you get through life," says Colvin, "is simply that the less you fight it, and the more you go through it *emotionally,* the better off you are. All cultures try to make sense of what they feel. And feeling doesn't have any black or white or right or wrong to it. Any kind of art tries to take different forms of communication and put them together in a combination that works; the goal is to *make* you feel."

On *Steady On,* Colvin mounted a sirenlike assault on the sensibilities, enticing with fair words and castle-building imagery, and then delivering concrete disclosures that ran dungeon-deep. Tracks like "Diamond in the Rough," "Stranded," "Cry Like an Angel," and "The Dead of the Night" each greeted the ears like the prettiest folk rock in ages, but their dreamy poetics soon grew into aggressive, stifling dramas, the songs' central characters impelled to admit the youthful self-deception on which they'd based their adult impressions of love.

" 'Cry Like an Angel' was real personal," says Colvin. "I wrote it in 1987 with John Leventhal, my frequent musical collaborator. It's about the healing power in the acceptance of a person, regardless of what they might hold in their heart. I won't beat around the bush—it came directly out of going to therapy and my rejuvenation through my discoveries. Growing up, I always felt like an orphan, and I had a pretty self-destructive lifestyle that I began to turn around starting in 1983. But I also found I had a big sense of gratitude about my angry high school days, because that was the last time I could remember when I'd had strong camaraderie with people. My real family was my friends, hence the line, 'We were raising each other.' "

The incremental volte-face from this rueful viewpoint is chronicled in "Polaroids" on *Fat City,* in which small mercies and furtive strides in

Colvin's emotional ripening are suddenly lifted into the sun and shared "like a lot of snapshots." The song's infectious tone of relief is a testament to the persuasive wiles of Colvin's writing, which continually produces the tug of universality while ensuring pathos remains secondary to plot. Indeed, Colvin inadvertently reveals her cleverly reflective storytelling technique on another *Fat City* highpoint, the caustic "Kill the Messenger," in which she confides: "You won't feel the chains/You won't see the moss . . . /There's an art to the game—/The aesthetics of love/The athletics of loss."

Some clues to the aura of apartness that pervades Colvin's compositions can be found in her itinerant background. One of a brood of four, she began life in remote Vermillion, South Dakota, but soon found herself carried from one college town to another across the Midwest and Canada as her ambitious parents ("They're academic nuts," she says affectionately) pursued advanced degrees in behavioral psychology (her dad) and law (her mom). The rather distracted nature of these activities, coupled with a certain impatience with Shawn's independent streak, left Colvin feeling like the odd sibling out. "It was as though I had been born and stuck into the wrong house. I wouldn't say I was discouraged, but I wasn't encouraged, either. It was like, 'We can't figure her out.' If a kid is prone to creativity, is it bothersome because they're not as containable?' "

Left to answer such questions on her own, she seized upon the least regimented talents common to her pedigree ("My father's a banjo and guitar player who still sings in university productions and my mother has a beautiful voice as well") and made them her profession. Adding the requisite Colvin restlessness, she became a traveling musician, playing solo in Illinois bars, fronting the Shawn Colvin Band in various heartland precincts, joining an Austin, Texas, C&W group called the Dixie Diesels, and finally staking out a stomping ground between New York and New England.

In 1988, she issued an eight-selection independent cassette from a Massachusetts concert, simply titled *Live Tape*. "It's been said that my songs walk the dark side of romance's street," she coyly told her *Live Tape* audience before launching into ineffably lovely acoustic versions of "Diamond in the Rough," "Stranded," and her folk-circuit cult classic, the bewitching "I Don't Know Why." The last title appears in a wistful new form on *Fat City*, and its presence as the concluding selection on her second major-label album signals a kind of closure for the first stage of Colvin's career—a crossing from the darkness into the light.

"I wrote 'I Don't Know Why' in 1981, and it's the first song I wrote in its entirety in one sitting. I was on the D train going up to the Bronx, where I was staying when I first moved to the city. I wrote it out of a need for comfort in myself, and I imagined I was singing it to a baby. It came so easily. Ten years later, I decided I would put it on *Fat City*. Maybe it's because I'm in love now and much stronger in my profession, and I have the recognition of those I admire, but I felt I could speak to that child with belief and understanding. If there's any philosophy in my music, it's that faith and hope are valid."

KEITH RICHARDS: ON THE "OFFENSIVE"

HE'S STILL A WANTED MAN, BUT NOW SOUGHT LARGELY FOR himself. And with the worldwide release on October 20 of *Main Offender* (Virgin), Keith Richards's third solo album, it should be self-evident that his sui generis guitar gristle has succeeded beyond all expectations in gaining him a raffish status wholly independent of the Rolling Stones.

There was a time when Richards, the Stones' notorious riffsmith–night watchman, had the 'round-the-clock task of either upholding or answering for the musical reputation of his primordial band. But, with a will as steely as the rant of his scuffed Telecaster, Keith has spent half a decade spurring his X-Pensive Winos ensemble toward a brashly separate sound and a following to match.

Granted, skepticism ruled five years ago when word first radiated that Richards and respected drummer Steve Jordan were co-producing a unilateral studio project for rock's rhythm outlaw. But, after the

Keith Richards

launch in 1988 of *Talk Is Cheap,* Richards and his new outfit became the fount of a cluster of album-radio favorites, including "Take It So Hard," "Struggle," "You Don't Move Me," and "Make No Mistake." The next step, in 1991, was a thirteen-track live journal, *Keith Richards & the X-Pensive Winos: Live at the Hollywood Palladium, December 15, 1988,* which confirmed that the road reputation of Richards's marauders was well deserved.

Now, *Main Offender* finds the brambly bray and corrugated riffs of rock's venerable party vertebrate converging with heightened discrimination. While Richards earlier exhibited a clear awareness of the leaps and limitations of his métier, the current record evinces an ingenious deployment of bare essentials to reach more sophisticated ends.

Critics like to accuse Richards of studied sloppiness, as if his modus wavered somewhere between Guns N' Roses at its worst and Nirvana at its best, but a careful examination of even the *Live at the Hollywood Palladium* record (the most able and engrossing concert memento since Jimi Hendrix's 1970 *Band of Gypsies*) puts that fable to permanent flight. The sole ragged factor is Keith's alleyway arias, which still resound with the free-round fellowship of a saloon keeper.

Meanwhile, the articulated space around the grooves and melody lines of Richards's *Main Offender* songs shows a faculty for synchronization that any Swiss chronographer would covet.

"The latest arrangements are more adventurous because we're really playing with time," says Richards, his leathery wheeze unfurling in a fat chuckle. "Rock'n'roll is a limited form musically, but we use a lot of percussion in a way that's technically not overemphasized, yet you still have the pleasurable feeling of getting up to your neck in it because it's all *ambient.*

"For this new record, the ten tracks were cut in specifically chosen rooms—chiefly Master Sound in Astoria, Queens, and The Site in San Rafael, California. We arranged the instruments to control the space—instead of vice versa—and then worked on the 'direct injection' of skilled musicians interacting in a single area instead of overlaying on tape."

Whether it's the springy cross-cadences of "999" ("a song about the cost of living"), or the intricate countervamps on "Bodytalks," the music joins the all-for-one R&B bonding of Chess and Stax studio quorums with the vintage judgment that the best rock'n'roll sessions are stud poker contests dealt from a clean deck.

"For me," says Richards, "the Winos band is a little miracle. We hadn't played together in almost four years—because everybody's got their own outside thing—and that prevented the latest music we made from being stale. I was always conscious of the possibility of us developing our own signature; and, knowing the loyalty of the Winos to each other, I definitely thought the new record would progress from the first one. But the *key* was the touring in between.

"Because to me, everything is based upon a rapport on stage; that's always been my criteria for growth. If you don't make it on the road, you never learn what to do next. So the fun of us getting back together as this performing unit to write and rehearse once again is where the present blossoming has come from."

The core Winos roster consists of Jordan on drums and traps; bassist Charley Drayton; keyboardist Ivan Neville (a scion of the Neville Brothers clan); guitarist Waddy Wachtel; and former LaBelle vocalist Sarah Dash, with additional harmonies provided by singers Bernard Fowler and Babi Floyd. The axis, of course, is Richards, grinding against the meter with his "Exile on Main Street"–era Telecaster, as well as "this great new Gibson I got, which is a copy of an old Robert Johnson acoustic." The cozy solidarity among these regulars also allowed Richards to cultivate a warmth and emotional proximity uncommon in his previous work. "Hate It When You Leave" borders on the confessional, while "Demon" and "Runnin' Too Deep" seem like eavesdropping on others' most confidential moments.

"You're hitting it on the head!!" he admits. "I'm really drawing on thirty years of experience, and I can tell stories and hint at moods and atmospheres that I know very well, looking at all these little secrets from a more detached point of view. Everybody's got demons, and the way I've always written songs was to try and put an intimate focus on something I've observed, so you don't feel so alone.

"A song like 'Wicked as It Seems' hints at a tense relationship ["I suffer the blow/So the bruises don't show/ . . . No broken necks/No broken hearts"] that may or may not blow up at any possible moment— which is the kind of subjects I'm very interested in. And if I come up with a pretty melody like 'Demon,' I immediately give it some of the hardest lyrics to counteract that mood. I'm looking for the *mystery* in how people relate to each other, rather than the *meaning* of the matter."

And what of band leader Richards's own intrapersonal obligations?

"With the Stones, you mean? Well, that's easy. The Winos will tour in December and January. Then Mick [Jagger] and I have got a date to meet somewhere remote—it could be New Guinea!—in February or March to do the Stones album."

Incidentally, is Bill Wyman officially an ex-Stone? "*No*," Richards rules, "it's not settled. I'm going to go over to London in a week or two and I'll have a chat with him to find out if he wants to go for another round. I don't want to change the lineup at all."

Last question for the ringleader: Why did he name his new album *Main Offender*?

"Oh, it was just one of those things that goes on *wherever* I am. When somebody's looking for a culprit, usually the finger points to me." Lacerating laughter. "It was a tossup between that title and *Blame Hound*. I'm an easy mark."

ARRESTED DEVELOPMENT'S "REVOLUTION"

GROWTH IS THE GRASPING OF AN UNWANTED CHALLENGE. IF that challenge is met, one learns the value of change. When change inspires others, it becomes an option. If that option seizes imaginations, it becomes an issue. If that issue touches hearts, it becomes a need. If that need invades the soul, it becomes a revolution.

And if that revolution furthers the growth of truth, no force can forestall it from becoming a reality.

"To me, revolution means a rebirth, a cleansing," says Speech, the twenty-three-year-old singer whose ardent but unaffected songwriting and production style are the prime attributes of his group, Arrested Development. "The word *revolution* is misconstrued, in America especially. But when you look at all the different problems that face African-Americans—or every American—I think revolution is a beautiful concept that gives people hope."

And now it also gives people a musical rallying point, since "Revolution" is the name of the Arrested Development song chosen as the first release off the soundtrack of director Spike

Arrested Development

Lee's much-anticipated *Malcolm X* movie. The "Revolution" single and its Lee-directed video will be issued by Chrysalis/EMI Records on November 10, with the film biography's full soundtrack to reach stores via Qwest Records when the picture opens nationwide on November 20.

"Malcolm X's basic thing was self-determination and pride," says Speech, who was born Todd Thomas in Milwaukee, the second son of Patricia O'Flynn-Thomas and Robert J. Thomas, who publish the *Milwaukee Community Journal* newspaper. "One thing the movie does that I'm really thankful for is that it gives a side of Malcolm that's also the perspective Arrested Development comes from, which is *caring.*

"The movie shows the sensitive side of Malcolm as a family man, a husband, and a person who made a lot of sacrifices. Malcolm X was a changing man; he always had the same goal, which was the freedom of African people, but he changed philosophies throughout his lifetime, and that really shows a very caring person—a person whose ego didn't get in the way of his objectives or his growth as a leader."

These same virtues are apparent in the demeanor and artistic ideals of Arrested Development's unassuming head man, whose music is equal parts colloquial rap, rustic hip-hop, festive incantation, and fearless spirituality. Speech's lyrics are the plainspoken cultural scrutinies of a conscience in action, wary of compromise and venality, while inviting candid dialogue with others (such as Aerle Taree, Speech's cousin and the confident female counterbalance in Arrested Development's choral web).

On record, cowbells, casual conversation, and the percussion of daily life mingle with scratchin' passages, bass drum thumps, and harmonic gospel-reggae hollers for A.D.'s two top-ten hits, "Tennessee" and "People Everyday," from the group's inaugural *3 Years, 5 Months and 2 Days in the Life of . . .* album (Chrysalis/EMI). As with "Revolution," whose boisterous cannonade will fill the film's closing-credits sequence, the A.D. method seems communal and extemporaneous, an automatic cohesion of oratorical charm and social alarm.

"When Spike Lee asked me to write a song," says Speech, "it was a privilege, but also a personal responsibility, because I needed to tell how a man like Malcolm could affect me. That's why in the lyrics I say, 'Am I doing as much as *I* can for the struggle?' My responsibility as an individual is to acknowledge that there *is* a need for struggle, because of all the bad things going on in the nation—high teenage pregnancy rate, high rate of black-on-black crime and homicide, high rate of crack babies, three-quarters of the black population living in the underclass—with most of them being experienced by the people Malcolm X was preaching to. As the song also states, 'Let's *talk* about revolution,' because this is a serious and timely moment to discuss it."

Arrested Development began some four years ago when Speech and DJ Headliner (aka Tim Barnwell) met at the Art Institute of Atlanta. "At that point, I was fighting a lot and doing terribly in school," says Speech. "I had just graduated from high school and moved to Atlanta when I heard Public Enemy's 'Rebel Without a Pause,' which was rebellious enough to catch my attention." After a half-hearted stab at gangsta rap, Speech and Headliner devised a more embracing fusion of "southern-folk-ethnic-rap" that they christened "life music." They brought two women (singer-designer Aerle "Early Ta-Ree" Taree and choreographer Montsho "Ee-She" Eshe) into the fold, along with drummer-vocalist Rasa Don, dancer-counselor Baba "O.J." Oje, and support personnel like singer Dionne Farris, whose fervent solo swept across "Tennessee."

But there would have been no "Tennessee" or Arrested Development as we now know it if not for an abrupt series of personal losses suffered by Speech in February 1991.

"My grandmother, who I had grown up with in Tennessee [in a small town off U.S. 51 called Ripley] and was extremely close to, had a sudden heart attack," he explains. "Then my brother Terry, who was the older brother who I had bounced ideas off of and looked up to for my whole life, died of an asthma attack that same week. Ironically, he had just become a doctor; he was twenty-nine, and had only been a doctor for a month, and he was engaged to be married.

"It put me through some soul searching," he continues somberly, "and the sole reason I wrote 'Tennessee' was to get through that pain. It was a rough, pivotal time, and a certain weight took over my body; not exactly a burden, but more like a sense of being awake for the first time, along with the wisdom that God gave me music as an outlet for feelings."

The plaintive, pastoral pull of "Tennessee" paved the way for the current platinum-plus sales of the *3 Years, 5 Months . . .* album; and the graceful musicality of A.D.'s recent live sets as tour openers for En Vogue have primed both rock and rap fans for the group's inciteful uplift on "Revolution."

"Historians' biggest and best examples of history are usually art," Speech counsels. "It gives the most complete story of a people's existence. Music is the same way. I'm not saying song is the only way that messages should be sent, but it's fascinating how it can reach across obstacles to tell others exactly how people are thinking and living.

"America only *seems* free in terms of freedom of speech," he adds, "and any conscious person is surely aware of the tactics that are taken to shut people up, whether it's the assassination of people like Malcolm, or the political imprisonment of others. Art is often one of the only ways you can slip challenging information into a situation, to tell people about their commonalities, and spread reality. That's why I've never looked at music as just entertainment.

"Song lasts for generations; in terms of revolution, it definitely serves its purpose."

STEVE MARTLAND: CLASSICAL ICONOCLAST

ENGLISH COMPOSER-CONDUCTOR STEVE MARTLAND IS OUT to intrude on the prejudices of the classical realm, to tamper with its neat sense of time and space, to meddle with its proprieties, to interrupt its aloof decorum and stilted traditions, and to interpose a new, contrapuntal democracy of sound and sensation.

In purely musical terms, Martland's approach could be likened to *hocket*, a medieval technique in which the melodic line is broken into alluring fragments by means of short rests. The ringing effect is simultaneously spasmodic and precise, and Martland's contemporary application of it is best heard on "Principia," an almost jazz-pop percolation of saxophones, trombones, electric violin, flügelhorn, and a conventional rock rhythm section that can be found on his new British album, *Crossing the Border* (Factory).

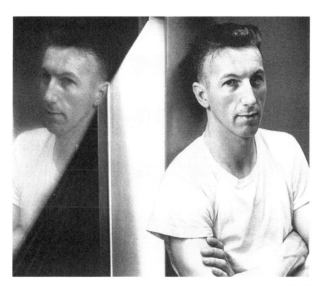

As the title would indicate, *Crossing the Border* exemplifies Martland's intense concern with the social role of the creative act, as well as his determination to expand the classical

Steve Martland

audience beyond the confines of a privileged elite. And, while the five original pieces on *Crossing the Border* betray a rhythmic bias and a range of instruments more typical of popular music, they also boast a dynamic bluster that mixes baroque orchestration with richly tonal rule breaking. Imagine a harmonious collision of the airy splendor of Purcell and the metrical complexity of Aaron Copland, with the influence of minimalists like Steve Reich and Terry Riley thrown in for—quite literally—good measure.

If this sounds like antiromantic classicism with a curious Stateside tilt, Martland figures that's just about right.

"I think my music is very American," says the Liverpool-bred Martland with a lilting chuckle. " 'Principia' reminds me of driving in America and honking your horn on a busy street. As with the title piece of the record, it's got this jazzy, aggressive American optimism that's a bit like Copland, although the string section does seem very English to a lot of ears, because everybody associates England with string music."

Martland wryly refers to the English classical world as "institutionalized mausoleum orchestras" and "symphony concerts where nobody comes out whistling." In contrast, portions of *Crossing the Border* were originally performed to highly animated audiences and critical acclaim in settings as unpretentious as the Old Town Hall in Gdansk, Poland, and the Cafe de Unie in Rotterdam. And when it came time to record the album, Martland chose to do it at Eurythmics' Church Studios in the Crouch End section of London, using his own roughly twelve-piece classical group, the Steve Martland Band. Consequently, *Crossing the Border* has an aural candescence and crackling pep closer to what could be called classical roll than any prim concerto form.

"The Eurythmics' studio, which is really a reconstructed church hall, has got the most perfect acoustics for strings," says Martland, "and that's why it sounds so fantastic. Plus, the band is so enthusiastic and dedicated; they've been together for two years, on and off, but since *Crossing the Border* they want to do more."

Isn't it unusual for a classical composer to have his own band?

"In England, yes," says Martland with a laugh, "but not in America. Steve Reich had to have his own band back twenty years ago because nobody performed his work. Now the practice is very much a feature of the new classical music being written, with people forming their own ensembles; it's like a theater director or a playwright having a resident company. I hadn't been played in England for about two years except amongst my students!"

But all that has rapidly changed for Martland. He recently drew raves for his conducting of the BBC Symphony at London's Royal Festival Hall in a performance of his own 1983 masterstroke, *Babi Yar* (Martland's sole work for large orchestra), whose gripping evocation of the horrors of that Nazi death camp outside Kiev was broadcast on BBC's Radio 3 on September 27.

Martland, thirty-three, is now writing a BBC-commissioned piece called "Patrol," which will be premiered this month by the Britten Quartet. There will also be a December performance by Martland's band of a series of six Martland-arranged Mozart opera arias that are the centerpiece of *Wolfgang,* his second new Factory album of 1992.

But how did this combative outlander (an amateur bodybuilder and outspoken socialist who's been known to conduct in a T-shirt and army fatigues) manage to penetrate the classical establishment without succumbing to respectability? And by what route did he get himself signed to Factory Records, that upstart bastion of Joy Division, New Order, Happy Mondays, and the cream of Manchester pop?

"Well, that's a strange story," assures Martland, one of two sons born to a Liverpool carpenter and his wife, a worker in a local clothing factory. "I discovered music and the piano when I was a boy in school, and I guess the first thing I learned to play on keyboards was 'Moonlight Sonata.' Liverpool is a port city, and I love ships, so my father's plan was that at sixteen I would go into the navy like my uncle had. But I rebelled and stayed at school to study music. The fact that my parents weren't remotely supportive made it more of a necessity."

After graduating from Liverpool University, Martland was accepted at Cambridge to study composition under Alexander Goehr. Still rebelling, he soon elected to move on to the Netherlands to work with Dutch post-minimalist composer Louis Andriessen (best known for his controversial *De Staat,* available on CD in the United States on the Nonesuch label). Afterward, Martland shunned the classical career treadmill to work with the postpunk Test Department, the Loose Tubes jazz orchestra, and ex-Communards singer Sarah Jane Morris, for whom he created the "Glad Day" song cycle. His signing to Factory Records in 1989 occurred via a chance meeting with label executive Tony Wilson, who agreed ("without ever hearing my music!") to record a performance of *Babi Yar* in Holland that February by the Resident Orchestra of the Hague.

Martland is currently completing a television documentary on Louis Andriessen for the BBC, and then plans more of the "cross-fertilization" common to his composing. "What I do," Martland explains, "is a crossover—although I hate that word—between formal classical composing, the instruments of common jazz, the rhythms and amplified sonorities of rock—and even the 'bop-bop-bop' hocketing I first heard when Andriessen brought his own band called Hoketus to Liverpool University.

"The process sounds intellectual, but I hope the results are always down to earth and inviting, particularly to the young CD-buying public that doesn't usually go to the symphony. I want to disrupt conventional ideas of classical music, create a new word-of-mouth following that's very like rock's core audience, and," he laughs, "maybe leave some listeners whistling!"

BOUKMAN EKSPERYANS: VODOU VICTORY

THERE IS A MUSICAL SAGA OF HIGH DRAMA UNFOLDING AT this very moment across our nation.

It concerns certain policies of the pope, the legacy of a beloved black revolutionary, and the dangerous crossroads at which a society may find itself when it must vote to either honor the polyglot heritage of its common people, or reject their needs and beliefs in favor of the cynical ambitions of a tiny elite.

However, the story in question pertains neither to Sinéad O'Connor and her outspoken anti-Catholic Church convictions, Spike Lee's new Malcolm X movie, nor the recent U.S. elections. Rather, this drama is embodied in a U.S. concert tour currently under way to promote an album on Island Records' Mango label by Haiti's Boukman Eksperyans.

If all this seems just a shade unlikely, well, you probably haven't yet been exposed to the provocative sights and sounds of Boukman Eksperyans and their arresting new record, *Kalfou Danjere* (Dangerous Crossroads).

The group is named for a native

Boukman Eksperyans

Vodou priest whose dream of liberation precipitated the overthrow of French colonialism in this hemisphere and the birth in 1804 of the world's first black republic. A former slave from Jamaica, Eksperyans was a natural mystic whose 1791 Vodou rite unifying the African and indigenous *Iwa* (spirits) on Haiti formed the symbolic turning point in its long history of native oppression. The band celebrates the daring lesson of Boukman's "experience."

"This is a time in Haiti when you see a freely elected democracy stopped by a coup d'état," says Theodore "Lolo" Beaubrun Jr., lead singer-songwriter and keyboardist for Boukman Eksperyans, referring to the military-supported toppling of the government of populist priest-turned-president Jean-Bertrand Aristide in September 1991. "So we are at a dangerous crossroads where the people have to decide for revolution, or face the dying of the country. In Vodou, we believe that the crossroads is the place where your soul will be judged."

In Haiti, the outlook of Lolo's band on the country's tensions is not taken lightly. Their music has often been outlawed by the local radio, and despite "Kalfou Danjere"'s status as the most popular song during the island's 1992 Carnival, Boukman Eksperyans was barred by the government from the annual competition. (In reaction, neighborhood street bands throughout Haiti adopted "Kalfou Danjere" as their anthem.)

"We are attacked in Haiti by fanatic communists as well as the capitalists, who both say we are political, and Catholics and Protestants also say we threaten them," says Lolo. "But we are singing about a state of life that is *above* politics and religion. We believe in what we call the 'balance of the three words,' where what you're thinking, what you're saying, and what you're doing is all one and becomes truth, love, and justice. For us, this message comes together in the spiritual alternative of the *lakou*."

Haiti's ancient Vodou folk religion has two syncretic strains: Vodou *hougan*, the much-romanticized form, which is centered around the spells and ministrations of local necromancers; and Vodou *lakou*, a more communal type of worship that takes its title from the African-derived peasant collectives that flourished around the turn of the nineteenth century.

Lolo sees a conflict between the Vodou way of life and French-derived Roman Catholicism in the decision of the pope to formally recognize the military regime of Prosper Avril.

"The Vatican made a big, big mistake in this recognition," says Lolo, "but then many people feel the Vatican [whose Salesian Order expelled Reverend Aristide for allegedly using the sacraments for political purposes] was involved in the coup. Some say Haiti is a Catholic country once ruled by a Napoleonic code, but Haiti has always been a Vodou country with a Vodou code, which is not a religion but rather a system of family life."

As Lolo notes, Haiti has long witnessed a tug of war between the foreign-imposed values of the city life and the pious African Creole credos of the peasant existence. The island's modern musical history, likewise, reflects these conflicting attachments. During the fifties heyday of the corrupt "Papa Doc" Duvalier regime, the meringue-flavored *compas-direct* sound of famed saxophonist Nemours Jean-Baptiste was favored by the government because of its escapism. In the mid-sixties, that music was eclipsed by *mini-jazz*, a rock-edged, hedonistic *compas* offshoot.

"The *compas direct* was encouraged by the Ton Ton Macoute [secret police] in the 1950s," says Lolo, "because it was uncritical of the regime and encouraged people to forget their worries. *Mini-jazz* also did this. In both cases, something good was exploited."

But a major shift in Haitian sociomusical emphasis occurred circa 1978, the year of Boukman Eksperyans' founding, with the band's bold popularization of traditional Vodou culture. Later, the additional influence of *rara* (rural festival music) *raborday* rhythms helped Boukman Eksperyans forge the winning song in the 1990 Carnival, "Ke-M Pa Sote" (My Heart Doesn't Leap/You Don't Scare Me)—which was featured on their 1991 Mango album *Vodou Adjae* (Vodou Music for Trances and Dancing).

Since the coup, Boukman Eksperyans has become the polestar of Haiti's hopes for a peaceful return to the deepest roots of Haitian spirituality, emblemized by the *lakou* path to the individual and collective defeat of life's greatest enemy: fear.

"When you find yourself inside and have an awareness beyond fear and the selfishness fear brings, we call this *Ginen*," says Lolo. "In *Ginen*, there is no battle between the side of reason and the side of mystery." And the primary intention behind Boukman Eksperyans' current road trip is to give the uninitiated a taste of what this sensation might feel like.

Onstage last week at Manhattan's Lone Star Roadhouse, the nine-piece band looked like a shy peasant family ironically attired in the collagelike riot of primary colors and playful chock-a-block patterns that are the festive social costumes of Haitian peasant culture. But, as Boukman Eksperyans' shimmering mechanism of bass-toned drums, tinkling bells, and guitar-propelled choral chanting exploded in "Kouman Sa Ta Ye" (What Would It Be Like), the packed house instinctively grasped the rippling rune of thanksgiving to the ancestral *lwa* that fosters the forces of community.

There is a juncture in each electrifying Boukman Eksperyans show when a band member—usually Lolo's vocalist wife Mimerose—steps forward to speak in heavily accented English to the crowd, describing the mood of the room. On such occasions, the audience discovers it has become a part of this dramatic musical saga.

Mimerose's statement last week was uncommonly moving for its devout simplicity: "If you look for love, you look for the truth. If you look for justice, you look for harmony. And if you look for love, justice, and truth, you will discover God, and you are *Ginen.*"

JUDIE TZUKE: U.K.'S *WONDER* WOMAN

ENGLAND HAS RECENTLY SEEN SOMETHING OF A RENAISSANCE in women singer-songwriters of a reflective pop persuasion, most notably Julia Fordham, Tracey Thorn (of Everything But the Girl), Nicky Holland, Beverley Craven, and Lauren Christy. Each pens pithy interior monologues about city-dwelling females in quest of a fiercely independent but romantically fulfilling existence. And each takes a slant that blends blunt stock-taking and sophisticated self-awareness with a certain London-at-dusk dolor; as such, their stuff usually works best when it's simply stated rather than somberly self-dramatizing.

Each of these artists also shares, to an often-startling extent, a stylistic link to a newly reemergent British cult figure who long ago perfected the frank, meditative tone for which they all strive.

The lady looming in the shadows is Judie Tzuke, whose 1979 debut album for Elton John's Rocket label, *Stay with Me Till Dawn* (issued in the U.K. as *Welcome to the Cruise*) is still a much-sought collectors' prize among aficionados of superior pop pensiveness. Her tenth U.K.

Judie Tzuke

release, *Wonderland,* recently issued by Essential Records, is highlighted by the piquant, disturbing "Man and a Gun," one of the year's best pop ballads.

" 'Man and a Gun' is about my best friend and also another very good friend of mine," says Tzuke. "They're both really bright, clever girls, but they always choose men who are just *diabolical* to them. Especially my best friend; she constantly ends up being beaten up, and then goes back for more. I wrote the song one day because I was so frustrated: No matter how much I try to talk her out of it, I can't."

Pretty and pungent, the unnerving, piano-centered vesper graphically delineates this predicament: "He'll beat you when you're up/He'll knock you to the ground/Well he'll hit you anyway just to keep your spirit down/I'm just so afraid of the way that this will run/And that your name might be written/On the bullet in his gun."

"The main criticism I get in England is that I'm a bit intense," Tzuke allows with a soft laugh. "*Wonderland* was such an emotional album, and while it's gotten good reviews, many people in England are so frightened of admitting they like any theme that's a bit distasteful."

Tzuke notes that another track, "She Loves His Hands," employs childhood impressions of tenderness to convey the betrayal suffered when an adult abuses a young girl's innocent trust. "I had to write it," she says, "because of something that happened to me when I was a child. While it did *not* involve my father, who died when I was fifteen, I used the powerful image of a father's hands because they're one of the main things I remember about him, and they seemed to work well with the subject I was writing about."

Although unrivaled for sheer saturnine effect, Tzuke's handsome-sounding tribulations are always leavened by a disarming directness, as illustrated on "Swimming," an ode to the stresses of self-preservation. To quote a rave *London Times* review of a legendary live concert that the seldom-touring singer gave at the Hammersmith Odeon in 1985, Tzuke is gifted at "combining a glacial poise with her innate sensuality."

She also possesses a winning sense of humor about her own work, freely confessing that a few detractors in the flavor-of-the-month British music press find her "rather naff or *wet.*" And while her loyal fans praise her blond, zaftig beauty, she insists—in reference to a *Wonderland* track called "Vivien"—that she "always wanted to look like Vivien Leigh: little, black haired, and waiflike!"

As for the striking impact she's had on a new generation of British songbirds, she shyly says she "hears that a lot," but confides that the only current English female artist for whom she feels a real affinity is Fordham.

"I've met Julia Fordham, and I quite like her music, and I've been told she likes mine too. Of all those women usually mentioned with regard to me, I prefer her records because they have an honesty and an intelligent tension that separates them from the rest.

"People in the States are far more receptive to my introspective sort of writing than they are in England, where you're rarely allowed to have a mature career beyond the first splash in the pop charts and fan magazines. It's difficult to break out of the 'pretty girl at the piano' mold that serious women songwriters here can get stuck with once they've tasted commercial success. When the single of 'Stay with Me Till Dawn' became a hit in England in the summer of 1979, people wanted me to be just that—a nice face at the keyboards—but my music has always grappled with a lot of touchy issues and topics that make many people uncomfortable.

"In the States, my two albums on Rocket [the second being *Sports Car*, (1980)] are said to be obscure favorites," she summarizes drolly, "but I'm still the best-kept secret in England."

That situation seems ripe for abrupt reversion, since she has recently been signed by Shakespear's Sister manager John Campbell; and John Reid, Elton John's veteran representative, has also pledged his support. Despite this upturn in her fortunes, though, Tzuke hasn't forgotten the sudden career decompression she underwent in 1980 when Elton jumped from MCA (which distributed Rocket) to Geffen Records. "MCA was angry," she recalls, "and the Rocket artists found themselves in an awkward state, with the MCA reps told not to do anything more for us. I opened for Elton in 1980 at a free concert for 450,000 in Central Park and went over really well—but there wasn't a single copy of my albums in the shops!"

There were no hard feelings, however, between Elton and Tzuke, who co-wrote material for John's *21 at 33* MCA finale. And, with her classic Rocket titles available on CD via PolyGram U.K., everything old is virtually new again. Since Tzuke controls the bulk of her back catalog, including the exceptional *Turning Stones* (Polydor, 1989) and *Left Hand Talking* (Columbia, 1991), a retrospective set is being considered for worldwide release.

But Tzuke's blue devils are not so easily dispelled. Maybe it's the split sensibilities of her upbringing, her late father Sefton Myers having been a resolutely practical, Piccadilly-based real estate agent, while her more lighthearted mother, Jean Myers Dishroon, is a retired television actress who appeared occasionally on such fond BBC fare as the *Rise and Fall of Reginald Perring* comedy series.

In explaining herself, Tzuke also describes the essential message underlying *Wonderland:* "All my life I've been an adviser and counselor for my friends, trying to sort out their personal pain, because I always had the attitude that everything will come out right in the end. Now, I'm at a stage in my life where I don't feel I can either believe or offer that advice anymore. I've come to realize that there are absolutely *no* guarantees for anything. But somehow that knowledge feels better than all the old assurances."

WHAT FUELS RAGE AGAINST THE MACHINE?

FURY IS OFTEN THE FLOWER OF DEEP DISAPPOINTMENT, AND IT can blossom most fiercely in the hearts of frustrated young believers. It's tough to placate the pupil who has been taught to care too much, and Rage Against The Machine is the sound of anger at the brink of heartbreak.

A Los Angeles–rooted hardcore band that grafts capacious punk compulsion with crafty political rap, Rage Against The Machine is also the deeply felt forum for the poetry of Zack de la Rocha, a twenty-two-year-old guitarist-songwriter of Chicano and white parentage.

"When I was younger, I had a weird image of myself as an all-American kid," says de la Rocha, whose unruly dreadlocks and boyish demeanor belie a personality toughened by a heritage of conflict. "I grew up moving back and forth between my father's place in East L.A. and my mother's home in the white suburb of Irvine, because I was the focus of a heavy custody battle between my dad, who was a first-generation Mexican muralist, and my half-Chicano, half-German mother, a teacher's

Rage Against The Machine

aide who eventually raised me while working at the University of California at Irvine. I was never able to communicate with my father, a talented but difficult guy, and while I couldn't adjust to life in the suburbs, I also found that I was not accepted by the *cholos*—the homeboys from the barrio of East L.A.—because I never learned to speak Spanish. Of course, the true language of my people is not Spanish but Nahua, the tongue of the ancient Aztecs, but these individual experiences of disenfranchisement fueled my political awareness of how our system has cut us off from the real sources of power in our nation.

"My political awakening came in high school when I realized you're only seen as successful in this country when you've been completely assimilated *and* you've achieved a lot monetarily. So the oppression that ordinary people are constantly subjected to is as much spiritual as political. If our music sounds angry, it's because we're fighting for empowerment on a spiritual level as well as a material one. And when I sing a song on the new album like 'Settle for Nothing,' it's a reflection of my inner self as well as my social philosophy."

The lead singer of Rage Against The Machine goes on to explain that the songs on the band's self-titled debut album (on Epic Associated) emerged from his "ambition to evolve as a poet as well as a musician. I started playing guitar when I was eight, and I played mostly punk at first, but then in junior high, a music teacher turned me on to Joe Pass and Charlie Parker. At the time, I was in a punk band called Juvenile Expression, and jazz opened me up to the possibilities of improvisation and hybrids. Later in high school I started listening to the Sugar Hill Gang, Grandmaster Flash, and Run-D.M.C., and this was a time when I was struggling to shape my own identity as a Chicano caught between two cultures."

Membership in hardcore bands with names like Hard Stance and Inside Out led de la Rocha to the conclusion that the conventional hardcore approach was "ultimately kinda limiting. I envisioned a fusion of punk, hardcore, hip-hop, and rap that would also be an outlet for this rap style of poetry I'd been working on, and over the course of two-three months I wrote all the material that would wind up on this album."

If this sudden burst of literary inspiration marked de la Rocha's arrival as a lyricist, the formation of Rage Against The Machine was an equally swift creative alliance of boyhood friends and compatriots from other L.A. bands. Zack had known bassist Timmy C since the sixth grade, drummer Brad Wilk had thundered beside Eddie Vedder prior to Pearl

Jam, and lead guitarist Tom Morello had previously been part of a local outfit called Lock Up. Just prior to their initial public performances in the fall of 1991, Rage Against The Machine recorded a homemade cassette album formidable enough to sell in excess of five thousand copies locally. (The Desert Storm–denouncing "Bullet in the Head" amply illustrates the trenchant allure of the indie cassette, thus that track was eventually transferred intact to the Epic album.)

From the start, Rage Against The Machine was a wildly precocious crowd pleaser, opening for Body Count, Public Enemy, Pearl Jam, and Perry Farrell's Porno For Pyros, as well as being showcased on the second stage for the Los Angeles leg of Lollapalooza II. And on the strength of the Epic album–co-produced by Rage Against The Machine and seasoned engineer Garth Richardson (Red Hot Chili Peppers, Ozzy Osbourne)— they must be viewed as one of the most original and virtuosic new rock bands in the nation, capable of a latticed wall of stridor so deftly woven that it's destined to be the standard for any audacious headbangers who dare follow.

Not since the first Led Zeppelin album or Motorhead's on-tour *No Sleep 'til Hammersmith* has a band rumbled and roared with such extravagant craft, compelling Rage Against The Machine's record company to circulate the following clarifier: "No samples, keyboards, or synthesizers have been used in the making of this album; *all* sounds are the product of guitar, bass, and drums."

But the ornery abandon of Rage Against The Machine's sound is leavened with a forte for intensely versatile arrangements that feature touches of incisive wit and vulnerable self-examination. Tracks like "Take the Power Back," "Know Your Enemy," "Wake Up," and "Freedom" commence with a martial wallop and then careen along a surprisingly cogent path from growling thrash metal to plaintive choral rap to rolling electric blues vivified with postpsychedelic guitar vamps.

In the space of a given song, drummer Wilk can hammer out a half-dozen tensile tempos in styles that incorporate pure swing, punishing funk, and dashes of hip-hop jazz. Meantime, wondrously adept guitarist Morello creates drenching cataracts of raw melody, his consummate runs and delicate organlike surges redolent of Hendrix, Jimmy Page, and Dr. Know of Bad Brains—yet none of it seems even remotely busy.

Interswirled with de la Rocha's elastic vocal howl and the riptide of Timmy C's bass, Rage Against The Machine generates the most beautifully articulated torrent of hardcore bedlam that one could imagine. And the hopes invested in these humming murals of urban din are equally visionary.

"Back in 1974," says de la Rocha, "my father's paintings were part of the first Chicano art exhibit ever organized at the L.A. County Museum of Art ["Los Four: Almarez, de la Rocha, Lugan, Romero"]. That accomplishment was really something to be proud of. I want to make music that gives people that same sense of identity, and lets them see that human rights, civil rights, and spiritual rights are part of the same struggle we all face: to take the power back."

DISCOVERING BELLY'S PERSONAL POLITICS

"SOMETIMES I THINK MUSIC IS IMPORTANT," MULLS TANYA Donelly, leader of the new group Belly. "Other times I think it's an entertaining distraction from things people should be paying attention to, like the healthy control of the world or their own families; the unresolved issue is the proper place of music in people's lives."

And it's precisely this sort of modern quandary that Donelly, formerly best known as a member of Throwing Muses, strives to explore in

Star, Belly's debut album, due for release on Sire/Reprise/4 A.D. Jan. 26. Like a beacon probing a breathtaking fog, Donelly's clear, hesitant voice moves through the dreamlike noise of her songs, posing questions about values and attachments ("Do you have a sister? Would you . . . step one tiptoe in hell for her?") in a song called "Someone to Die For" or asking unfeasible favors ("Heal me by a river") in the song "Slow Dog." Shifting between folk-rock anxiety and garage-band assertiveness, the music is dulcet and droning, and its inquiring lyrics sound innocent, but the

Belly

sum effect is of rising alarm about the groping way in which we continue to live our lives.

"The inspiration for 'Slow Dog' was this magazine article about an adulteress in ancient China who, for penance, had to have a dead dog strapped to her back until it decomposed," says Donelly. "*That* was her punishment for sleeping with someone other than her husband. Can you imagine?"

The power of a song like "Slow Dog" is that it actually tries, in its own impressionistic way, to imagine such cruel absurdities, as if the resurrected figment of them will rehabilitate the past and restore tenderness to the present. As with most of the fifteen consistently entrancing tracks on *Star*, we come upon the richly agitated instrumental drive of "Slow Dog" as if the song were already in progress, Donelly and fellow guitarist Tom Gorman's tinkling acoustic-electric chords passing by us in a spectral procession. By the time the tough, frolicking rhythms of Chris Gorman's drums and Fred Abong's bass join in, the phantomlike movement of the track has been transformed into a flesh-and-blood parade. The listener is left with the sense that, in times of doubt and disbelief, emotions are the only lasting truths. And they can be harder to take than all the facile lies we've been told.

"People think they want to be in love," says the twenty-six-year-old Donelly with a girlish guffaw, "but they don't want all the responsibility it entails. Another song on the new album, 'Low Red Moon,' is my favorite, because it's my first accessible love song." Yet it's a melancholy, almost draining, evocation of a "strange moon," a "strange man," and the exhausting nature of deep sensual endearment.

Meantime, the appearance of Belly and its first album marks a fond move for Donelly away from the security of her long association with Throwing Muses, the eccentric alternative pop outfit headed by her stepsister Kristin Hersh. "The decision really became necessary out of the blue," she explains. "Previously I'd written maybe two songs a year with Throwing Muses, and suddenly, about a year ago, I found I now had twenty of my own I wanted to record. It's just not possible to unload that much stuff on the Muses because, really, it's Kristin's band." Moreover, Donelly had become a virtual free agent within the Muses fold, forming the Breeders as a side project in 1990 with Kim Deal of the Pixies, while also recording with the ever-transmogrifying ensemble known as This Mortal Coil. "I actually quit the Muses back when we were making *The Real Ramona* album [1991]," she confides, "but we didn't want anybody to know until I left officially in June of 1991. It was a comfortable decision as far as Kristin and me. She's always been my closest and dearest friend, dating back to when we'd get stoned as kids [Kristin's mom was once married to Tanya's father] over at her house, and write our first songs."

And what were Donelly's earliest compositions like?

"Well," she chuckles, "the chorus of my very first song was 'Steal me a car/And I'll love you.' That should tell you something."

If anything, it suggests a craving for excitement, along with some secondary interest in escape. Growing up as Donelly did in the attractive resort town of Newport, Rhode Island, she found the right measure of both desires fulfilled in nearby Providence, whose club scene has encompassed such legendary showcase haunts as Lupo's and the Living Room.

"Providence is a great place if you want to start a band," she says. "It's very urban but very relaxed, and there are so many different kinds of good players there that it's pretty difficult not to discover musicians with common interests, or at least someone unexpected."

Which also describes how Tanya's father, a plumber-guitarist-actor, encountered her mom, a legal secretary. "They met at a church social in 1965, when they were sixteen. Dad was a Christian, my mom had on a red leather miniskirt, calf-high boots, and fishnet stockings. Basically, she dragged him down with her."

Years later, their rock'n'roll daughter is able to write wistful quasi–folk ballads like "Untogether," that encapsulate as well as anyone has the "impossible demands" and frustrating tears of an ill-fated but blameless romantic pairing.

If there is a common thread in Donelly's work, whether with Throwing Muses, the Breeders, This Mortal Coil, or her own group, it's the sure, observant tone of a songwriter whose work transcends any easy gender categorizations. Although Belly is led by a woman, it is, like Throwing Muses, neither overtly feminist in spirit nor uncomfortable with its occasional erotic impulses. Whether imagining the secret intimacies of Solomon or recognizing the puppetmaster side of Pinocchio's Gepetto that lurks in many of us, the moody, brilliant material burns with the strength of its own unconditional will.

"The music on our new album has a fragile, melodic, and even honest thing to it that I can confess I really appreciate," says Donelly, who mentions her admiration for Janis Joplin. "But I don't think much about any symbolism in my role as the songwriter or front person for Belly. And in Throwing Muses it never really occurred to us that it was unusual because females were the main creative forces. We were never self-conscious about that at all. I started playing a cheesy Guild acoustic when I was fourteen, and I was nineteen when Throwing Muses was signed, so this work is the only kind of job I know. I do have strong personal politics, as far as being female and feeling it's important for a woman to be onstage with a guitar. And if that has a positive effect on people that's gratifying.

"But the main thing I want to do with Belly is make powerful guitar-oriented music that could never be considered just"—she can't hold back a big laugh—"creepy pop songs! When music *is* important, it's because you can make useful connections for people, instead of hiding behind the noise."

LORD KITCHENER STILL RULES CALYPSO

THE YOUNG RELISH THE EXCITEMENT OF EXPERIENCE, AND the old savor the might of remembrance, but it takes a true sophisticate-sage to fuse discovery and memory into a timeless new force.

Carnival season in Trinidad and Tobago is just commencing, yet seventy-year-old living legend Lord Kitchener, aka Aldwyn Roberts, has already captured the loyalties and libidos of much of the populace with several songs from his just-issued *Longevity* album (J.W. Records). Chief among the singer-songwriter's candescent new crop of rug cutters are "Mystery Band," a ligament-stretching soca yarn about an incorporeal rainy-day *mas* combo, and "Roll Your Abdomen," a torso-cossetting ode to carnal dance traction that's steamy enough to take the crease out of a cricket pitch.

Lord Kitchener, 1962

"Calypso is like a news report, observant and universal," says Kitch, as he is affectionately known. "The story behind *Mystery Band* is that in Port of Spain we have what we call the Dry River, which passes through the city. And I know for a fact that when there's a strong rainfall, a sound comes from it that seems like Carnival music." Or to quote the lyric: "Pan beating all night in the Dry River/Darling we all hearing but can't see this orchestra . . . /Some say the music sound like the late Forties/ Some say it sound like a band from space/But however it sound every man was pleased/For it surely had we shaking we waist!"

Come sunup on the riverside, the perplexed/partying revelers peer out from under their crumpled umbrellas to solve the riddle of the torrential racket: "Milk tin coming down in the flood water/With all kind of old bottle and old can/A-tink-a-ling-a-ling, they bouncing off each other/And they'd mistaken it for a steel band!"

Kitchener's cagey stanzas are a gentle reproach to the tame generation of steel pan ensembles in the annual road march competitions, while also satirizing stagnant imaginations within the dance-obsessed ranks of the leading soca (i.e., "soul calypso") performers. But the triumph of Kitch's allegorical censure lies in the galvanizing gait of the track, its sambalike vigor sharpened by palpitating scat vocals ("Paloon-ting! Paloon-tong!") that are as pendulous as they are pungent.

Which brings us to "Roll Your Abdomen," a rapt cantata to lower-anatomy calisthenics (courtesy of an assertive character named Cindy) that might seem utterly profligate were it not so uproarious in its caricature of standard soca dance couplets: "Kitch, I don't want 'jamming,' I don't want no 'wine'!" So he counsels, "Roll your belly and cool your mind!"

As the Solomonic old calypsonian explains, "In the early days of ca-lypso, you had more lyrics and less music. Today with the soca, you have more music but less lyrics. Soca excites the dancers, yes, but it doesn't say as much. For the last two, three years, all the calypsos were about nothing but the 'wine' and 'jam.' The whole thing was monotonous and unimaginative, so I decided," he says, giggling with sly glee, "that now 'the action is on the *abdomen.*'

"Really, I wanted to create another big jump in the soca sound, in its brains and vitality, just like back in the forties," Kitch assures, passing the afternoon in his comfortable home near Diego Martin on Trinidad's northwestern peninsula while wife Betsy Howell Roberts gets a meal under way. The veteran troubadour is referring to his revolutionary move in 1946 to organize his own calypso tent under the heading "The Young

Brigade," he and compatriots the Mighty Killer, Spoiler & Viking, and Lord Ziegfeld electing to intensify the rhythmic structure of calypso, adding more horn-accented Latin swing to its festive folk-based street tempos. He also sought to expand its post–World War II themes, featuring less of the old *picong* (improvised) judgments on local politics or domestic gossip (such as his own girlfriend-denouncing "Green Fig" [aka "Mary I Am Tired and Disgusted"], 1944, and "Tie Tongue Mopsie," 1945), and increasing the apologies of ethnic pride and civil rights commentary, including an epochal song he first performed in 1948 during his extended (until 1964) stay in England—"Black or White (If You're Not White You're Black)."

That track and "Africa My Home" would later be huge hits circa 1953 on the U.K. Melodisc label, with the former, statesmanlike treatise on colonial racial stratification remaining one of the most admired in modern Caribbean history: "Your father is an African/Your mother may be Norwegian/You pass me when you say good night/Feeling you are really white/ . . . No, you can never get away from the fact/If you not white you considered black."

Born on April 18, 1922, to blacksmith Stephen Roberts and wife Albertha, Aldwyn was raised with his two brothers and three sisters in the crossroads town of Arima, St. George parish. Taught guitar and the oral calypso tradition at the age of ten, they became his sole source of income four years later when the death of both parents compelled the six-foot-two teenager to seek full-time employment as a salaried serenader of Water Scheme laborers in Trinidad's San Fernando Valley. By 1939, Aldwyn (also known as "Bean" for his height) was able to score his first calypso hit, "Shops Close Too Early."

Come 1944, when the wartime ban on Carnival was rescinded, he won the celebrants' hearts with "Mary, I Am Tired and Disgusted." The Growling Tiger, greatest of the first golden era (1920–40) of folk calypsonians, saw that a new talent had seized the psyches of his countrymen, and Tiger christened him Lord Kitchener for the famed British field marshal and war minister.

In 1978, Kitch conquered calypso anew, notching the first international smash in the ascendant soca style with his "Sugar Bum Bum." He's enjoyed steady hits ever since with songs like "Iron Man" and "Parkway" (both 1990). In 1989, he was inducted into calypso's Sunshine Awards Hall of Fame. And since Lord Kitchener is one of the foremost living contributors to the literature of modern song, Caribbean observers trust the

University of the West Indies will one day bestow an honorary Doctorate of Humanities on this Woody Guthrie of the Lesser Antilles.

"In my time," says Kitch, "I've sung for Harry Truman at Waller Field in 1945, and for Princess Margaret at London's Chesterfield Club in the fifties. But in the early days at home, performers like me were outcasts. It's only in recent years that our own country has given official recognition to calypso, but I'm thankful."

Like the towering *immortelle* trees imported to Trinidad and Tobago in the eighteenth century to shelter its delicate coffee and cocoa shrubs, the calypso of Lord Kitchener has foreshadowed and nurtured key rhythmic and vocal strains of popular music in this hemisphere, from jump blues and dance to rap. Indeed the various lineages of these genres would make no logical sense without calypso, just as the 1993 Carnival would be poorer in spirit without "Roll Your Abdomen" and "Mystery Band."

"For fifty-five years, I've tried to make calypso more intelligent, and make soca more danceable," says Kitch quietly as his wife calls him for lunch. "Long ago, today, and tomorrow, that is my job."

STING: INSIDE THE SUMNER'S TALE

AMONG ALL LIVING CREATURES, ONLY HUMAN BEINGS ARE endowed with a sense of humor, and their worthiest attribute may be the will to laugh at themselves.

"You're supposed to have a smile on your face—or I do, anyway—after you hear this record," says Sting of *Ten Summoner's Tales* (A&M, due March 9), confiding that his sixth solo album is "mostly a series of musical jokes." Yet this is levity with a sense of heritage as well as humanity. "What interests me about songwriting is that there is some kind of lineage between the tradition of songwriting and the tradition of storytelling."

Hence, the lighthearted template for Sting's latest release is one of the most cherished strokes of rhyme and whimsy in the English literary tradition, *The Canterbury Tales*, which medieval poet Geoffrey Chaucer wrote between 1386 and 1399. In Chaucer's time, the practice of making pilgrimages to holy shrines was a popular and unusually egalitarian practice that brought together citizens from every station of medieval life, whether noblemen, peas-

Sting

ants, or those of the midtier civil and religious services, such as friars and summoners. It was the summoner's job to notify citizens of impending civil or ecclesiastical court appearances. As one of Chaucer's pithy wayfarers puts it in "The Friar's Tale": "A summoner's one who runs about the nation/Dealing out summonses for fornication."

"Yeah, he's a rascal, basically," laughs Sting, aka Gordon Sumner, "and if you didn't want to go to court, you just paid the summoner. In England at this time, everyone wanted to earn blessings and indulgences by making pilgrimages, but both the church and civil societies would also sell these blessings. The more basic joke at work here is that this is actually where my surname came from! Over the centuries *summoner* became *sumner.*

"The stories in *The Canterbury Tales* are romantic, bawdy, funny, sad, and the characters tell them in different styles. I think my record is a lot like that. It's a mixed bag of character sketches connected only by the journey it took to complete them, meaning that for the first time in my solo work the songs—which actually number *eleven*—are simply a record of my labors over a particular period."

Just as Chaucer's *Tales* were the fruits of a picaresque career as a courtier-clerk for the royal houses of King Edward III and Richard II (whose company he was privileged to entertain by reading aloud, versifying, and singing in the vernacular English), so former schoolteacher Gordon Sumner has found his calling as a worldly wise chronicler of the social commerce of his own era. And since last April, Sting's been conceiving and recording his music in the chapel-like vaulted dining room of his sixteenth-century manor house in Wiltshire (built in 1578 for a West Country wool merchant).

A visit there last summer found the bass-playing laird laboring over the final touches of the first single from *Ten Summoner's Tales*, the gliding, gorgeously sung "If I Ever Lose My Faith in You." As a pale pastoral sun spilled in through the tall, leaded-glass windows, co-producer Hugh Padgham and Sting stood at a portable sound board and tinkered with the track's imposing knell, bringing a chapel-like warmth to the cathedral-sized sound.

"That song is interesting," Sting now reflects, "because while it's very easy to define what one may have lost faith in—and you can list them: governments, the church, all the things you're supposed to have as crutches in our society that have proved to be fake—I found that it's not so easy to define what you still *have* faith in, so the song doesn't. It's very uplifting when you get to the chorus, but I don't state whether it's God, self-acceptance, or romantic love that I'm optimistic about.

"I think a lot of ghosts were exorcized on my previous record," he notes, referring to *The Soul Cages*, which was dedicated to the memory of his late father. "That album was very personal, confessional, and therapeutic in terms of facing death and loss. But I guess you could say the therapy worked, because now I have a new sense of freedom, a desire to move on and make songs solely intended as entertainments, designed to amuse."

Hearkening back again to Chaucer, Sting aimed to concoct what the author of *The Canterbury Tales* had called "some comedy," a phrase that six centuries ago meant a narrative poem in the common tongue with a pleasurable conclusion.

While Sting could never be accused of resembling in aspect Chaucer's own Summoner, whose features are described as so pockmarked they frightened small children, the singer's startling wit is equal to that of his fictive namesake as he skewers the false piety of our world in other new songs like the hilariously theatrical "Saint Augustine in Hell" or the hard-rocking "Heavy Cloud No Rain." Throughout the record's varied array of musical character studies, royal astrologers and witchcraft-reliant farmers do their best to redirect the forces of fate, but the only power that prevails is sincere faith in the mystery of one's own potential.

Though Sting insists *Ten Summoner's Tales* is a "traveler's rag bag of tunes" it actually is his most uniformly engaging effort yet at conjoining dramatic musicality and sonic storycraft. Simply by recognizing the depth latent in the patterns of ordinary ritual—how the suits of common playing cards are derived from the turbulent symbology of the tarot ("spades are swords . . . clubs are weapons . . . diamonds mean money")—he constructs a bedazzlingly handsome ballad about the intrinsic specialness of love on "Shape of My Heart." Within the innate poker of the track itself, plucked acoustic guitar, chromatic harmonica, delicate drums, cello, and Sting's imploring vocal comprise a masterly wager on the power of control versus the sweetness of probabilities. The effect is so subtly euphonic it must be heard to be believed.

"We all know that the shape of the heart on the playing card is not the actual dimensions of the human heart," says Sting. "And yet we gamble all the time as if things really are that neat and precise and familiar. On this album, I've looked around at the most normal things in my life: the cowboy movie on my TV, the golden fields of barley beyond my house, and tried to see the subtle stories within them. Yet on the record's final song, 'Epilogue (Nothing 'bout Me),' I say you can search them all and still not know anything about me, the storyteller.

"But maybe that's not true, because being whimsical is an essential part of my personality and my own searching. I want to be a good pilgrim on the road to Canterbury, but I want to ignore all the signposts along the way. As I quote him on the album, St. Augustine had a prayer for all the rascal summoners of the world: 'God, make me pure, but not yet!' "

RAY CHARLES'S
BRAVE NEW *WORLD*

"THE MIND IS ITS OWN PLACE, AND IN ITSELF/CAN MAKE A
heav'n of hell, a hell of heav'n," wrote blind poet John Milton in his fiercely
vulnerable epic poem of free will, *Paradise Lost.* But it was Satan who was
doing the talking in that particular passage from Milton's tale, the ancient
archfiend trying to put the best face on his fabled fall from grace.

For his part, the legendary Ray Charles proffers no similar rationales
about life's shifting fortunes or his own tug of war with eternity. "I don't
go through rituals and shit,"
rules the nondenominational
musician, in reference to both
his art and its spiritual consequence. "I don't mean no harm
by that, but I just do whatever
comes natural!

"I've loved music ever since I
come into the world, and that's
why I'm never gonna retire,"
explains the feisty sixty-two-
year-old Genius of Soul as he
begins another full day's work
at the offices of R.P.M. ("which
means Recording, Publishing,
and Management"), the Los Angeles headquarters Ray built to

Ray Charles

his specifications thirty-one years ago. "God knows I have enough money to last me the rest of my life—I'm not bragging or trying to be forward, I'm just telling the truth—so it ain't about money. I know how to play music, I know how to write music, I know how to try to sing songs. And I'm gonna do that 'til God says otherwise."

Sightless since the age of seven due to the depredations of glaucoma, Charles has also endured the isolation of being orphaned, the humiliation of homelessness, the self-deception of drug abuse, and the craven racist animus of the Ku Klux Klan. Along the way, he taught himself the basics of big band and orchestral arranging by age twelve, had a number-two national hit on the R&B charts with his self-penned "Confession Blues" before his nineteenth birthday, and at twenty-five was skilled enough in backstage card playing with guitarist T-Bone Walker to turn numerous winning hands at blackjack into a 1955 hit named after the game. In that same year, Charles mingled gospel fealty and profane rhythm into a wickedly effective amalgam on "I've Got a Woman," a number-one R&B smash that forever altered the landscape of rhythm and blues.

"I just want to play good music every day of my life," says Charles with a husky chortle. "I've been out there forty-eight years, and I swear to God, what I'm about is to be my best. That's what I call soul: when you make the public *believe* in what you're doing." And the enveloping aura of Charles's no-fuss creative drive is in full effect on the forthcoming *My World* (Warner Bros.), a ten-song dose of street ecclesiastics and pew-pounding backtalk that burns with Charles's surliest fire in a decade.

Working with producer Richard Perry, an unerring studio band that includes Eric Clapton, and backing singers of the caliber of Mavis Staples and June Pointer, Charles is able to devote himself vocally to an almost memoirlike range of material. The title track, "Let Me Take Over," "So Help Me God," "A Song for You," "I'll Be There," and "One Drop of Love" are disarming, "let's-cut-the-crap" slices of the saloon sermonizing Charles has specialized in since his 1952–59 bible 'n' brimstone period on Atlantic, with Perry often lending modified hip-hop momentum.

The pillars of the project, however, are three transporting performances that reactivate the edgy emotional vibrance that made Charles such an invincible artist from the start. The first is "None of Us Are Free," a hard-rolling exhortation—heightened by Clapton's turbulent solo—that deserves to be a multiformat radio anthem for these morally faltering times. The second standout track is "If I Could," a simple statement in defense of the defenseless, reminiscent in its tender consonance of "I Can't Stop Loving You" and "You Don't Know Me" from Charles's pioneering *Modern Sounds in Country and Western Music* album (ABC-Paramount, 1962). "If I Could" can be construed as anything from a love pledge, to a parent's lullaby, to a prayer of requiem.

And the last of this trio of stunners is Charles's humble, unsettled reading of Paul Simon's "Still Crazy After All These Years," the deep personal parallels in Simon's pragmatic verses ultimately reducing the author's version to a virtual demo.

"I always liked that song, the chord structure, and of course the lyrics," says Charles, "and I figured, 'I'll put my own little thing to it.' If you notice, the arrangement on it is very much like my small bands [his Atlantic-era septet and octet].

"I'm basically a sentimentalist," he continues, "so I like the slow stuff. It's strange how you mention 'I Can't Stop Loving You.' When I went to Sam Clark, who was the president of ABC at the time, and I told him I wanted to do this country-and-western record, he thought I had lost it! He said, 'You're gonna lose a lot of fans, because people know you for your rhythm and blues.' I said, 'Yeah, Sam, you may be right about that. But if it works right, I may *gain* whatever fans I lose!' So we did it, and you know what happened." The album became Charles's first gold record and "I Can't Stop Loving You" sold three million singles.

"I've been very lucky," says Charles. "People who I figure had an impression on me when I was younger, or who I looked up to, well, there was a lady when my mom died [circa 1945]. Her name was Lena Mae Thompson, and her husband was Alfred. They was just friends of my mom, but they took me in just like I was their own kid. They fed me, gave me housing, put clothes on my back. And then there was Mr. Wylie Pittman, who took time with me to show me the difference between hitting on the piano with both hands, as opposed to playing the keys with one finger at a time. I mean, he could have shooed me away."

Asked about private favorites in his vast catalog, whether written by himself or others, Charles answers, "Oh, my goodness, I'm not trying to be modest, but I don't think I wrote anything all that great. But things I wrote were successful, like 'Hallelujah I Love Her So'—I enjoyed writing that. I think my favorite song that I wrote, and it was a slow song, was called 'A Fool for You' on Atlantic." As for cherished material generated by others, Charles cites "Baby Grand," his 1987 duet with Billy Joel.

"I really dig him a lot," Charles confides. "We hit it off real good, and the song is very fitting. If you listen to the words ['I've come far/From the

life I strayed in/I've got scars/From those dives I played in'] you can tell
he wrote it exactly about what goes on out there on the road. It's very true
to life—take my word for it."

Ray Charles will soon be on the road again, bringing his band and the
Raeletts to a town near most of us, sharing a bit of *My World*. How much
heaven can he still make out of the hellish grind?

"I'll leave you with this one message," he says softly. "I never, ever
record or play anything that I don't genuinely love. See, I wish I could if I
had the talent, meaning that some people can just take *any* song and go
on ahead and do it. But anything that you hear of Ray Charles's, you can
believe me, he *loved* it when he did it."

AIMEE MANN:
WHATEVER MATTERS

TO SPEAK FROM THE HEART REQUIRES COURAGE, BUT TO SING from the heart can take something more valiant: a desire to share one's deepest vulnerabilities.

"Telling what you feel, trying to talk about what's important to you, does not make you weaker," says blonde, winsome Aimee Mann with a calm smile, by way of discussing *Whatever*, her first solo album (on Imago/BMG, due May 11). "That's the big secret that nobody seems to get. I think the role of artists and songwriters is to say, 'Maybe you can't do this, but I'll do it for you.' In other words, I'll try to sing, out loud, the truth of what you and I both feel. I have nothing but disdain for people who spend a lot of energy trying to protect their emotions."

And Mann's many fans have nothing but respect for the singer-song-

Aimee Mann

writer's forceful output since 1985, which appeared on three albums (*Voices Carry, Welcome Home, Everything's Different Now*) by the Boston-based group 'Til Tuesday, and is now displayed on her own free-standing debut. One of her staunchest admirers is Elvis Costello (with whom she wrote the wistful "The Other End [of the Telescope]" on *Everything's Different Now*), who has pronounced her among the fore-most songsmiths in popular music today. She's also an intensely expres-sive vocalist, her tangy, insistent phrasing and the pressing tone of her lyric lines converting each silvery melody line from a covert notion into a kindred necessity.

And while Mann is still best known as the embodiment of "Voices Carry," the top-ten hit 'Til Tuesday enjoyed in the spring of 1985, her rep-utation in critical and cult circles rests on the unshakable spell of subse-quent efforts like "Coming Up Close" and "Rip in Heaven," each a searching oath of romantic self-scrutiny that is unstinting in its seasoned frankness.

What protects Mann's music from the traps of pop self-pity or trifling bathos are its impertinent wit and coolly suggestive structure, the player and arranger taking over from the writer to insert devious and sly instru-mental touches to sharpen her messages. A perfect example of this able balance occurs at regular intervals throughout the *Whatever* album, whose parallel themes are the rewarding difficulties of self-redemption (on the first single "I Should've Known," "Put Me on Top," "Way Back When") and the surface temptations of self-defeat ("I've Had It," "Could've Been Anyone," "Jacob Marley's Chain.")

Theme-wise, are these tracks lovelorn exercises, poison-pen letters, rapt reaffirmations, or caustic manifestos? Stylistically, are they intricate pop ballads, wrenching rock confessions, sly folk-punk outbursts?

Turns out they're all of the above and more, performed with a Beatles-esque disregard for the improprieties of mixing irate power chords, folkish strumming, sighing mellotrons, and a snare drum that sounds like it's ringing from the recreation room of a mental ward. Her enticing singing winds its way through the flawless counterpoint like a cunning waif, whispering and prodding and rising in a trenchant warble that leaves no insight unspoken.

"Songwriting can take on any amount of separate lives according to the treatments you give it," says Mann, "but it should never be a dodge or a disguise for the central issue of telling the truth. Even pity and com-passion and gratitude, although very noble impulses in themselves, can be very destructive in too great amounts because they become narcissistic, a way to cover up inadequacies or fears."

Professionally, the facts Mann chose not to avoid on *Whatever* were the personal regret and discouragement she felt after reaching a commercial and artistic impasse with former label Epic following the release in 1988 of *Everything's Different Now* (her then-finest and least-known album). After years in and out of lawyers' offices and showcase clubs—grappling with the possibility that her career was permanently crippled—she reached a diplomatic agreement and a new beginning. Deciding to strike out on her own, she found a new manager willing to help put up the money for her to make *Whatever* entirely under her own flag—right down to its cover art—and then presented the finished product to Imago. While risky, it was a strategy that turned Mann from a virtual lost soul into one of the year's most dramatic new faces.

But it also parallels the struggles and sorrows of her own background, including the part about being "lost."

"My parents split up when I was about three years old," she explains. "And my mother and her new man, he concocted this plan to kidnap my brother and I and go off to Europe with his kids from a previous marriage. They couldn't get my brother, but I went with them. My father, an advertising executive, was searching for me with private detectives for a year! That's probably why I don't like to travel," she notes, laughing.

"I was returned to my father and the divorce was made final, but then I didn't see my mother again until fifteen years later."

At this point, Mann was eighteen and had decided to leave her home in Richmond, Virginia, to attend the Berklee School of Music in Boston. In between stints baking croissants at an Au Bon Pain shop in the Prudential Center and working at the counters of Strawberries and Newbury Comics record shops, she grew from a shy member of the Young Snakes to the leader of the successful if beleaguered 'Til Tuesday.

In the intervening years, Aimee, now thirty-two, has resumed contact with her mom ("She's very soft spoken and intelligent, with a somewhat introverted, analytical thing I recognize in myself; she now works finding foster homes for disturbed children"), and taken control of her own destiny.

"The best thing that anyone can ever do—and that I certainly did—is make a choice not to be afraid anymore. I was a very fearful person, and leaving Richmond to go to the big city of Boston by myself for music school when I knew nothing but four Neil Young chords on an acoustic guitar—that completely changed my life.

"This is embarassing to admit, but I find it useful in times of stress to imagine I'm talking to the most perfect, loving, understanding person I can envision, and say, 'Well, what should I do in this situation? I'm completely upset.' I then have that ideal person talk to me and say, 'It's not really this that you're upset about. It's because it reminds you of this *other* thing.'

"In short, I know the right thing to do, but I had to learn to give myself those answers. The realization that I could be so objective about myself is what's made me a good songwriter."

And it's what makes Aimee Mann's *Whatever* such a great achievement.

DONALD FAGEN'S
EPIC *KAMAKIRIAD*

THERE IS NO REST FOR THE WEIRD, AND HISTORY PROVES IT.
While Belgian master violinist Joseph Merlin may have originated roller
skaites in 1759 in order to make grand entrances while playing at costume parties, he never learned to brake them properly, shattering both
his violin and various ballroom mirrors in the process. Horticulturist
Johnny "Appleseed" Chapman became famous sowing his free seed-
lings throughout the Midwest, but the poor ninny died of pneumonia in

the winter of 1847 because he
always made his wilderness
rounds barefoot. Richard M.
Hollingshead Jr. built the first
patented drive-in theater near
Camden, New Jersey, in 1933,
but since sound travels slower
than light, cars in the back rows
found the primitive foreground
speaker tower dangerously out
of sync with the screen lust
their occupants scrambled to
emulate.

Reflecting on these rather
checkered modern sagas of
techno-musical acceleration, ecological wanderlust, and the cinematic dawn of Virtual Carnality,

Donald Fagen

observers may someday decide such efforts never quite achieved overlapping cruise control until 1993, when ex–Steely Dan singer-songwriter Donald Fagen unveiled the surreal sedan extolled on his second solo album, *Kamakiriad* (Warner Bros., due May 25).

As Fagen explains, "Kamakiri is an invented car. The word in Japanese actually meaning 'praying mantis,' but a Kamakiriad would be a journey, like the Iliad. The story takes place a few years in the future, when this guy gets this environmentally correct car, a multiscreen magical exploration vehicle with a bionic backseat vegetable garden.

"It's a hero story in which this guy's depressed and suicidal until he arrives at a place called Flytown, where he hears this strain of music and encounters old friends that enable him to go forward into the unknown. The songs represent his sensual adventures."

Each of these exploits bespeaks an emotional spin cycle of an atypical sort, beginning with the rousing instant the hero first takes possession ("I was born yesterday/ . . . When they handed me the keys") of the utopian conveyance in the album's sweetly oscillating opening track, "Trans-Island Skyway." And it is plain to anyone along for the ride that no past mishaps in the annals of technology, musicology, *or* autoeroticism will be repeated. This is prime Steely Dan terrain, an exuberantly batty orbit of cabaret funk, proto-jazz, sci-fi boogaloo, and hallucinatory pit stops wherein harpies and satyrs crash an end-of-the-world rent party cohosted by LTD and the Ohio Players. Memories of veteran R&B hedonists may even stray to those overheated sirens on the Players' outrageous LP dust jackets when they hear the sybaritic first single from *Kamakiriad*, "Tomorrow's Girls."

As produced by bass-playing former Steely Dan partner Walter Becker, the album's fluctuant fantasy environment overflows with bantering horns, beckoning female backing harmonies, and a tremulant keyboard sound that sustains Fagen's amorphous vocals with the ease of an Eames chair.

Who would go to the intemperate trouble of making turnpike groove music so grievously kooked out? As far back as Becker and Fagen's 1967 introduction while students at Bard College, what could have possessed these two rock eccentrics to travel together in the first place?

"Hey now," chuckles Fagen, "we just liked writing funny songs! We were both jazz fans, had begun an interest in Chicago blues, and liked the Byrds. We were pretty ironic kids, and we used to just laugh a lot while we were writing. So we ended up with a bunch of songs and tried to unload them on somebody. We placed a not-very-good song with Barbra Streisand for one of her less popular albums; it was called 'I Mean to Shine.' Then we moved to L.A. in 1972, where we were staff writers for ABC-Dunhill, but we were terrible pop songwriters.

"On his first solo album, John Kay of Steppenwolf did a tune of ours— this will give you an idea of why we had trouble writing pop songs— called 'Giles of the River.' We soon realized that to play the material we really liked, we'd have to have a band, so we started rehearsing, and just before Dunhill fired us, we put out a record [*Can't Buy a Thrill*, ABC Records, 1972]."

The original group, which was named for the steam-powered dildo in William Burroughs's novel *Naked Lunch*, had Fagen splitting lead-vocal responsibilities with David Palmer. Following two Fagen-sung hits ("Do It Again," "Reelin' in the Years"), Palmer departed and Fagen became the reluctant interlocutor of the act. In a perhaps unconscious attempt to bolster that role, Becker's glib bass assumed an almost conversant presence and Fagen's keyboards followed suit ("I never had regular piano lessons, but after I listened to Ray Charles and Thelonious Monk, I devised a way of playing it like a solo saxophone.").

And since both Becker and Fagen were somewhat shy personalities, they made the music into an ambivalent commentary on the passing parade. "A lot of the songs are about relationships that have gone wrong," says Fagen. "And we'd deliberately use the wrong music—like something very cheery with the gloomy lyrics in 'Peg.' It had a very strange, distancing effect."

After a decade's worth of peculiarly imposing albums, including *Pretzel Logic* (1974), *Aja* (1977), and *Gaucho* (1980), rock's most entrancingly weird wiseacres suspended Steely Dan to pursue other interests. Fagen issued the acclaimed *The Nightfly* (1982), Becker produced China Crisis and Rickie Lee Jones, and both joined briefly to assist singer Rosie Vela on her 1987 *Zazu* album. Now they've reconvened for the chronicle of the Kamakiri—which not coincidentally is also "steam powered"— and a possible summer tour. What got this stalled alliance back into gear?

"When I was finally about to go in to record," says Fagen, "it just seemed like it would be more fun if Walter was there to help me out, and it was. The new album's not strictly autobiographical, but in the ten years since *The Nightfly*, I had to somehow adjust to the middle of my life and figure out a new place to draw energy from after my long post-adolescence," admits this son of a Passaic, New Jersey, accountant and a onetime Catskills dance-band singer. "My mother used to sing all day long in the house, and she'd backphrase like Martha Raye or the Andrews Sisters. I've always loved swing music because it's very propulsive, so I tried to get that feel, even though I'm using a *much* heavier backbeat. Meanwhile, setting the new album in the future and putting it on a mythic level enabled me to detach from it."

Since Fagen finds a measure of impartiality useful in his work, does he endorse the same bent for fans?

"Yeah! To me, music shouldn't always carry a lot of tired accoutrements. I want the listeners to bring their *own* imaginations, and be collaborators."

HORNSBY'S CHESAPEAKE HARBOR LIGHTS

IT IS AMERICAN REALISM, INSIGHTFUL BUT UNASSUMING,
as it explores the interludes between light and shadow, silence and
sonance, seclusion and connection. Exposing both inner verities *and* the
elusive values of the outside world, it portrays a stillpoint of quiet clarity
in a transitory realm, as if to show that the character of a nation's culture
can still be felt in its most commonplace tableaux.

What's being detailed here is *Rooms by the Sea,* famed twentieth-
century expressionist painter Edward
Hopper's sunlit 1951 study of an
empty oceanside bungalow, which
adorns the cover of Bruce Hornsby's
new album, *Harbor Lights* (RCA, due
Tuesday, April 6). But these words
could also be an explication of the
music of Hornsby, who happens to
be a blood relative of Hopper's.

Whereas Hopper ("My maternal
grandfather Pete's first cousin,"
says Bruce) was born in the Hudson
River port town of Nyack, New
York, and ultimately divided his
time—and sites of stimulus—between Greenwich Village and coastal
Massachusetts (where *Rooms by the
Sea* was done), Hornsby was reared

Bruce Hornsby

in the Virginia Tidewater area of the Chesapeake Bay and spent roughly a decade in Los Angeles' urban sprawl before resettling in his birthplace of Williamsburg, Virginia.

Hopper's best-known depression- and World War II–era paintings, including *Nighthawks, Office at Night, Summer Evening, Hotel Room,* and *Solitude,* are formal attempts to fix the fleeting daily atmosphere of the most ordinary civic environs, exposing the loss of faith in technological advance and economic self-interest that appeared to resound from every structural shadow and human surface. The late painter (1882–1967) perceived his work as part of a movement toward a "native art" that contained "the tang of the soil" in this country. Hopper described his own heavyhearted style as "My most intimate reaction to the subject as it appears when I like it most—when the facts are given unity by my interest and prejudices."

Like his renowned relative, Hornsby is a modern American regionalist whose output is distinctly introspective and values-directed in nature, concentrating on objective yet metaphoric images drawn from his immediate surroundings. "I've always tried to have a real strong focus in my work," says Bruce, "like southern fiction in a sense, with a real sense of place, whether it's southeast Virginia, or Los Angeles as viewed by someone from my background. So if you'd look back on all my records, they would be of-a-piece."

Hornsby ascended to pop prominence in 1986, a time when the avaricious economic manipulation of the Reagan-Bush years was slowly becoming unraveled by the sheer volume of the stricken have-nots. Hits like "The Way It Is" (1986); "Mandolin Rain," "Every Little Kiss" (1987); "The Valley Road," "Look Out Any Window" (1988), and "Lost Soul" (1990) were casually heard as beatific acoustic piano ballads, but more attentive fans of the albums from which the songs sprang (*The Way It Is, Scenes from the Southside, A Night on the Town*) knew them to be intensely saturnine plaints against racist cynicism, rampant joblessness, and rank dejection in the face of a calculated New Depression.

Now Hornsby returns after a three-year respite with *Harbor Lights,* his first record without his longtime band the Range, his first without an outside producer, and his first to be cut in his home studio. Centering on a trio of Hornsby, Yellowjackets bassist Jimmy Haslip, and Range drummer John Molo, this fourth album is more free spirited and jazz tinged than Hornsby's earlier outings, drawing from keyboard influences such as Bill Evans, McCoy Tyner, and Leon Russell that date to Hornsby's college days at the University of Miami music school. *Harbor Lights* freshest textures are further contoured by the guest artists (Phil Collins, Jerry Garcia, Branford Marsalis, Pat Metheny, Bonnie Raitt) who are on board. The social conscience of *The Way It Is* is reaffirmed on an upcoming single, the astringently funky "Talk of the Town," whose story of interracial love will be shot for video by Spike Lee. And the Hornsby knack for pop collaboration previously heard on his and Don Henley's "The End of the Innocence" is exhibited once more on "Pastures of Plenty," a scintillating session with Garcia that's obviously been informed by the one hundred tour dates Bruce recently logged with the Grateful Dead.

Even so, *Harbor Lights* has the largest measure thus far of the regional aura Hornsby desires in his sound, especially on the title song, "Fields of Gray" and "The Tide Will Rise." Reared amid the colonial residue of the seminal American settlements of Williamsburg, Yorktown, and Jamestown, Hornsby's creative disposition still hews closest to the working-class egalitarianism of his lowly settler forebears, rather than the aristocratic bias of the actual Founding Fathers.

"The first Hornsbys reached here from England in the 1770s or 1780s and ended up in Virginia and Kentucky," says Bruce, "with the ones I'm most aware of coming to Yorktown and Williamsburg from the eastern shore of Virginia around the 1830s. All these people were simple fishermen who I don't think fought in the Civil War. They were real 'watermen,' as they're called around the Chesapeake, tending their crab pots and oyster beds. Today they're a dying breed because of the dwindling shellfish population in the bay. I wrote 'The Tide Will Rise' about them, and I played it with a local symphony orchestra last spring; the Working Watermen's Association bought tickets to this high-brow affair, and all these old fishermen marched past these hoity-toity symphony types and sat in the front rows dressed in their Sunday best." The six-foot-four, thirty-eight-year-old Hornsby beams with boyish pluck. "It was a really good thing."

Spring has come again to the Chesapeake basin, carp, and *cooters* (box turtles) spawning in the coastal streams and tributaries, and millions of migratory waterfowl (snow geese, whistling swans, goldeneye ducks) departing via the Atlantic flyway above the Gloucester Peninsula, while the upland woods are alive with vireos and thrushes that flicker between the wild violets and mountain laurel. The Chesapeake is itself a microcosm of transition, the largest estuary in North America, where salt and fresh water converge and mingle, and myriad living creatures of seemingly conflicting habitats find a way to accept and even fortify each other.

Inspired by this seasonally changeful setting, and with a painterly hand worthy of Edward Hopper himself, Hornsby's "Fields of Gray" lifts *Harbor Lights* to a gently heartening highpoint.

"It's a song about guiding my little twin boys, Russell and Keith, through an uncertain world," Hornsby confides with an intent smile. "Its basic sentiments are that you try hard to be a realist, but you still hope that you can do your very, very best."

WYNONNA'S
SEARCHING
TELL ME WHY

THE ONLY WAY TO CURE LONELINESS IS TO DEFEAT THE DREAD of being alone. Yet this fear often can't be conquered without facing a separation from all things familiar.

Such dilemmas retain a special poignance when expressed in country music, whose cultural ethics are as old as the pioneer life that produced them—whether the frontiers to be crossed lay in the Scottish Highlands, across an Irish moor, or upon the hostile seas between Britain and southern Appalachia.

"I felt like I was leaving home but still going back for meals and laundry," says singer Wynonna Judd with a laugh, alluding to her self-titled solo debut of 1992. "With this second record, I'm a little more adventuresome," she assures, describing *Tell Me Why,* her subsequent effort on MCA, due May 11, as well as the traditions from whence her music springs. "My solo records are chapters in my life; they're very autobiographical in terms of what I've been through," she adds, by way of acknowledging

Wynonna Judd

her former status as one-half of the Judds, the hugely successful mother-and-daughter country vocal duo that dissolved after parent Naomi's forced retirement due to a rare, incurable strain of hepatitis.

"Every decision I ever made in my life was a team effort, since my mom and I did everything together," explains Wynonna "and orchestrating Mom's professional funeral so to speak, the farewell tour [in 1991], was devastating to me. I'm twenty-eight, but I feel like I'm eighteen. Right now I'm starting to feel my rebirth; I'm starting to understand what it's like to be alone."

It is the rudiments of that emerging comprehension that color every song on *Tell Me Why*, with each probative experiment in personal autonomy having both familial and historical antecedents. Born, like her mother, in Ashland, Kentucky, which straddles Boyd and Greenup counties in the Appalachian Mountains of northeastern Kentucky, Wynonna is a product of a broken home. Neither she nor her mother—whose parents divorced as she turned thirty—has known an upbringing untouched by emotional turmoil. Wynonna's high and plaintive leads, plus the mournful edge of Naomi's contralto harmonies, on such Judd laments as "Change of Heart" and "Mr. Pain" (each authored by Naomi) were electrifying onstage alloys of youthful trust and the scar tissue of experience, that is, the Judds always embodied the aggrieved generational travails of their music. For Wynonna's latest solo record, her mother presented her with the conspicuously knowing verses for the song "That Was Yesterday," which her daughter describes as being about "the hell" her mother went through with her second husband during their courtship: "She threw him out like forty times or something . . . she would put his clothes in a garbage bag and throw them out in the yard . . . but she loved him so much that she hung in there, and now of course they're married."

Such torment and disarray have long been the grist for country songwriting, but they are also grounded in the punishing social orthodoxies of pioneer America, in which young people would frequently pass immediately from the crib to the plow or its hard-scrabble equivalent. Those uncushioned by sure family cohesion lacked the calm moral judgment that allows a balanced diet of romance and duty, responsibility and impulsive pleasure. Wynonna's first release had a number of guilt- and regret-ridden supplications, including "When I Reach the Place I'm Goin'" and "My Strongest Weakness" (written by Naomi and Mike Reid), but the new record elevates this dour outlook to near-devotional degree. That "Father Sun," "Only Love," "Is It Over Yet," and "I Just Drove By" are as lovely as any country hymns you'll hear this year is no alleviation of the sadness and soul-vexed searching they detail.

"We've forgotten where we come from," says Wynonna, "and the song 'I Just Drove By' really hit me right between the ears when I first heard it, because I thought, 'My God, I've done that.' I live about five miles from the home that mom and I and my sister Ashley lived in when we first moved to Nashville. Whenever I'm having a real bad, emotionally weird day, I go by this house and I sit there and think back to when it was just the three of us together, to find out why I am the way I am. I don't write yet; I'm still trying to dress myself, but I choose songs because they affect me."

And this kind of material, borne of pitched battles of the self, runs as deep in Western culture as the poems of William Dunbar and Robert Burns. Whether shaped by Scottish Presbyterianism, Puritan dissent, or the Calvinist pessimism that cast a noble pall upon their marginal status, many of the immigrants who gravitated to the American South in the seventeenth, eighteenth, and nineteenth centuries brought with them a secular sort of plainsong that warned of the perils of freedom from care. Youthful independence is a sorrowful state as adjudged in the ancient British "forsaken maiden" folk balladry of "Trooper and Maid," "The Nightingale," "Apron Strings," "A Fair Beauty Bride," "Pretty Polly," and other lyric predecessors of the tragic "Barbara Allen."

When the blue minor sevenths of "Here We Go 'Round the Mulberry Bush" and the Scottish "Cradle Song" combined with African idioms to produce seminal Southern shouts like "Get Along Home, Cindy" (a cautionary tale of an overly precocious young girl), the folk evolution of the American country blues became as frank as the civil and spiritual conflicts it reflected.

In recent decades, the poverty, upheaval, and social uncertainty that bedeviled much of the American South has come to permeate the entire nation. At the same time, the hybrid vulnerability of the narrative song-making traditions of this region have slowly come to epitomize the unwanted isolation felt by much of our citizenry. The bare candor in Wynonna's cover of Karla Bonoff's "Tell Me Why," in which a bystander frets over having too much time on her hands and heart, cannot fail to strike a chord in a society that can no longer see itself in its daily mechanisms.

"Just recently, for the second time, I took my Harley out and cruised to this secret, secluded place about forty minutes from my new house," says Wynonna. "It overlooks some water, and no one knew where I was.

It was a sunny day, the water was very, very musical, and it was so quiet you could almost hear your heart beating. If everybody had a hiding place where they could sit, and scream if they liked, we'd all be better off."

Why did she ride there?

"I was preparing, psyching myself to go back on the road, to cross that frontier again. I'm not really thrilled about coming back out into this crazy world when I'm so safe at home. But I'm learning that the problem with this country is also the problem with ourselves. Solitude is fine, but when you're lonely, that's because you're separated from *you*. Like I sing in the song, it's 'only love' of who we really are that can get us to the other shore."

PLANT: THE SONG REMAINS THE AIM

IF ONE TRULY BELIEVES THAT LOVE OF ADVENTURE IS synonymous with the adventure of love, then no restless urge is improper, no hidden knowledge is off-limits, no secret place is inviolable, and all journeys are greater than their inner or outer geography.

"I have a fascination with other cultures, other places, and especially other feelings and sensations," says singer Robert Plant. "Because of this, I love the road, the blue highways of the United States, the ruins of Welsh Bronze-Age settlements, and the sun circles and misty mountains of what I call the *other* Britain. I read a lot about Celtic lore and religion, and the lives of the great European explorers and traders throughout the years—these fantastic souls like Sir Richard Francis Burton, who traveled all over Asia Minor and Africa in a Victorian period when no outsider dared to. Such people were shunned and called pornographers and mad poets because, in Burton's case, he translated the wonders of the *Kama Sutra, Arabian Nights,* and *Ananga Ranga: The Hindu Art of Love* for us in the West."

The occasion for Plant's passionate meditations is twofold, embracing his forceful, forboding

Robert Plant

Fate of Nations solo album (Atlantic/Es Paranza, due June 1) and his zesty identification with *The Devil Drives,* the engrossing biography of Sir Richard Francis Burton by author Fawn M. Brodie, which Plant just finished devouring.

The book quotes the storied Sir Burton's letter to a friend, dated 1863, in which Burton asked himself why, despite inviting constant outrage and censure from Victorian society, he pushed himself to such flagrant lengths as an explorer, scientist, and literary light. Burton's own half-whimsical reply: "Damned fool . . . the Devil drives!" As his biographer judiciously noted, "Though Burton scoffed at all forms of religious superstition, he dwelt fascinated upon all things accounted devilish in his own time."

Contemporary admirer Plant, being former lead singer–lyricist of Led Zeppelin, the source of eight rather rakish solo records, *and* the endlessly emulated prototype for the restless rock saturnalian, feels he knows what it is like to be a figure of comment and fanciful speculation. But Robert likewise discounts any occult overtones to his intrepid temperament, stating, "None of the process of simply investigating these ideas and places is macabre. What it is, though, is sensuous and transporting—and thank God for that!"

Whether whooping Zep's "Whole Lotta Love," the inevitable "Stairway to Heaven," or howitzer-fired solo rhapsodies like the 1988 hit "Tall Cool One" and the new "Calling to You" from *Fate of Nations,* Plant is an appealingly confounding symbol of surly virility and substantial tenderness.

His now-clement acceptance of such paradoxes as well as the improbable distraction of competitors like Coverdale Page ("Just separate artistic points of view," he allows, "and I respect them as that.") have conspired to amplify the enviable weight of Plant's own music and impose a safe distance from rivals or antagonists.

Certainly it would be difficult to identify a track more intrinsically Plant-like than "Calling to You," its mythic tabernacle of seduction built around Pete Thompson's volcanic drum salvos, Robert's rich treble head tones and the gothic-classical duel of Nigel Kennedy's violin and the guitars of Kevin Scott MacMichael and Francis Dunnery. Equally transfixing is "Come into My Life," a rapt fable of romantic consecration that features ghostly hurdy-gurdy, Richard Thompson's cascading chords, and an angelic vocal descant from Clannad's Maire Brennan.

This is rock'n'roll contexture of a high order, redolent of early experimentalists like the Incredible String Band or Moby Grape on its first album, with Plant's vocals recalling the deep-soul entreaties of James Carr. And that's exactly what Plant intended.

"From the very beginning of this project, around January 1991, right after the 'Manic Nirvana' tour," he reflects, "I knew what I was going to do: go back into my past, listening to Grape, the Airplane, Tim Hardin, Quicksilver, Traffic, and other turning-point artists in rock. These people were trying to tell the listener something, joining various traditions, with the sense of a quest being insinuated and bandied in their acoustic and electronic themes.

"I'm also very proud of what I've attempted to do lyrically, trying to tell vivid tales that come from a hearty tradition of prose. Things have changed since the glory days of teen lust. We've gone from Jerry Lee Lewis's 'Great Balls of Fire' to Julian Cope's 'Jehovahkill'; our culture has grown more expansive and you need a facility for ambiguity and abstraction to comment on it. If 'Stairway to Heaven' had just been about cruising in a convertible, it wouldn't have endured in a meaningful way."

Plant sees his solo songwriting as a steady progression from his Zep lyricism for, say, "The Rover" and "In the Light," and informed by his cerebral avocations—but also salted with his full range of travel experiences. The devilishly sexy drive of "29 Palms" ("My ideal love-affair-gone-wrong song") emerged from some personal backroads motoring through "rural Pennsylvania, the Outer Banks of North Carolina, on through to Boulder, Colorado" during the "Nirvana" concert swing, while his version of Hardin's "If I Were a Carpenter" came about when he remembered that "in the Band of Joy, before [future Led Zep drummer] Bonzo [Bonham] and I ever met anybody from London, let alone Jimmy Page or John Paul Jones, that was one of the best songs we used to do."

Viewed as a whole, the solitary portion of Plant's career trek is quite cogent, starting with his ballsy 1966 rendition of the Young Rascals' "You Better Run" for a fictive studio group called Listen, followed by his obscure 1967 CBS Brit R&B singles (["Our Song"/"Laughin', Cryin', Laughin'," "Long Time Comin'"/"I've Got a Secret"]), and such un-matched late-sixties sessions as his bluesy Alexis Korner–backed raveup on "Operator"—whose falsetto fulminations are sufficiently propulsive to put a new part in any diehard Zep fan's hair. Add a generous dose of tracks (["Burning Down One Side," "Big Log," "Little by Little," "Heaven Knows," "Hurting Kind [I've Got My Eyes on You]"]) from Plant's modern solo outings, plus treats like "Let's Have a Party" from 1990's U.K. "The Last Temptation of Elvis" charity tribute, and you've got the boxed-set–sized sequel to the Zep denouement that cultists have craved for more than a decade.

"The man wants to wander, and he must do so or he shall die," warned Sir Richard Francis Burton in an 1865 journal of his pilgrimages, but Robert Plant glimpses a clear goal to his own collateral rambles: "I've roamed, loved, shook my ass for fun, but my aim as a singer is still honesty. People should feel the *song* is the point."

LIZ'S *GUYVILLE:*
ALL IS PHAIR
IN LOVE

SEXUAL AWAKENING AS BOTH FACT AND POETIC EFFIGY HAS stoked the arts since the twinkling of human self-awareness. And rock-'n'roll has been the favored forum in recent decades for youthful fertility's most intense public representations.

"I've always found that people are very concerned with erasing from their memory the parts of their life where they feel fragile or defeated," says singer-songwriter Liz Phair, whose ethereally explicit compositions on her *Exile in Guyville* debut (Matador, due May 17) employ the protocols of puberty to evoke the mysteries of sex and socialization. "There should be a finishing school for human relationships, to understand why you have these urges and what they mean, because life is *about* experiencing emotions.

"My own life is just one long thread of mischievousness," adds the Chicago-based Phair, who giggles easily and often. Especially when divulging that her official Matador bio—describing a skin-diving neurologist dad, a mom in the diplomatic corps who read aloud to her daughter from Henry

Liz Phair

Miller's *Sexus*, and Liz's own rebellious involvement with both Scien-
tology and a beau who was a hazardous waste engineer—is "all made-up
garbage I got talked into!"

Adopted in infancy, the twenty-six-year-old Phair is actually (or so she
insists) the daughter of Dr. John Phair, chief of Infectious Diseases at
Northwestern Memorial Hospital, and wife Nancy, a historian in the
museology department at the Art Institute of Chicago. Phair calls her
parents "warm, honest, and intelligent" and states that she "dragged
them through living hell from eighth grade onward," this protracted
cycle of turmoil peaking just prior to her hard-won graduation from
Oberlin College ("Oberlin takes people who are creative and in crisis, or
look like they're going to be.").

If surviving higher education settled much of Phair's psychic hash, the
decision in the nineties to issue her affectionately uncouth songs on the
cassette-only GirlySound label (the first collection was called *Yo You
Buddy Yup Yup Word to Your Mother*) earned the Matador contract.

Exile in Guyville was cut last year at Chicago's popular Idful Studios as
a co-production with former Shrimp Boat drummer-bassist Brad Wood.
While Phair calls live performing "brutally, mortally embarrassing," she
was convinced the slatternly glow of her "quasi-slutty" pop was coalescing
when she saw "Brad cracking up with laughter in the control room."

"I'm very female," says the slim, winsome Phair, "and I *go* with it, but
too often you can go for something and then find yourself inexplicably
diverted from your goal. I was definitely a late virgin—I didn't lose my
virginity until college—but the truth is we're taught very early that sex is
not about who you are and what you want, but how other people will perceive those issues."

This is turbid creative terrain that artists such as Prince have spent
careers trying to penetrate. As a fallen Episcopalian, Phair doesn't seek
transcendence through carnality, though—just a solid understanding of
its consolations. That Phair soars where the sovereign of Glam Slam has
lately stumbled is owed to her touching humility—principally the mettle
to admit the loneliness that makes desire so debilitating—on tracks like
"Flower" and "Fuck and Run." The former song is a bare-mattress offer-
tory ("Every time I see your face/I think of things unpure, unchaste . . . /
Everything you ever wanted/Everything you ever thought of/Is everything I'll do to you . . .") that makes Prince's dirty mind seem like a
prelate's Mass missal, while the latter song is a museful miscellany of

drum beats, Fender Duo-sonic riffs, and slapped tambourine that ascends to the achingly alarmed refrain: "I can feel it in my bones/I'm gonna spend another year alone."

With a pleasing vocal assonance midway between the trilling surrender of Judee Sill and the skewed pastorals of Miranda Sex Garden, Phair reports on the deliciously broody inclinations of the heart vs. the libido. The deeply vulnerable motifs are undogmatic and justly disturbing in their unconstrained aural caress, as when the singer responds to a bedmate's morning-after insincerity by stage-murmuring: "I heard the rest in your head."

"America has a way of disconnecting you from sexuality from the beginning, making you think you have to perform," says Phair, "so that when you finally achieve a sex life, you find yourself at a loss to comprehend what's going on. If our culture embraced sex rather than rejected it as a danger, at least you'd have a connection to your feelings once you have them. Instead, we wind up war torn, as if we blew a qualifying heat in a weird athletic event."

While Phair is ingenious at restoring sex and other ceremonies of self-revelation to an ordinary, freshly affecting scale ("Whatever happened to a boyfriend/The kind of guy who tries to win you over?"), she assembles her material on such topics the way Rage Against The Machine guitarist Tom Morello constructs his gape-inducing solos: with a genre- and structure-shifting knack that borders on sorcery. That the vast range of prurient psalms in *Exile in Guyville* truly adheres is due to the austere recording recipe employed by Phair and Wood, the album's ingredients so close to the basic household acoustics of instrumental/vocal rumination that listeners may wonder if the songs aren't demos of their own soul-kitchen subconscious. There's a touch of Circe in Phair's singing too, her fragile gifts far greater than her urge to apply them, the emphasis more on extemporaneous force than tonal refinement.

"I fixed on the Rolling Stones' *Exile on Main Street*," she explains, "and treated it like a thesis, compiling the songs I'd written years before I ever heard that Stones album, which worked best as coincident parallels. The term 'Guyville' comes from a song of the same name by Urge Overkill. For me, Guyville is a concept that combines the smalltown mentality of a five hundred-person Knawbone, Kentucky–type town with the Wicker Park indie music scene in Chicago, plus the isolation of every place I've lived in, from Cincinnati to Winnetka."

The record opens with the endearingly off-balance "6'1"," swerves into the assured throb of "Help Me, Mary," recedes for the solemn whisper of "Glory" and the impishly pretty "Dance of the Seven Veils" (which manages to drop such delicate asides as "Johnny my love . . . I'm a real cunt in spring"), and then leaps into the palatially pounding first single "Never Said," followed by the funny "Soap Star Joe," forlorn "Explain It to Me," etc.—the full gamut, feeling as unimpeded as a great conversation.

"To be able to share things which are extremely private requires either the grace of a natural performer or the willingness to beat the shit out of yourself," Phair notes with a final simper. "It's a second puberty, a passage unlike any other." And by the end of Phair's courageous eighteen-song rite of displacement and restoration, there's no doubt she's led alternative rock's postpunk nineties naturalism to a captivating new pinnacle.

BILLY JOEL: OF TIME AND THE *RIVER*

IF THERE IS AN IRVING BERLIN IN ROCK'N'ROLL, HIS NAME IS
Billy Joel.

In his thirty-odd years in music—twenty of them spent recording for Columbia Records—William Martin Joel has authored many of the most cherished songs in the canon of American popular music, ecumenical odes to the hard knocks of self-realization that have few rivals in their flair for depicting our Age of Anxiety.

Like his Tin Pan Alley predecessor, Billy is a scion of immigrant stock, imbued with the deep unease of an epoch that could make refugees or specters of several generations of his ancestors. Berlin's family fled czarist Russia's persecutions of Jewish peasants in 1893, while Joel's father, Howard, was a Jew born in Nuremberg who escaped Nazi persecution in the 1930s, migrating to New York City by way of Cuba (although Hitler seized the family business, Waschemanufaktur Joel, the largest mail-order textile firm in the country). Howard later returned

Billy Joel

as an American G.I. to liberate the Dachau death camp near Munich in April 1945.

The teenage Irving and Billy would transform their inherited fears and secret shortcomings into stubborn refinements of the spirit, striving to report on humanity from the best part of themselves.

"I've been referred to as a writer in that Tin Pan Alley sense," says Joel, talking at home in eastern Long Island. "Maybe I am, because I don't believe in completely breaking with the past. When something new is going to happen, it comes from a desire not to kill off everything that came before, but to improve on it vastly."

As brooding idealists graced with a common touch no cynic could grasp, both Berlin (who also recorded for Columbia) and Joel would borrow liberally from the vulgate of their times to envision an idealized universal dialogue. Akin to whistling in the dark, Berlin's "Blue Skies," "White Christmas," "Puttin' on the Ritz," and "Let's Face the Music and Dance" were quasi-brash affirmations meant to quell interior qualms; likewise, Joel's "Just the Way You Are," "Tell Her About It," "Only the Good Die Young," and "A Matter of Trust" are fierce appeals from a soul too apprehensive to pray.

"In the past," Joel continues, "I had always written as an onlooker, from a journalistic sense. And while I was never being detached, I also worked in the old days because I had to deliver albums. Now, I've reached a point in my life where I'm not going to write unless I have something to say—and on this album"—meaning *River of Dreams*, his fifteenth record, due July 27—"I *did* have something to say."

Which was that he was "an angry, disillusioned, bitter person who had lost faith in everything because I had lost faith in myself, in my ability to form any discerning judgment about what the hell was going on around me." This disabling malaise had descended in the wake of Joel's $90 million lawsuit in 1989 against former manager Frank Weber.

By the time Joel met with veteran guitarist-producer Danny Kortchmar (James Taylor, Neil Young, Hall and Oates, Don Henley) in December 1992 to play his work tapes, Joel had begun to win various bouts in his ongoing court battle. "I was writing each song in sequence and as I did I was actually living through these feelings, working things out and coming to grips with what was troubling me." The first demos that Kortchmar and Joel recast in the studio were the album-opening "No Man's Land" and an instrumental segment the singer was calling "The Motorcycle Song."

"There's a line in 'No Man's Land,' " says Joel, "where it says, 'I see these children with their boredom and their vacant stares/God help us all if we're to blame for their unanswered prayers.' I didn't realize how pissed off I was about everything in our culture. I mean, this is a guy who thinks that—as my father used to say when I was a kid—'Ahh, life is a cesspool.' "

Kortchmar sensed that the bold melody of Joel's bumpy "Motorcycle Song" was potentially the regenerative antidote to "No Man's Land," so he suggested Joel slow the tempo down. "I did," says Billy, "and *boom*, I hit the essence of what the melody was: soulful. I was getting to the stage where I was looking for things I did believe in, and one of them is deep, substantial love." Thus, a throwaway track instead became "All About Soul."

From there, Joel went on to tackle "The Great Wall of China" ("A wounded, mocking account of betrayal, with a primal scream at the end that I'll never be able to hit again"), "Blonde over Blue" ("A sardonic song where the guy's grasping at something—sex, I think"), "Minor Variation" ("About giving in to the fucking blues"), and "Shades of Grey" ("An ironic, purging, Cream-influenced song about ambiguities").

Hired to supply a thorny thrust to Joel's demon bashing, Kortchmar summoned a studio brigade that included legendary Mountain guitarist Leslie West, drummers Steve Jordan (of Keith Richards's X-Pensive Winos) and Zachary Alford, plus Mellencamp/Springsteen vocalist Crystal Taliefero.

Visiting Joel at the end of March as he was winding up his writing-recording with sessions at Cove City Sound Studios in Glen Cove, New York, the now-bearded piano warrior was but two songs short of finishing the album, whose "watershed" had been the just-completed title track, a gospel strut in which Joel uses "the emotional resolutions that go on in our sleep" as an allegory for the "instinctive continuity" of life.

"I literally woke up singing the refrain, 'In the middle of the night/I go walking in my sleep!' " Joel exulted. Once again in fine humor, he shared anecdotes about his somewhat "smart-ass" father, Howard, a classically trained pianist and longtime resident of Vienna who regards rock as "trash music." Joel confided that his contrary parent finally had seemed proud of his offspring when witnessing a recent encounter between Joel and violinist Itzhak Perlman, who flattered Joel with a fan's warmth. "My father turned to me and said, 'Diz man likes your stuff?!' *That* impressed him."

And what of Billy's own status as a living link between figures like Irving Berlin and the next rhapsodist of the common folk? "Well," Joel chuckles, deflecting any direct comparisons, "I've come to the conclusion that these things of mine aren't collections of pop tunes; what I've been writing are all these musicals!"

Yet what left the biggest impression on Howard Joel's wayward son as he put the last touches on *River of Dreams* was a sudden awareness that the "Lullaby (Goodnight My Angel)" track crowning the finest album of a remarkable career also had unconsciously captured the continuity of his own mortal path. Composed by the devoutly atheistic Billy to allay his seven-year-old daughter's dismay at the inevitability of death, its chorus contained a wordless fragment of "Mighty Like a Rose," the lullaby his mother, Rosalind, had sung to him as a toddler. "I was trying to comfort my child," says Joel, his voice trembling, "and I got choked up when I realized I was passing along the 'loo loo loo' that had once reassured me. I guess we both needed comfort."

WINGS OF DESIRE: *ANGEL* AND THE STORY

IF GOD WAS CAPABLE OF CREATING ANGELS, WHY DID HE bother concocting humanity? Maybe seraphim were meant to inhabit the myths that we should most avoid.

Winged spirits crop up repeatedly in the title song and other tracks on *The Angel in the House,* the superb second album (Elektra/Green Linnet, due July 20) from the Boston-based vocal duo known as the Story. While normally seen as guardians or sacred go-betweens, the celestial creatures in the Story's compositions most often appear as agents of tragic delusion, messengers "terrible" and misleading.

"I grew up in a pretty religious household—Christian Science," explains Jonatha Brooke, chief lyricist and Jennifer Kimball's vocal cohort in the Story. "It's totally a spiritual way of life, devoid of ritual, ornamentation, and priests, so you're not dealing with angels, you're dealing

the Story

with a *direct* path to the deity—there's no mediator." And while Brooke no longer practices that faith, she admits that "it's still a part of me and something I can't get rid of."

But what has been tougher to dispense with, she finds, are the extrareligious qualities that society can ascribe to those it stipulates as angelic.

"The original inspiration for *The Angel in the House*," says Brooke, "is a Victorian poem by this guy [Coventry Patmore] professing to understand women and to know what the ideal female virtues were: Take care of your husband, keep the house clean, always have a cheerful countenance. [English author] Virginia Woolf gave a speech [in 1931 at the London chapter of National Society for Women's Service] to a group of females who had trouble getting into professions they were pursuing. She explained 'The Angel in the House' as this archaic vision of women that we're fighting against, and that it was even harder to kill the angel because it was a 'phantom.' I think that I and my generation are still messing with this stupid angel that says 'Why don't you take care of your house before you write a song!' "

If the strangely stirring music of the Story were overtly spiritual or feminist in mood, it might be easier to quantify the issues of dignity and faith that it addresses. And if the pair's uniquely penetrating aural idiosyncrasies could be described as rock or folk or acoustic pop, it might aid in measuring the potential of their steadily expanding audience. But such simplifications fall short. Structured as drawing-room ballads with a sometimes jazzy Celtic tinge, the Story's subtly dissonant sound has less to do with matters political or pious than with the epidemic loneliness of a culture that can no longer reason in private. And what makes the Story's salon pieces so poignant is the tolling tenor/soprano twine of Brooke and Kimball's voices, an intersecting hum that is less a harmonic mesh than an airborne metaphor for heartache. Almost cruelly pretty, the tiered tones of *Angel* call to mind a lover's atonement drowned out by a train's departing whistle.

"My mother is a big part of the song," admits the blond, girlish Brooke, twenty-nine, over lunch in a Boston restaurant, as shy Kimball, a thirty-year-old brunette, looks on sympathetically. "It's about me and my mother, and anyone's mom and her mother, and any woman who's been torn between desires and what they're supposed to do as a female in this world." The song's verses fill in the rest of the scenario: "My mother moved the furniture/When she no longer moved the man/ . . . She wanted to be a different person/ . . . And he walked away."

"The hardest thing of my past," adds Kimball in support, "was probably *my* parents separating and then divorcing when I was fifteen. That was an awful time; they were very friendly, almost too friendly, and I wanted them to be more angry at each other and more separated. I couldn't understand why it couldn't be worked out if they were so friendly." In performance as in conversation, Kimball's deeper-pitched, bassoonlike passages are the kindly counterpoint to Brooke's clarinet-crisp declarations.

The two met in the early eighties at Amherst College at a stage when beliefs in religion, lasting parental relationships, and personal self-reliance were at a mutually low ebb. Brooke is the daughter of writers Nancy Nelson (whose pen name is Darren Stone) and Robert Nelson, who both worked for the *Christian Science Monitor,* and Kimball is the Manhattan-bred offspring of Geoffrey and Carol Kimball, two staunch Presbyterians who worked in finance.

After a cursory, high-soprano stint in a campus doo-wop act, the duo's joint songwriting-arranging experiments commenced during the 1983 school year, such efforts as "Always" and "Over Oceans" first surfacing on the indie Apropos Productions tapes that attracted interest from the ethnic-folk Green Linnet label.

Both women had maintained day jobs, Brooke becoming an accomplished professional dancer and Kimball a graphic artist at Little, Brown publishers in Boston, and both married (with Brooke's husband, noted keyboardist Alain Mallet, later co-producing their music). But the Story's fortune's were transformed when the June 1991 Green Linnet release of its debut album, *Grace in Gravity,* quickly led to regional acclaim and a licensing deal with Elektra.

Fans of the fragile gleam of *Grace in Gravity* will find the *The Angel in the House* a darker prism. The song "Mermaid," as Brooke asserts, "is based on the original, sordid version of Hans Christian Andersen's 'The Little Mermaid,' in which—unlike the movie—she dies, doesn't get the prince, and she turns into sea foam." And then there's the album's initial single, "So Much Mine," a mesmerizing hymn to an adolescent runaway, and "The Barefoot Ballroom," which Kimball describes as a moonstruck vision of an ideal realm, complete with barefoot (and in this instance, benign) cherubs: "One strong thing about Jonatha's writing is that it transports people in an unconscious way to somewhere else, their own childhoods or their own Barefoot Ballrooms."

"I guess," mulls Brooke, "I've always been obsessed with subjects and words that twist my heart, like a sob, and lose me in some way. We enter these characters, and sometimes it's difficult when you see audiences being overcome by emotion. It's hard to know why we do it; we're both sort of well adjusted and solid."

"Speak for yourself!" laughs Kimball, gently nudging her partner at the conclusion of lunch.

As the pair disappears down Newbury Street, it's plain the chance bond that repaired their youth and became a creative rudder is also their music's tacit subject and most powerful trait. Seventeenth-century poet Edward Young, another English writer who critiqued seraphim, myth, and humanity's hunger for belief, probably said it best: "Angels from friendship gather half their joy."

UMAR BIN HASSAN'S POETIC JUSTICE

WHAT UMAR BIN HASSAN HAS TO SAY IS SCARY. BUT THE FACT that his expressions have been so necessary for nearly twenty-five years is far more frightening.

"Number-one tunes on the hit parade. Daddy came and then was gone. Made a move that left a pawn. Boys in the hood. They test the waters and dance the flames. They hear the whispers but never their names. Looking over shoulders trying to look ahead. Overlooking paranoia to hear what's said. The only enemy becomes the only friend. The only way out becomes the only way in. Indecent exposure to legendary fame playing with stacked decks while destroying the game. The divine becomes tempting and then cocaine addiction becomes subtle and then profane. Wearing the streets like they wear a crown. Wearing their dreams like they wear a frown. I can't quit. I can't quit. This is all I've got. There's plenty of drama but where is the plot?"

The preceding passage is a splenetic ex-

Umar Bin Hassan

cerpt from "Bum Rush," a typically searing "spoken picture" from the forthcoming album *Be Bop or Be Dead* (Axiom/Island, due July 20), by Umar Bin Hassan, once and future member of legendary rap progenitors the Last Poets.

If the track seems hypercritical of any home slice acquiring fame from speech set to the beat of ghetto stance, Umar has been making his living in that once-undefinable field since the summer of 1969. Back when Kool Herc had just traded Kingston for the Bronx and was mixing his breakbeat funk at sound-system block parties, Umar was already inside Manhattan's Impact Sound Studio cutting Douglas Records' *Last Poets* debut.

Before Afrika Bambaataa coined the term hip-hop, before Doug E. Fresh became a human beat-box; before Public Enemy revived message rap with *Rebel Without a Pause*, before Arrested Development paid soundtrack homage to Malcolm X and Digable Planets helped pave the way for *Jazzmatazz*, the Last Poets had been there, done that, with Miles Davis and Nina Simone lampin' backstage like the fans they were.

The Poets pioneered the premise—but never the pose—of gangsta shootout scenarios on the 1973 Douglas album "Hustlers Convention" (with musical accompaniment from the likes of Kool and the Gang, Eric Gale, and Julius Hemphill), and dropped science with Nikki Giovanni, Amiri Baraka, and Rap Brown. Onstage and off, they enjoyed street currency to a degree more intensely dope than any hops before or since. Yet none of these things were ever the goal, because, as Umar takes pains to remind his most rabid young emulators, "The only point was to be a poet."

"I'm comfortable being called a rapper," says Umar, "but if people want to understand our music or my latest work on *Be Bop or Be Dead*, they have to know the ancient purpose of the poet in a society. Poets mirror the pain and the misery around them, to help make listeners politically and spiritually aware. To do that, you have to first be honest with yourself.

"In my past, I've been through heavy dues with drugs, but you never conceal your mistakes, because people are always watching the poet. And while they may see that you have misgivings and weak points in your character, if you're trying to be real, you can get that respect. So the poet is not an actor, does not wear a costume or a uniform, does not play a role or assume a character. The poet must always be himself, nothing less.

"Lastly, you have to be conscious of your surroundings, or you can't make a contribution. If you feel it's OK to knock women down and call them bitch, or shoot up some grocer and blame him for your troubles after the Reagan-Bush era, you're not conscious. But if you're aware, you know what's really happened is that we've lived through a time of robber barons who have ransacked the S&Ls and government agencies like HUD for evil political purposes. The enemy is too strong, the job ahead is too hard, to have anybody behave as if guns are toys and music is a game.

"As for me," adds Umar, who was born Jerome Huling in Akron, Ohio, in 1948, the son of journeyman trumpeter Gilbert "Sonny" Huling, "being a poet means everything, because the Last Poets was the only real job I ever knew."

Growing up watching his father strain to hold a family together with wages from a shoeshine parlor and pickup gigs with passing bands such as Count Basie's, the younger Huling resolved to avoid compromise in his choice of vocation. Umar was a black-nationalist militant visiting the Antioch College campus in 1969 when he caught a show by a then-unrecorded contingent of the Poets (whose flexible ranks have included Felipe Luciano, Gylan Kain, David Nelson, Abiodun Oyewole, Suliaman El-Hadi, Alafia Pudim aka Jala Nuriddin, and conga player Nilaja).

"I followed the group back to Harlem," he recalls, "and found them at the East Wind, their loft on 125th Street. All I had was twenty-two cents, my suitcase, and a book of my own poetry. And I wasn't gonna leave"— he laughs—"until they let me join. My poetry with the group was naive at first, but my influences were Miles Davis and Marvin Gaye singing 'Stubborn Kind of Fellow.' Abiodun and the others helped me mold my style into something explosive. Six months later, Abiodun and I were sitting in Mount Morris Park and he said, 'What have you learned as a poet since you came to Harlem?'

"I looked at him and answered, 'I've learned that niggers are scared of revolution.' He said, 'Oh my God! *That's* what you gotta write!' " Within weeks, the "Niggers" poem was completed and cut for the Last Poets' inaugural album, an agitated Nilaja thumping his conga while Abiodun and Alafia lent cowbell and churning chant backing. A seething discourse on humanity's capacity for apathy and self-exploitation, "Niggers Are Scared of Revolution" became a fulcrum of the flowering rap ethos. The original version was featured in *Malcolm X*, the acclaimed 1972 Warner Bros. documentary, and Umar offers a caustic new on-camera performance this July in film director John Singleton's *Poetic Justice*, starring Janet Jackson.

All of the aforementioned compositions and more (including "AM" and the giddily crafted ghetto/African-village canticle of "Pop") are contained on *Be Bop or Be Dead,* an incomparable treatise by a true pioneer of our modern oral traditions. The brawny band assembled by producer Bill Laswell for *Be Bop* is anchored by Hammond B-3 genie Bernie Worrell, guitarist-bassist Bootsy Collins, drummer Buddy Miles, and an array of guests such as kora ace Foday Musa Suso and conga-chatan percussionist Aiyb Dieng. But ultimately this record is about one man's belief in words.

"The poet," says Umar Bin Hassan, "is entrusted with something very important: the language. It's a gift, to make you think. If you destroy the language, you destroy yourself. It's the best weapon an honest person has."

JAMES TAYLOR, AMERICAN TROUBADOUR

WHEN JAMES TAYLOR'S FOREBEARS FIRST ARRIVED ON THESE shores in the second half of the 1600s, America was an idea only recently added to most maps. Yet if melody be destiny, as the Scottish balladeers of the time believed, the Carolina-bred Taylor's future status as a modern troubadour of the New Land and the Old was practically preordained.

A typical centuries-old Scottish air collected in North Carolina is "The Maid Freed from the Gallows," and other American tunes of Scottish origin that inform the folk culture of that region include the "Loch Lomond"–derived "Amazing Grace," "Rye Whiskey," and "Shady Grove." With the merest stretch of the imagination—triggered by exposure to the exquisite thirty-song *James Taylor Live* (Columbia, due Aug. 3)—this list might be expanded to include "Something in the Way She Moves," "Country Road," "Sweet Baby James," "Secret o' Life," "Walking Man," and "Shower the People." Similarly, those with an awareness of classic Scottish verse would perceive more than a passing spiritual kinship be-

James Taylor

tween "Fire and Rain" and Lord Byron's "So We'll Go No More a Roving,"
or "Don't Let Me Be Lonely Tonight" and the Scottish minstrel tragedy of
"Clerk Saunders."

And anyone hearing the mesmerizing new arrangement of "Mill-
worker," with its fifelike touches and martial lilt, could be forgiven for
assuming it began its life in the Highlands, rather than on Broadway in
the 1978 musical *Working.*

"I'm relatively illiterate about my Scottish musical roots," laughs
Taylor, who has played and traveled in Scotland, "but if you asked
Kathryn [Walker, Taylor's erudite actress-wife], she could stand up and
make a good showing for me, and really give us some nice references!"

For the sake of history, the original Taylors came to the American
colonies by boat from Marykirk, a Highlands village near the North
Sea–bound stream of West Water in the County of Kincardine. Marykirk
also was in the path of mid-seventeenth-century brawling between Scotland and England, Church and State, and Catholics and Protestants.

"I'm told it was an Isaac and a James Taylor that made that passage to
North America," says the singer-songwriter, "and I understood that they
left Scotland under some pressure for some political reasons. There is
also some sense in our family history that James was washed overboard,
and so they now relate that to my song 'Frozen Man' [from his 1991 *New
Moon Shine* album, about a drowned sailor who's revived a century after-
ward], although I wasn't aware of that story when I wrote it."

What's certain is that Isaac Taylor, at least, made landfall at the port
town of New Bern, North Carolina, thus establishing the Taylors'
southern ties and not coincidentally enabling James to sell out concerts
in his boyhood home of Chapel Hill just as often as he cares to book
them. Taylor was born in 1948 and reared on a generous sampling of
Hank Williams and the Grand Ole Opry, white gospel, and the late-night
strains of Slim Harpo and Howlin' Wolf courtesy Nashville's WLAC. By
his teens he could play Weavers' material as well as his favorite guitar
funk with a plucked picking style equal parts Doc Watson and Brownie
McGhee.

These days, Taylor is quite literally a folk hero to a new generation of
country stars, who craft their own writing in the long shadows of his
most eloquent work.

"I like what's happening to country music these days," he enthuses.
"The best stuff is unpretentious, straightforward, with no arrogance and
not overblown." And it was this practical brand of esteem that embold-

ened him to cover the sixties country gem "She Thinks I Still Care" on *James Taylor Live.*

"It's a *great* George Jones tune," says Taylor, "and it wasn't a regular part of our rotating set, but the night that we did it at a show in Virginia, it turned out that we wanted to keep it."

Taylor says the other twenty-nine tracks on the career-comprehensive *James Taylor Live* (including the previously unrecorded "New Hymn") were selected with equally unstudied enthusiasm, and even veteran fans may find themselves becoming more attached to the finer textures the arrangements attained over the years.

"Performing live brings an energy," says Taylor, "a commitment that's a quantum thing, making the leap into real time. You can hit or miss in the studio because it's an odd, abstract, artificial place to get an emotional connection with the material. Live, you are elevated."

Given Taylor's legendary pride in his concerts, which have earned him annual sellout guarantees on a par with the Grateful Dead and Jimmy Buffett, the issue of assembling an unimpeachable live collection from his 1992 touring season became a serious objective.

"We didn't overdub a single lick," he explains. "There are some edits to make it all uniform as you skip from night to night, because we did fourteen gigs and used stuff from North Carolina, Long Island, Boston, Lowell, Massachusetts, and elsewhere. And we mixed the sound and faded the audience in and out. But [co-producer] George Massenburg and I agreed it was gonna be *live,* and accept whatever roughness as part of the bargain."

The album is one of the most impressive performance documents imaginable, but its core accomplishments outstrip such logistical accolades. Rarely does a songwriter possess the grace and balance to bring his early material to a mature peak without overreaching, yet Taylor also is able to make the tacit case that his output in the second stage of his career rivals or outranks the songs with which he first forged his reputation. From the live evidence, there can be no more inspirational contemporary ballads in the chromatic parlor idiom than "I Will Follow," "That Lonesome Road," "Shed a Little Light," "Copperline," nor ones that follow in such an effortlessly unbroken line from Robert Burns to Stephen Foster to Woody Guthrie and beyond. This is American balladry of the first artistic rank, and if Leadbelly could recast "The Lass of Rochroyall" as "Blind Lemon Blues," it's time the stylistic hybrid of "Steamroller Blues" preserved on this record is also appreciated as the zestful transcultural fusion it's become.

A bonus treat on *James Taylor Live* is the man's wit and modesty, which are on display in equal measure—sometimes in the same onstage rejoinders. When a female fan shouts out "I love you!" at the close of "Something in the Way She Moves," he responds with a coyly noncommittal, "Good." There's an impeccable pause, and then he confides, to explosive audience laughter, "I think it helps us not to *know* each other."

"You, know, there were a lot of other names that came to mind for this live project," Taylor concludes, as he prepares to depart on a nonmusical family trek to Tibet. "For a while I wanted to call it *Must Ride on Wheels,* and another was *Now This!* but in the end I decided to just keep it simple and true. I hope people hear it that way."

TERRANCE SIMIEN
MAKES *ROOM*
FOR ALL

IT WAS A TOUGH NIGHT FOR TERRANCE SIMIEN AND THE Mallet Playboys. Every chair was empty on a recent Manhattan Tuesday at Tramps, and the capacious club's idle bartender was free to catch up on his bottle washing—yet neither circumstance was cause for concern. Rather, the evening's trials centered on the fact that it had taken nearly five songs for Terrance and company to pack the dance floor.

But no matter: Virtually every bouncing patron in the bustling establishment had finally abandoned the sea of tables to huddle buttocks to belt buckles before the bandstand (and that's not counting the nine spectators spontaneously welcomed onstage, who received tambourines, cowbells, and washboards to augment the revelry) as a maniacally flailing Simien and band thrashed out the thrilling "A Moi

Terrance Simien

Maison" from his upcoming album, *There's Room for Us All* (Black Top/ Rounder, due September 15).

"Where we come from, if people don't dance it's an insult!" said the Eunice, Louisiana–born Simien with a husky guffaw the following afternoon. "The real deal is: We a lot of times get people in the crowd who are kinda shy and really wanna dance. We kinda *force* things so the ones that should dance will come up."

Most nights Simien accomplishes this wholesale feat of funky levitation by means of frantically fluttering hand gestures interspersed with bursts of his diatonic button accordion—as well as the undeniable uplift of his rib-rumbling zydeco sextet. Just as late zydeco king Clifton Chenier incorporated the bluesy twenties Cajun-Creole synthesis pioneered by accordionist Amade Ardoin and fiddler Dennis McGee into the mongrel that is modern zydeco, so Simien has furthered Chenier's open-stewpot approach by adding parboiled portions of the Jackson 5's repertoire, Bob Marley's reggae, and the smooth sizzle of the early Commodores.

Roughly half the album's thirteen cuts are bewitching laments like the title cut or "Come Back Home," but Simien and company also provide terrific adaptations of "Zydeco Boogaloo" (which Terrance embellishes with sly fragments of the Jackson 5's "I Want You Back"), and Bob Dylan's "I Shall Be Released." The woe-stricken treatment of the Dylan hymn is redolent of such early Cajun dirges as "J'ai Passé Devant Ta Porte," sounding as though it emerged during *Le Grand Dérangement* that brought Simien's ancestors to Louisiana.

"The Simiens are a mixture of Acadian and Creole; they went from France to Canada, and then straight to Louisiana in the early 1800s, I think," says Terrance, alluding to the French-Canadian colonists expelled from the Maritime Provinces of Nova Scotia and New Brunswick in 1755 for refusing to swear allegiance to the Crown of the conquering British Army. Many of these Acadian, aka "Cajun," refugees (they'd named their colony "Acadie" in homage to the rural utopia of ancient Greece) wandered for decades before reaching the Attakapas region west of New Orleans.

"Zydeco is the music of my people and the music that I love most, and it's from the heart, not from the head," asserts Simien, son of bricklayer Matthew Simien and the former Ethel Rene. One of four children, he was born September 3, 1965, and grew up watching his mother sing in the choir of St. Ann's Catholic Church.

"They used to have record hops at the church hall at St. Ann's for teens," Simien remembers, "but the top-forty music was 'kiddie' and uptight for me. Instead, at thirteen I used to sneak into clubs like Slim's Y-Ki-Ki in Opelousas, where a guy named Wilfred LaTour was playing. The zydeco dance was 'come as you are, do what you wanna do,' and mainly an older crowd, but there was a lot of kids my age that would come with their parents. A better scene than St. Ann's—pretty loose!"

At this point, Simien had spent three years studying jazz and classical trumpet at Lawtell Elementary, but his interest in the school orchestra faded as the zydeco saloons intensified their century-old siren call. The word zydeco is a Creole modification of *les haricots* (pronounced lay-*zah-ri-co*), or snap beans, as popularized in the traditional Cajun one-step "L'haricots Sont Pas Sales" (The Snap Beans Aren't Salty).

The music itself grafts Acadian folk songs onto the Afro-Caribbean rhythms brought to Louisiana by French-speaking slaves and free men of color in the wake of the Haitian Revolution (1791–1804). The accordion was introduced to fiddle-focused Cajun instrumentals in the 1870s by German immigrants, and the vivacious "black Cajun" Creole form called "lala" gradually overlapped with Cajun two-steps at community dances known as *fais-dodos* (an alloy of "go to sleep," i.e., advice given underage children, and "fete de Dieu" [festival of God]). Clarence Garlow scaled *Billboard's* R&B charts in 1950 with "Bon Ton Roula" (a French revision of Louis Jordan's "Let the Good Times Roll"). Clifton Chenier's mid fifties sides for Specialty and Chess clinched zydeco's R&B repute.

As for Simien, another illicit trip in 1981 to Slim's Y-Ki-Ki exposed him to zydeco's squeeze-box monarch: Chenier himself. Clifton's set turned Terrance's heart from rock to *roula*. Glued every subsequent Saturday (11 A.M.–noon) to Lou Collins's Black Zydeco Special on Eunice radio station KEUN, Simien taught himself the music of Fernest Arceneaux, the Sam Brothers, and Chenier, practicing on a $250 Hohner single-row diatonic he'd gotten for his fifteenth birthday. He used these skills in 1982 to anchor the initial, short-lived incarnation of the Mallet Playboys ("The group was an older clan," explains Simien, "that didn't want to learn more than five songs").

After another decade and several recordings (including the 1986 Grand Point single "You Used to Call Me" with guest vocalist Paul Simon, *The Big Easy* film soundtrack, and the 1991 Restless album *Zydeco on the Bayou*), Terrance Simien and his younger and wiser Mallet Playboys are well poised for the release of *There's Room for Us All,* a collection that captures, in co-producer Jeffrey Greenberg's words, "all the diversity of traditional forms of zydeco and other southern rural musics"—plus the raucous authority of the finest vanguard house rockers. And the presence on the "Room" project of such distinguished sidemen as bassist-producer Daryl Johnson, pianist Art Neville, and the Meters only deepens the peppery kick of this cutting-edge *étouffée.*

Simien feels "the album's title says it best: There's a lot of musicians on this record that came from different bands and different backgrounds, and there are a lot of different people in this world that we gotta learn to love and accept."

CATCHIN' CAB: THE MAGIC OF CALLOWAY

NO LIVING PATHFINDER IN AMERICAN POPULAR MUSIC OR ITS jazz and rock'n'roll capillaries is so frequently emulated yet so seldom acknowledged as Cabell "Cab" Calloway. He arguably did more things first and better than any other band leader of his generation, a fact exemplified by *Cab Calloway—Best of the Big Bands* and *Cab Calloway—Featuring Chu Berry* (both Columbia/Legacy), two exceptional new installments of the ongoing Legacy Big-Band reissues series.

Half a century since his heyday, most of Calloway's accomplishments remain preeminent.

"You see this rapping they doing today, I did that twenty-five, thirty-five, forty-five, *fifty-five* years ago!" exclaims the eighty-five-year-old White Plains, New York, resident with the thunderclap cackle fans will recall from vintage films like *The Big Broadcast* (1932) and *The Singing Kid* (1936). "I did a rap thing on 'Minnie the Moocher's Wedding Day' and 'Hi-De-Ho Man, That's Me.' Call it rap or scat, singing for me was just a *feeling* that you got. I forgot the lyrics to 'Minnie the Moocher' one night [in 1931, on

Cab Calloway

a live radio concert] and out of the clear blue sky it came out of my mouth: hi-de-ho!"

The most vocally proficient performer ever to front a true jazz orchestra, Calloway had prankish pipes that bridged the full breadth of bass, baritone, tenor, and soprano—randy yet always refined.

Calloway's expert troupe, comprising such paragons as Berry, Ben Webster, Illinois Jacquet, Milt Hinton, Mario Bauzá, Sam "the Man" Taylor, Danny Barker, Doc Cheatham, Ed Swayzee, Cozy Cole, Eddy Barefield, Dizzy Gillespie, and singers Lena Horne and Pearl Bailey, commanded a demanding repertoire, each arrangement characterized by inspired soloing. Calloway never hogged the spotlight, a deferential instinct atypical for the time.

Nonetheless, Calloway was an eye-widening figure before the footlights: trim, well tailored, debonaire with his pencil mustache as he swayed atop a stepped podium, adroit drill teams of female dancers stomping and swiveling before him. He whipped his jet-black mane with each surge of the breakneck beat, leaping into full airborne turns, slow-motion breaststrokes, or a pre-Moonwalk glide called the Buzz.

These days, Calloway's ingenious groundwork glows beneath the late Louis Jordan's witty boogie shuffles in Broadway's *Five Guys Named Moe* (Jordan having molded his forties merrymaking around the Calloway prototype), and it also shadows the saltatory grooves, videogenic style, and double-entendre storytelling of Prince circa *Sign o' the Times* and *Diamonds and Pearls*.

Calloway's melodic/percussive jazz mastery of word sounds and scat singing was complete by the thirties, surpassing that of early mentor Louis Armstrong and fully anticipating the complex instrumental approaches that Lambert, Hendricks and Ross, Ella Fitzgerald, or Bobby McFerrin eventually would bring to the party.

"What I expected from my musicians was what I was selling: the right notes, with *precision*, because I would build a whole song around a scat or a dance step."

And, naturally, there had to be a racy musical setting to complement each agile physical stunt. Within the drumbeat of modern musical history, Calloway quickly became the human rimshot: vocalist as choreographer, dancer as comic, humorist as percussionist, social critic as rhythmatist, maestro of a maelstrom.

Calloway came to life on Christmas morning 1907, the son of Rochester, New York, lawyer Cabell Calloway and college-educated public-school teacher Martha Eulalia Reed. Cab was a crap-shooting teenage choirboy, with a few voice lessons and a drumming hobby, when he found work as the timekeeper in a ten-piece Baltimore Dixieland outfit, Johnny Jones and his Arabian Tent Orchestra. Further chance employment as a substitute singer in the support crew of "Plantation Days," a touring revue in which his older sister Blanche starred, got him as far as Chicago.

"The first band I had was at the Sunset Café: the Alabamians," says Calloway. "It was a corporate band, meaning everybody was the leader, and they wouldn't listen to *any*body. I had ideas that were really explosive ideas—like jazz. They played novelties, and that's why we bombed when we came to New York. They sent us back to Chicago."

But Calloway opted to stay behind in New York after Louis Armstrong got him a job in *Connie's Hot Chocolates*, a Broadway show whose score, by Fats Waller, Andy Razaf, and Harry Brooks, was notable in part for juvenile lead Calloway's vocal contribution: "Ain't Misbehavin'."

"I went over very, very well," says Calloway. From there he moved to the Savoy Ballroom, where he took over regular second-tier attraction the Missourians. The Savoy was the most famous African-American dance hall in the world, a wide-open Harlem frolic box rocked regularly by the bands of Count Basie, Jimmy Lunceford, Chick Webb, and Duke Ellington.

"With the Missourians, we were working our way to the Cotton Club," Calloway continues, "but we first had a gig down at 126th Street at a new club just about to open called the Plantation Club. We had been down there during the day and rehearsed and everything, and we went back there that night and everything was in shambles! Gangsters who ran the Cotton Club had walked in, took over, and broke up the joint!" Within a few months, the Cotton Club offered Calloway's Missourians a rotating substitution slot for Duke Ellington's outfit, which had Hollwood film commitments. The new job turned permanent in February 1931. Calloway was twenty-three years old and making fifty thousand dollars a year in the depths of the depression. He rechristened his lineup the Cotton Club Orchestra, signed a recording contract with Brunswick Records, and had his first number-one smash with "Minnie the Moocher." Radio banned his next hit, a reefer-laced "St. James Infirmary" fit for Cypress Hill.

In the years immediately after World War II, the dilemma among jazz giants of the era was whether to court jazz orchestra enthusiasts or jump-blues dance ravers. Since his maverick music satisfied both camps, Calloway saw no need for such midcourse adjustments. His sound was a pure, pixilated spectacle of self-conception, and by 1945 it was pushing jazz, rhythm, blues, and his own improvisations nearer the polymetrical palette of Bop.

Listeners to the *Cab Calloway* installment of Legacy's winning reissue series will discover beautiful music between antics, while those who treat themselves to *Cab Calloway—Featuring Chu Berry* will find the fearless leader's sides with tenor sax scientist Leon "Chu" Berry were leavened from the start with a sly measure of mutual accommodation. "Before he came on," Calloway says, "I was playing saxophone, and it was very *weak* saxophone. So Chu said, 'I'll join the band on one condition: You put down that saxophone.' I said, 'Awww, alright. You got a job!' "

RICKIE LEE JONES
REACHES *PARADISE*

IN THE REALM OF RICKIE LEE JONES, NOTHING IS GUARANTEED.
Lovers arrive too late to link up. The wind lifts urgent letters from mailboxes and whisks them to oblivion, unread. And, in the afterlife, one's destiny can be missed as though it were a lost trolley.

"When I began one song, I pictured a woman accompanying a man to his death; they're sitting there waiting, and no one comes," says the vocalist-composer, explaining another of the poignant daydreams that fed the conception of "Pink Flamingos" and the rest of the tracks on *Traffic From Paradise* (Geffen, due September 14), her latest and most indelibly imagined album.

"The title of the album came from a line in a short story I was writing about an abortion I had in Washington State when I was eighteen. The clinic was right by an airport, and they treated me like I was a terrible person, didn't

Rickie Lee Jones

give me painkillers, and it hurt real bad. I felt like I was standing under 'falling traffic from paradise.' "

Talking softly in the remote home in Ojai, California, that she shares with her five-year-old daughter, Charlotte, Jones details the emotional building blocks, born of separation and loss, that make up the new record. Destiny is its implicit theme, dark tremors of reluctant partings rebounding through ten folkloric songs. Like the valedictory of a vagabond, they convince and dismay; when will this eloquent pilgrim know peace?

Then, just before nightfall, the sun breaks through, brilliantly.

Nearly fifteen years have elapsed since the soul-crooning Jones first sauntered into the foreground of contemporary songwriting, each boppin' sigh of her bluesy beat-sonnets culled from a hand-to-mouth life of street singing, coffeehouse jazz, and the childlike cantatas of the Southwest, in which she spent segments of her shattered youth.

She was signed to Warner Bros. in 1978, and an adult nursery rhyme called "Chuck E.'s in Love" became a dark horse top-five hit from her 1979 debut, *Rickie Lee Jones*. Critics praised the rash originality of her eccentric sound (although she herself was quick to credit Van Morrison, Leonard Cohen, and Laura Nyro as motivators), yet many also questioned her bohemian credentials. When her background (broken home, tragedy-gnarled family tree, destitution as a teenage runaway) proved far more distressing than anyone could have guessed, skeptics next suggested that artistic longevity was unlikely for a performer whose songs seemed so tightly stitched to her sorrows.

Six often-superlative albums later, the self-produced *Traffic From Paradise* is her most concise, droll, and persuasive synthesis of the dulcet melodies and dire moral divinations that demarcate her output: a near-perfect record about human imperfection.

"I've been involved in a two-year divorce," Jones explains, referring to the recent deterioration of her 1985 marriage to musician-producer Pascal Nabet-Meyer. "It made me want to write these short stories about my life; they got too personal, like writing a diary, and I haven't [worked on them] since I started the record last July, but those stories freed me, got me confident again. [Guitarist-songwriter] Leo Kottke, who I met last June and kind of got a crush on, was a big inspiration and participated in most of the songs. And so I was able to make a really friendly record that's like the beginning of my life now."

Not that the pained panoramas of the past are ever entirely dispersed. Entering the world in Chicago on November 8, 1954, Jones was the third of four children by failed actor-musician Richard Loris Jones and Bettye Jane Jones, a practical nurse. Both of Jones's parents grew up in orphanages, victims of parents unwilling or unable to raise them. In time, the footloose Richard Jones would leave his wife and family behind.

Following Jones's initial success, her alienated dad resurfaced to actively resent and revile it. A reconciliation was finally achieved just prior to his death in the late eighties. Later, during 1989–1993, Jones witnessed Bettye Jane Jones's attempts to forgive her own absentee mother, who passed away this summer. Glimpsing anew the effort required for such acts of charity, its lessons helped heal a breach between the singer's life and her work.

"My mother's childhood was so horrific," Jones says. "My grandmother, Peggy Glen, and my grandfather had no means of support. My grandfather was arrested for stealing chickens; he had also been gassed in France in the First World War, so he wasn't really well. The orphanage in Mansfield County, Ohio, took their children away. They got the boys first, but my grandmother ran away with my three-year-old mother through a cornfield, and hid. She was at work one day when the county welfare person came for my mother."

Once a month during the brief span before she remarried, Mrs. Glen would stop in at the orphan asylum to see her daughter. But a virtual lifetime passed without further contact.

"In the late eighties, my mother [who now lives in Washington State] started to go to Ohio to visit her [mother] once or twice a year," says Jones. "I have a picture of them together, and my mom sits next to her and looks just like a little girl; her posture and her face are like she's ten."

These sagas of disconnection swam in Jones's imagination as she strained to keep her personal roles as parent and provider on course. "I wrote a song for the album that's really a family photo: 'The Albatross.' It's about looking at your disastrous family, the legacy your parents give you, and you give your kids. You finally go, 'OK. I carry this pain proudly. This is our banner, who we are. I accept it.'

"I now think," she adds, "that there is only this *moment,* and we must try to extract everything from it that's good about ourselves. All you can do is give your children the best, and let them see you learning as well."

All residents of the Ojai Valley know that on certain unclouded evenings at sunset the waning light strikes the quartz crystals on the slopes of the surrounding Topa Topa Mountains, banishing the gathering darkness in a sudden flush of unearthly clarity called the Pink Moment. And when it doesn't happen in the hills, it can still occur in the heart.

On "Stewart's Coat," the ravishing acoustic epistle that crowns *Traffic From Paradise*, Jones sings about an eternal twilight in which fear vanishes and adults petition Heaven for a last chance to understand love, mercy, and death—in essence, to appreciate each pink moment before it's gone.

"A few months ago, as I was finishing the album, my daughter was talking to me about these profound questions," Jones concludes. "I said something about God, and she said, 'You know who God is? God is the *first* person who died.' I'll be thinking about that for quite a while."

MARIAH CAREY'S STIRRING MUSIC BOX

MANY SAY IT'S THE UNIMPEACHABLE POWER OF HER HIGH-coloratura vocals that assured Mariah Carey's success, but after hearing her heart-piercing *Music Box* album (Columbia, due August 31), some may hereafter maintain that it actually was the perceptible hurt in her voice.

"I always used to sing when I was a little girl if I was upset about something," says Carey, sitting alone in mix room A of Sony Music Studios, on Manhattan's West Side, after listening for the first time to the final mastering of her much-anticipated third full-length album. "Some kids go outside and play basketball or something, but I would take a walk by myself in the woods, or wherever nobody else was, and I'd sing to myself."

The enduringly reflective pangs in her singing are perhaps the most absorbing aspect of Carey's four-octave abilities. Whether it's "Vision of Love," from her 1990 self-titled debut, *Make It Happen*

Mariah Carey

from 1991's *Emotions* collection, the savvy exuberance of 1992's *MTV Unplugged EP*, or the current "Dreamlover" single, Mariah's earnest interior monologues convey the doctrine that belief is its own dominion/ sanctuary.

As a consecration of this view, *Music Box* is easily the most elemental of Carey's releases, her vocal eurythmics in natural sync with songs that examine the personal ferment of faith, particularly fidelity to one's most private emotional ideals. Unlike her previous studio efforts, technical perfection has been downplayed in favor of feel and flow—a move aligned with her decision to tour this fall. "I'm just more comfortable about being myself and letting go," she says.

Music Box treats trust as a secular sacrament. Yet the album confronts an era when constancy and its sensual value have been despoiled by meanness of spirit, any hint of devotional candor automatically decried as déclassé. One must venture back to the best Motown work of Tammi Terrell to find singing so instinctive in its exaltation of vulnerability as (arduous) virtue.

Nonetheless, the material is marbled with admissions of "disillusion," "loneliness and emptiness," and the dread that "everything fades away." To understand why somebody would put such feelings on the public record (Carey is the lyricist and co-composer of almost all the songs), one must consider the background of the singer herself.

The youngest of three children by aeronautical engineer Alfred Carey and the former Patricia Hickey, a vocal coach and onetime mezzo-soprano with the New York City Opera, Mariah was born on March 27, 1970. It was the iffy onset of an uneasy decade, as fighting raged in the Middle East, Simon and Garfunkel's "Bridge Over Troubled Water" was the most popular song in America, and four students at Kent State University were six weeks away from being slain by National Guardsmen during an antiwar demonstration.

Unbeknownst to the infant Mariah, the Carey household had its own troubles, her family soon to rupture into two separate camps, Mariah fated to be reared as if an only child.

"My parents divorced when I was 3," she says, "and after the divorce my older sister lived with my dad. My brother moved out when he was sixteen and I was six, so I grew up on my own with my mom. I was always singing around the house because *she* was always singing, so I would try to mimic her." A subtle grin. "She couldn't shut me up. I was like a little tape recorder."

Patricia Carey was the impressionable Mariah's inevitable exemplar, but the economically pressed parent preferred to regard her daughter as a cohort and comrade-in-arms. "She wouldn't let anybody talk baby talk around me," Mariah says. "She had me around all her friends as a kid, and she used to say I was like a little adult. All I wanted to do was sing for my mom's friends, so I would memorize every jingle on TV, and whatever records were playing around the house, like Stevie Wonder, Aretha Franklin."

Those soul songs, commercial ditties, and the mother who lovingly praised Mariah's execution of each, were the only touchpoints in Carey's unsettled existence. Mrs. Carey and her daughter moved some thirteen times ("I always felt the rug could be pulled out from under me") before Carey reached her teens. Carey's mounting sense of detachment from her ever-shifting surroundings was reinforced by the schoolmates who criticized the striking looks afforded by her interracial heritage.

"My father is Venezuelan and black, and my mother's Irish—her parents came from County Cork," Carey explains, "so I guess I was seen as being different. I felt like an ugly duckling, but if I didn't think I belonged, I at least knew I had a special thing: I could sing."

It excited Mariah to discover that her maternal grandfather also had been a singer and musician. Unfortunately, Patricia Carey could share only sketchy details. "He died a month before she was born," Mariah says, "so she didn't know him."

Religion was another link to her ancestry, but Patricia Carey was a fallen Catholic of conviction, so all issues of belief centered on self-reliance. An instance of personal pluck that still produces giggles for Carey was her appearance, while still a first grader, in a high-school production of *South Pacific*, during which she sang "Honey Bun." Subsequent attempts to open up to adults other than her mother usually met with disappointment. "In my third-grade class at an elementary school in Northport, we got assignments to write poetry," she recalls. "My teacher, a Mr. Cohen, wouldn't believe I wrote them, and embarrassed me in class, telling me I copied them out of a book!

"People try to drag you down and shatter your dreams a lot of times," she shrugs, more bewildered than embittered, "maybe because their own dreams haven't been fulfilled. It was funny how no teacher ever supported my singing; they would always tell me, 'What's gonna make *you* different?' That's why I wrote 'Make It Happen' on my second album. I was trying to inspire the people that nobody encourages."

At age fourteen, Carey began a secret after-school life as a demo singer for several Long Island studios, and six of the songs (including "Vision of Love") she penned at sixteen with early collaborator Ben Margulies wound up on her debut album. But the period before she signed with Columbia was a lean one, Mariah leaving home shortly after her mother's second marriage, supporting herself at seventeen with assorted gigs ("I hat-checked, sold T-shirts, waitressed in the Sports Bar and at the Boathouse Café in Central Park") and backup vocal stints for supporters like Brenda K. Starr. "I walked and worked and waitressed in a pair of shoes with holes in them in the snow and slush," she laughs, "living on one plate of pasta a day between three people.")

The ultimate lessons of the distance traveled are preserved in "Hero," a moving highlight of the refreshingly open *Music Box.*

"The song is saying you don't need someone to say, 'It's OK for you to do this,' " Carey says softly as she rises to go. "If you look inside yourself, and you believe, you can be your own hero."

COCTEAU TWINS' EXPERIENTIAL CALENDAR

LIKE POP GLOSSOLALIA FROM A PRESBYTERIAN MINARET, the vaporous invocations of Scotland's Cocteau Twins resemble the rapt musical pastiche of a ruined world. To hear the trio's forthcoming *Four-Calendar Cafe* album (Capitol/ Fontana, due November 4), one would think the prettiest sonic and mental rubble of Western culture's tragic past has been piously reassembled by a collage artist. And while a mood of requiem infiltrates every note and image, there is also a soaring sense of relief, as if the collapse of history permitted a bold new spiritual scavenger hunt.

"We felt so painfully cut off from our surroundings in Scotland when we began that I really can't think of a single specific influence," mulls the Twins' Robin Guthrie, a multi-instrumentalist who has played a guiding role in the group's opaque production style. "It was all internal, and what we worked on most is *feel* and *flow*."

Cocteau Twins

It's been more than a decade since the Twins bowed on the British 4AD label in 1982 with their *Garlands* album, whose ethereal wiles would render it the alternative-scene equivalent of *Astral Weeks*, so great was the penetrating spell it would cast (whether they concede it or not) upon such acts as the Smiths, Throwing Muses, the Sundays, and the Cranberries. The original trio of Guthrie, Will Heggie, and heavenly vocalist Elizabeth Fraser was formed in their native town of Grangemouth, an oil-refining and textile center on the south side of the Firth of Forth in Central Scotland. Heggie quit a year later, and was replaced (after Guthrie and Fraser had completed the 1983 *Head over Heels* album) by Simon Raymonde of The Drowning Craze. Over the course of a score of albums and EPs, numberless initiates to the cult of the "Cocks" (as the group calls itself) have experienced the slow-dawning realization that most of the beautiful elegies in the group's repertory resist either identifiable time signatures or lyrical dissection, so ineffably fluid is the uninflected celeste of Fraser's singing voice. The Scots term such techniques *Port-a-beul*, or mouth music.

Four-Calendar Cafe (whose title is taken from the book *Blue Highways*) represents another entrancingly tentative step into the daylight of self-revelation. The Celtic–back country twine of the climbing guitar figures in "Bluebeard" preface a plainspoken refrain ("Are you the right man for me?"), while "Oil of Angels" and "Squeeze-Wax" actually boast whole sentences of accessible verse, plus springy tempo turns that could qualify as grooves. For intent devotees, such profferings are postcard installments of the Rosetta Stone.

Background details and artistic determinants regarding the Cocteau Twins have remained no less mysterious, band members long dissuading any substantive inquiry by means of charmingly vulgar (and customarily pub-situated) putdowns of their best work. But the birth four years ago of Guthrie and Fraser's daughter Lucy Belle, and Raymonde's own growing family (one child, another imminent) has softened some of the old guardedness. Taking time out from an uncommonly merry session at their September Sound studio in the Middlesex section of North London ("We're recording 'Winter Wonderland' for Christmas," Guthrie giggles, "and last year we did 'Frosty the Snowman,' as fun things now that Simon and us have kids"), Robin and Liz agreed to explain themselves.

"In a way," confesses Guthrie, "our music has always been a reflection of our desperate desire to get as much distance from where we came from as possible. Grangemouth is like Elizabeth, New Jersey, a great chemical-refining works that's not at all picturesque. I was an apprentice in the British Petroleum oil refinery!

"It was a post-punk sort of time when Will and I bought our first drum machine," he continues, "and in 1979 we met Liz, who we'd seen getting up to dance in pubs. Grangemouth is such a small place that Liz and I have even got the same [registrar's] signatures on our birth certificates. We figured if she could dance so well she could probably sing, and when she did she blew us away."

Fraser then held a staff post in a local whiskey bond (distillery), labeling and boxing the bottled spirits. "You have to understand," she says, "how few the choices were. Most of the women worked where my mother did, in a sewing factory called Racke's. And most of the men worked for B.P., but my father was a tool grinder in a wood yard."

Seeing the enervating effects such toil had on parents William and Wilma Fraser, Liz gravitated instead to the leisure activities that seemed to revitalize them. "My mother had been a drummer in a pipe band, and my father played accordion. There were hundreds of British pop records at home—the Beatles, Petula Clark, Lulu—and I got shanghaied into singing hymns at Beancross Primary School when I was six. It was wonderful growing up with music in the house, because there was so much tension just outside the door, like our Protestant segregation from Catholics. My brother and grandfather were in the Orange Lodge, and you weren't allowed to cross the road when they marched. Religion left me numb."

The move to try music as a livelihood came at the very crossroads of adolescence, as schooling fell away and the sentence of factory life threatened. "I was just nineteen and Liz was seventeen when we made our first album, and it was rough making it," says Guthrie who regrets that his father, Gordon, died without hearing it. "Liz and I had to leave our apartment in Falkirk because we couldn't afford it, and we went on tour just to feed ourselves." The first two gigs performing the music that became *Garlands* were at a club in Stirling, and at a groggery in Glasgow where they supported budding Scottish actor Peter ("Local Hero") Capaldi's band, the Dream Boys. Soon came international cult status—and its attendant insecurities.

"I would often think a new song could only be good if the old stuff was shit," admits Guthrie, "and about a year ago it got to where it took loads of drugs and alcohol for me write and record 'Bluebeard' "—maybe the most spellbinding Twins composition thus far. "I was a bit off my nut,"

Guthrie says, "and I've cleaned myself up, but creating these things can hurt so much."

As for the formerly shy, stage fright–plagued Fraser, she fairly belts, "There is no going back/I can't stop feeling now/I am not the same/I'm growing up again/ . . . I had to fantasize just to survive," on the new record's affecting first single, "Evangeline." Like the rest of the captivating *Four-Calendar Cafe*, it's a modern construct of what her pipe-band playing mum would call *Ceol Mor*, or "big music." Liz also discloses that watching Lucy Belle discover the world has rekindled her own sense of curiosity.

"Before, I just stumbled through in my own inimitable way," she says, "and that included my singing. Starting next week, I begin studying with a vocal teacher, to keep fresh and keep learning. The fans are fine, but we'd always feel disappointed in ourselves. Our music started as an escape from the grayness and emptiness of our town, our past, but now it feels very healing. The kind of music that complements the emotions you're feeling, it's like a friend."

STAYIN' *COOL:* WAILING SOULS' STORY

"SUCCESS DEMANDS SACRIFICE," SAYS WINSTON "PIPE" Matthews of Wailing Souls, sitting pensively in a Manhattan hotel room, the latest in a three-decade continuum of transient havens stretching from First Street in Trenchtown to the simmering urban tangle of Los Angeles. "When reggae first come out, everybody thought it was just a little two-chord local rhythm for fun, and many just treat it like that. But we always worked hard to create thoughtful ideas to reach the vast majority of people, telling them to think a bit about the other man: to be more sharing and caring."

Matthews is discussing the untold trials he has shared with Wailing Souls cohort Lloyd "Bread" McDonald in their improbable pilgrimage to popular acceptance, but he could just as easily be recounting the plot of *Cool Runnings,* the Disney Pictures release opening nationwide October 3 that recreates the unlikely exploits of the 1988 Jamaican Olympic bobsled team. Wailing Souls' music dominates the multi-artist companion album (Chaos/Columbia, due September

Wailing Souls

28), whose pan-stylistic uplift earmarks it as the nineties screen-reggae equivalent of *The Harder They Come*, the 1971 riddim syllabus that incurred the first international caress of Jamaican roll.

Participants in the *Cool Runnings* record come from the top ranks of Jamaica's conscious reggae and dancehall infantry: Tony Rebel ("Sweet Jamaica"), Tiger ("Cool Me Down"), Super Cat ("Dolly My Baby"), and the irrepressible Jimmy Cliff, who lends a surpassing reinterpretation of Johnny Nash's "I Can See Clearly Now." A secret weapon onboard is nineteen-year-old Jamaican newcomer Diana King, whose sexy raga-muffin modification of Bob Marley's "Stir It Up" takes that Caribbean oldie to a rapturous new plane.

Still, Wailing Souls prevail over the proceedings with their jubilant reconditioning of Talking Heads' "Wild Wild Life," plus two choice tracks from their recent, Grammy-nominated *All Over the World* album: "Picky Picky Head" and "Love You Want."

Most observers took lightly Jamaica's bid to qualify for the bobsled competition at the Winter Olympiad in Calgary, but the purposeful four-man team passed muster in the trials and was adopted by millions as derring-do incarnate, in the finest Olympic tradition. The parallels of dis-regard and underappraisal run still deeper for Wailing Souls, however, who were present at the West Kingston creation of reggae and its risks.

"We saw every type of negativeness that youths could have when we were growing up in Trenchtown," says Matthews. "There is no degree of poverty or violence or humiliation today that we as youths did not see. But Bread and I decided that everything that would come out from us would be better than what we saw. If it was evil, we would make it warm, loving, and tender. If some other music sounds thin, we would put a much richer flavor into ours. And if it took more years than we could count to be heard, we would make whatever song we played seem like it just come out."

The son of Lila Johnson and Alfred Matthews, a supervisor in a small chemical factory that manufactured pesticides for bananas and other island crops, Winston grew up at 6 First Street in Trenchtown, counting Cliff, Bob Marley, Peter Tosh, and Joe Higgs as his boyhood musical com-panions. He says, "The first song I ever wrote and recorded was 'Little Dilly,' for Prince Buster, with a group called the Schoolboys," back when Matthews was attending Denham Town Secondary. The song appeared in 1963 on the U.K. BlueBeat label, but it wasn't until 1965 that Matthews resumed recording, uniting with McDonald and chum George "Buddy" Haye as the Renegades for "Lost Love," on Federal.

A half-dozen other Renegades sides emerged on Federal. Meanwhile, Pipe and Bread engaged in various formal and informal singing sessions with Marley, Higgs, and other members of the Wailers' extended brood. It was not until they joined ska-era Marley producer Clement "Coxsone" Dodd's Studio One operations under the Wailing Souls banner—issuing "Row Fisherman Row" (1970) and "Mr. Fire Coal Man" (1971)—that the group (with singers Oswald Downer and Norman Davis sometimes contributing) finally began to gain some commercial visibility. Yet the Souls were so poor that it took donations from seven musicians to purchase one acoustic guitar for use on studio dates.

Talent was never an obstacle; both Pipe and Bread were strong songwriters and, as the earliest Wailing Souls tracks reveal, they boasted one of the most luxuriant vocal sounds in the history of JA's top harmony units. Their fertile three- and four-part melody geysers were every bit as fine toned as the best outbursts by the Mellowlarks, Techniques, Gladiators, Meditations, or Heptones. Problem was, Pipe had a lead tenor whose adolescent reediness rendered it a virtual ringer for Bob Marley's, causing producers to pass. At Coxsone's urging, they sought career distance by donning aliases such as the Classics and Pipe and the Pipers, using the latter for a seminal treatment of "Harbor Shark" for Marley and Co.'s Tuff Gong label. Finally, though, both Matthews and McDonald resolved that only the Wailing Souls name *felt* right. Come 1976, with the advent of Ernest and JoJo Hoo-Kim's Channel One label, Wailing Souls (with Haye and Rudolph "Garth" Dennis filling out the quartet) were seasoned enough to excel in the ascendant rocker mode. "Things and Time" was the beachhead in a string of Souls smashes ("Very Well," "Fire a Mus Mus Tell," "War").

Singers Haye and Dennis were replaced in 1985 by Winston Thomas, and by 1991 assorted producers (Delroy Wright, Linval Thompson, Sly and Robbie, Junjo Lawes) had helped bring the Souls' total album output to a radiant fifteen titles. But it was *All Over the World*, produced by Richard Feldman in Los Angeles for the original duo of Pipe and Bread, that finally gripped the whole planet. The "Shark Attack" single was a global favorite, while the title cut and "If I Were You" became radio and dancefloor standards wherever reggae is heard, the swirling glisten of Pipe and Bread's ravishing grooves an unshakable experience.

With *Cool Runnings* as a capstone, the relentlessly touring/recording Wailing Souls have achieved their own paramount ambitions. While giving props to their storied predecessors, the simple fact is that Wailing Souls are the preeminent contemporary reggae group in Jah's creation. As for *All Over the World*, it is the most irresistible new reggae record of the last ten years; like the rest of an enviable catalog, it will stand.

"Jamaica is a little island that has been able to compete internationally in music and sports," Matthews says quietly. "What is most important in the competition—in the movies, or on a record—is morality. From the beginning, Wailing Souls has tried to put itself on the right road. Conscious reggae will always be here because people will always want to hear about truths, and rights, and the greatest victory to come: of Good over Evil."

YEARWOOD: A NIGHTINGALE REMEMBERS

LEGEND TELLS OF A SOUND SO SWEET IT CAN SEDUCE DEATH itself, filling the Grim Reaper with such longing that he is lured away from his appointed rounds. This song of the impossible—immortalized in the Danish folktales of Hans Christian Andersen, the British balladry of the seventeenth century, and the operatic and symphonic works of Stravinsky—endures in our culture simply because, every so often, one more person's most unlikely hopes are fulfilled.

The supposed source of this supernatural music is the nightingale, the Old-World thrush whose nocturnal melodies in nesting season have become synonymous with answered prayers and sudden grace. "The Nightingale" is also the spiritual axis of *The Song Remembers When*, the third and finest album (MCA, due October 26) by acclaimed country singer Trisha Yearwood, and the origins of this latest version of the fable fit the time-honored mold of an unforeseen gift.

"I'm engaged to Robert Reynolds [bassist for the Mavericks]," says Yearwood. "I usually don't volunteer that

Trisha Yearwood

information, but in this case my friend Jude Johnstone, the songwriter who also composed 'Hearts in Armor' and 'The Woman Before Me,' wrote 'The Nightingale' and sent it to my producer, Garth Fundis, at a point this summer when Garth and I were really up against the wall finding material to finish the album. I made Garth take me to his office and play it immediately—like at midnight."

What Yearwood discovered on the demo tape was a stark lyric narrative that seemed to sum up the lonesome last six years of her life, whether it was her advancement from record company receptionist to recording artist, the dissolution of her long-unsteady first marriage to a former college classmate, the chronic isolation of her sudden, tour bus–powered éclat, or the budding relationship with a country musician that she steadfastly discounted to friends ("He's too good-looking . . . There are all those skinny girls out there; he could have any of them") until Reynolds surprised her in March 1993 with a silver engagement ring. Like that moment, the words of "The Nightingale" seemed to stop time: "Yesterday I thought that I walked alone/And that love was just a memory/But a nightingale followed me back home/And my love was waiting there for me./I had lost my faith, as lovers often do/When the storm clouds gathered overhead/But the nightingale sang a note so true/That I knew I'd lost my fear instead."

"I was so moved when I heard it," says Yearwood. "It just really struck me, and I said, 'We *have* to do this.' I called Jude, and she said, 'I'll say this now that you've already decided to record it, but I had you guys in mind'—Robert and I had recently spent time together with Jude and her husband—'while I was writing this down.' She was very touched by our relationship, and that made it mean even more to me, because no one's ever written *for* me."

And nothing in Yearwood's background ever quite equipped her for the demands of her career path. Born in Monticello, Georgia, September 19, 1964, the second daughter of third-grade teacher Gwen Paulks and local bank VP Jack Yearwood, Trisha initially considered herself too commonplace to excel. She was a high-school honor student who later landed the lead in a junior-college production of *Little Mary Sunshine,* but her brassy vocals in a top-forty mixer band called Straight-laced made her status as a business major seem a prudent choice.

It wasn't until the postgraduate Yearwood, while moonlighting in a Nashville demo session, replaced a laryngitis-sidelined Barbara "Teddy Bear Song" Fairchild that she summoned the vocal moxie necessary to impress the professionals surrounding her. By 1989, Yearwood was a respected demo singer for many Music City songwriters, besides appearing with local songsmith Pat Alger's Algerians group and supplying backup vocals at showcases for hard-striving fellow aspirant Garth Brooks. Another Garth, a producer buddy of Alger's named Fundis, came down to check out Pat's much-touted female belter and became her indefatigable champion, a role he assumes to this day.

Fundis guided Yearwood to MCA, cutting the speculative tracks (including a willful townie tomboy's ode called "She's in Love with the Boy") that formed her first album. "The Boy" would be the first number-one debut solo country single by a woman since Dottie West's daughter Shelly scored with "José Cuervo" in 1983. Yearwood next reached number four with "Like We Never Had a Broken Heart," a tune co-written by Brooks and Alger. When the *Trisha Yearwood* album and its *Hearts in Armor* follow-up both went platinum (thanks to subsequent singles like "The Woman Before Me," "Wrong Side of Memphis," the "Walkaway Joe" duet with Don Henley, and "Down on My Knees"), she seemed established as a sure bet.

It is to Yearwood's credit that each successive release has grown more thoughtful and open souled, the certain route to acceptance supplanted by an intent to craft albums hewn as closely as possible to the substance of her own evolvement. Yearwood's singing is as fervent and foursquare as a solo woodwind within the simple yearnings of "Mr. Radio," the free-spirited flow of "If I Ain't Got You," and the vulnerable distress of "Lying to the Moon." Ranged against the sympathetically percussive time pieces of Fundis's production, the material uncoils with a calm rightness connoting the "Court and Spark" of country music.

During concert dates on a recent European swing (England, Ireland, Switzerland), audiences repeatedly were bestirred by the fundamental fire in her live performances of "The Song Remembers When," a tune about the mental touchstones an errant song fragment can trigger. "I was answering telephones at MTM [Records] when Hugh Prestwood was a staff writer there," explains Yearwood, "and 'The Song Remembers When' was a song of his I knew about when I made *Hearts in Armor* in 1992. It gives me chills, because it's a reflection of how you change as a person, or how you're able to see things in a different light. These have to be songs that move me as a singer, because I expect people to believe what I'm singing about.

"My eyes were pretty wide open when I started, but I've learned a lot and grown up some in the past couple of years. I was raised in the South, where you try to make everybody happy and you don't want conflicts. But I've learned what my own limits are, and how to balance things. I've also learned how women in country, like Kitty Wells and Patsy Cline, fought for things; women like them are the reason we have it easier, with some control over our careers.

"But the bottom line," she adds softly, "is that I learned I really do just flat-out love to sing. On my first album, I was a little conservative in my singing, because I wanted it to be perfect. On something like 'The Nightingale,' I just want it to be real. If you really feel it, other people will hopefully feel it too. But even if nobody's listening, I will do it forever."

HEARTSOUNDS: NYMAN'S *PIANO* MUSIC

THE HEART MUST SPEAK, AND ITS SEARCH FOR THE PERFECT
outlet is the premise of all artistic expression. When words are insuffi-
cient or impossible, and physical gestures fall short, music is a language
by which the soul can be heard. But when music itself is unattainable,
the silence can be more than one spirit can stand.

"These are things that actually are so unquantifiable, so unconscious,
and so deep, because it's very difficult to say where the brain, the ear, and
the power of speech give way to the soul," says Michael Nyman, the exper-
imentalist British classical and soundtrack composer whose poignant score
The Piano, due Tuesday (19) from
Virgin Movie Music, informs such
issues with a subliminal force that
startles all who hear it—including
the composer himself.

The Piano is the fictional story
of Ada, a mute young widow
of meager means who is trans-
ported via an arranged marriage
to nineteenth-century New Zealand's Maori-dominated coastal
wilderness. The journey forces Ada
to relinquish all but the two things
she holds dearest: her nine-year-
old daughter Flora, with whom
she communicates by way of sign

Michael Nyman

language; and Ada's piano, the means by which she addresses the rest of the world.

To Ada's horror, her emotionally remote new husband elects to leave the beloved but cumbersome piano on the beach where Ada made landfall, eventually selling it to a local *pakeha* (white) trader. The proper but desperate Ada conceives a covert bargain: As payment to reclaim the instrument, she will allow the lonely trader to admire her and her playing however he wishes during a number of private, increasingly sensual "lessons."

Written and directed by New Zealander Jane Campion, *The Piano* earned the 1993 Cannes Film Festival's highest honor, the Palme d'Or, as well as the Best Actress award for Holly Hunter, who portrays Ada. Meantime, the praise for Nyman's score has begun to mount, since it functions, as the composer puts it, "as a substitute voice, because Ada does not speak."

Fans of Nyman's music know him as an author (the definitive *Experimental Music—Cage and Beyond*), former critic (he coined the term "minimalism"), and increasingly prolific creator of operas, string quartets, choral work, cabaret songs (for German singer Ute Lemper), and orchestrations for numerous Peter Greenaway films (including *The Draughtsman's Contract; The Cook, the Thief, His Wife and Her Lover;* and *Prospero's Books*). Nyman's early commissioned music was characterized by a scholarly and often ironic flair for reimagining symbolic fragments of vintage classical works (Mozart, Purcell, Leporello, Brahms, Schumann), employing their enhanced harmonic systems to augment/ animate his larger themes. There's rarely specific borrowing evident, only haunting stylistic tremors. And most surprisingly, especially for the film scores, Nyman's compositions succeed in a sphere distinct from their cinematic origins, which may be why they lend so much on-screen dimension.

A supporting player remarks in *The Piano* that Ada's keyboard passages are "like a mood that passes through you . . . a sound that creeps into you," and while they fit trenchantly into the Victorian scheme of the film, neither the movie's principals nor its audience can dispute the uncanny sense of displacement they convey.

"Even people who like my music find it difficult to escape," says Nyman with a bashful chuckle. "I've heard so much New Music where you admire ideas and technique, but you're left with an emotional vacuum. For me, what's important is the emotional content.

"For Ada," he continues, "I not only had to find music for her voice, but also an internal and external reality for that voice. She was a female living in 1850 who was Scottish, so I decided she came to New Zealand with a repertoire of her own pieces, which would have been composed after the Scottish folk and popular songs of that period." Still, Nyman's sensitivity transcends such allusions.

"An A-minor piece I wrote for Ada is called 'The Heart Asks Pleasure First,' " he notes, "and it recurs in three or four forms throughout the film. When she first plays the piano on the beach, the piece is extremely upbeat, but it later becomes darker or more menacing. Yet it retains the validity of this eccentric, independent woman."

In Nyman's world, we are all creatures of memory, impulse, and fleeting insight, never certain if our longings come from romantic reverie or real experience. As with Ada and the rest of the people within *The Piano*, we are hungry for change, yet anxious for the safety of even the previous instant; we crave original experience but cringe as it arrives.

"What I concentrate on when I write is structure," Nyman muses, "but the emotion seems to rise of its own accord. Maybe something hot blooded in those old Polish genes of mine spills out."

And *The Piano* is not the first motif that's unexpectedly moved Nyman, whose stunning chamber opera, *The Man Who Mistook His Wife for a Hat*, was based on American neurologist Dr. Oliver Sacks's case study of a patient suffering from visual agnosia (pathological loss of sensory comprehension). "When I performed that piece for the first time in October 1986, I came offstage shaking with emotion," Nyman says. "My attitude when writing it was very cool, analytical, yet I somehow injected the material with great empathy."

Born in London March 23, 1944, Nyman is the middle child of three siblings by Mark and Jeanette Nyman. "They were lower-middle-class Jews in the fur trades, both children of immigrants. They were very open, very kind, but were raised with the social and financial limitations of their class. And my mother hadn't had the education her intelligence demanded, because she had to get a job at an early age."

Nyman's musical gifts were "discovered" at the age of eight by instructor Leslie J. Winters at Chase Lane School in Northeast London. "I couldn't sing or play, but he saw some quality in me no one had noticed before," Nyman says bemusedly. "It's one of the mysteries of my life."

Another personal puzzle is the quality of mercy in his music. "I guess I try to preserve the magic of certain moments: my crush on a girl at twelve, or something passionate or unreciprocated in my life," he says pensively. "When I write a film score, initially I'm being an abstract composer. But emotionally it comes alive in concert as an independent listening experience. For example, there's a crucial, bittersweet piece called 'All Imperfect Things' at the end of *The Piano*. Just a month after the film was given the Palme d'Or, [director] Jane Campion's baby died. I was playing this piece in an open-air concert in Italy, and my affection for Jane and the terrible tragedy of her losing a child aged just ten days all melded together, and became inexplicably contained in my impressions of this piece.

"Some people who encounter me personally might see me being not particularly empathetic, yet I find my music's impact on *me* to be overpowering. With *The Piano*, this one's from the heart."

ZOOP:
REMEMBRANCE OF
THINGS PAST

THE FEELING CONVEYED ON FIRST EXPOSURE TO THE FOLK
music of the United States Virgin Islands is best summarized by a sign
that once hung near the old seaplane dock at St. Thomas Terminal: "It's
fun to land on water."

Anyone who has ever caught a rickety, single-engine shuttle prop
bound for St. Croix, forty miles to the south, knows what it's like to
circle low over a fluid, aquamarine expanse empty of further traits: The
sensation is of seamless, formless floating.

But with the crisp impact of plane pontoons creasing the limpid St.
Croix tide, the camouflaged will of the rhythmless void is firmly revealed
as a restive pitch and sway.

And it's the same with the Crucian (i.e., St. Croix–rooted) sound
of the local "scratch band" music. One must be a breath away from the
bands themselves
to perceive their
fierce, rolling pull.
But once you've ex-
perienced it — as
folklorist Mary Jane
Soule did during
the first two years
she spent hopping
bygone Antilles Air-
boats flights be-
tween the harbors

Blinky & The Roadmasters

of Charlotte Amalie, St. Thomas, and Christiansted, St. Croix—you'll know why it was so necessary to preserve their near-extinct charms.

The musical treasures Soule retrieved can be found on the thirty-one-track *Zoop Zoop Zoop: Traditional Music and Folklore of St. Croix, St. Thomas and St. John* (New World Records), an unprecedented project that took some fifteen years to refine for the unique, award-winning New World label, which is committed to the care and reconnaissance of obscure American music.

Soule, a Connecticut-born, Cambridge, Massachusetts–based field recordist and documentary producer, had done work for National Public Radio, Nickelodeon, the Children's Television Workshop, and the Smithsonian Institution. But it was while creating a multimedia presentation in 1977 for the tourist board of the U.S. Virgin Islands that the then-thirty-year-old social archivist chanced upon the vestigial legacy of the region's musical heyday.

"A small portion of the tourist-board show dealt with oral history," she says, "and I remember someone sang me a story—an a cappella folksong they called a *cariso*—and I was deeply moved and intrigued."

What struck Soule about the cariso (a call-and-response form customarily sung by women and accompanied by a man tapping cadence on a barrel drum) was its complete absence from even the most festive public and private rites in the region. In 1978, she obtained a grant from the National Endowment for the Arts to begin investigating this riddle.

Located on the northwestern cusp of the Lesser Antilles, the islands of St. Croix, St. Thomas, and St. John had been divided in the eighteenth century into plantation parcels by the Danish West India-Guinea Company. Their subsequent sale to European planters of sugar cane resulted in British overseers importing slaves from what are now Senegal, Gambia, Ghana, and Nigeria. With emancipation in 1848, many croplands on St. Thomas and St. John were bequeathed to the free chattel by the departing plantocracy, but the more persistent feudal conditions on St. Croix led to labor uprisings, economic decline, and general depopulation.

The United States bought the archipelago in 1917 for $25 million, granting its residents U.S. citizenship in 1936. Post–World War II development in the late forties, plus the Cold-War isolation of Cuba in the fifties, provided the Virgin Islands' luster as a vacation alternative.

"However," notes Soule, "during its rapid fifties development into an American tourist mecca, outsiders made fun of the 'primitive' or 'naive' customs, to where residents were finally influenced or embarrassed into setting them aside."

It was into the "evasive, protective" byways of these hotel- and resort-engulfed Caribbean cays that Soule embarked in the summer of 1978. "I found," she says, that "three visits to each place was the magic number to make contact, prove myself," and induce the long-dormant musicians and singers to revive their buried bounty of *bamboula* tunes, quadrille dance calls, "massing" (masquerade) string-and-drum patterns, and the ascerbic *quelbey* party repertoire of the horn-centered scratch bands—whose name is owed to percussionists' metrical scraping of ridged *guiro* gourds.

Setting up "in bathrooms, kitchens, bedrooms," Soule and frequent coengineer Thom Foley accumulated four hundred hours of material. It took ten more years of erratically funded return trips and research missions to fact check and catalog the content of each song. The entire undertaking, of which the *Zoop Zoop Zoop* album represents just a glimpse, is a musicological milestone whose feats resemble those of Alan, John, and Ruby Lomax in their picaresque pursuit of the song traditions of North America.

Witness St. Croix's Maude Andreas and Jamesy and the Happy Seven's joyful recap of the traditional "Zoop Zoop Zoop" children's ring song. Or the sure, rhythmic alacrity of alto saxophonist Sylvester "Blinky" McIntosh and his scratch-band cohorts as they scold the fortune-teller who proved a faulty judge of horse flesh in "Cigar Win the Race." Or the keen faith in one's imagination that Eulalie Rivera displays as she offers her awed girlhood hints of "the Devil" masquerader who once cornered her as she hung over the fence at Ebenezer Orphanage: "I'll never forget that day; I thought I was gonna pass out."

As a consequence of Soule's intrepid zeal, McIntosh received a National Heritage Fellowship Award from the National Endowment for the Arts, as well as a recording contract with Rounder Records (the marvelous *Blinky & the Roadmasters: Crucian Scratch Band Music* was issued in 1990, with a new album planned). Moreover, the last several years have seen the emergence of new, young St. Croix scratch bands, and the various forms of the music rescued on *Zoop Zoop Zoop* have returned to the Virgin Islands' radio airwaves after decades of disregard.

Rivera herself wrote to Soule: "Congratulations for such a wonderful idea. It really has helped our people islandwide to become aware of what is being lost in our culture."

A fond keepsake of Soule's is a clipping from the *St. Thomas Daily News*, in which Blinky McIntosh reflects on the remarkable turnaround that *Zoop Zoop Zoop* effected upon his career and homeland. "It's made in St. Croix," he proudly asserted of the resurgent Crucian scratch-band sound. "And with this type of music, it never changes, never dies." The newspaper inquired how often the band now practices. "Never," said McIntosh with a laugh.

The shared remembrance of any moment of self-realization is a restoration of both the commonplace courage and the fond human mystery at the core of all vital communities. To hear the previously foresaken musicians on *Zoop Zoop Zoop* as they are coaxed back into reaffirming the contours of their folk heritage is to experience a profound reawakening. The record has touched and transformed all those who participated, and it leaves anyone who listens with the sense of alighting on water.

ROCK BUDDHA: THE
SINGULAR BOWIE

COMPOSING IS BOTH A MUSICAL AND PAINTERLY VERB, connoting the arrangement of artistic parts to form a unified whole. But it also can refer to a state of mind and body in which opposing forces are reconciled, anxieties are quelled, and a poised level of alertness is achieved. A master portraitist of himself and his times, longtime musician-painter David Bowie has attained an enviable degree of calm in his own creative makeup—quite a feat, considering his favorite raw materials are random selection and pure chaos.

"One thematic quality, right from the beginning, that is a strain that's run through the majority of my work is the juxtapositions of ill-suited information," says Bowie with a serene chuckle. "And it's not really surreal, some of it's more abstract. A realist would paint what he sees, whereas an abstract expressionist would paint what an object *feels* like. And when you work the way myself and a lot of my contemporaries have

David Bowie

worked, a lot of the imagery comes from what is just in the air at the time. None of it necessarily makes linear sense! But the overall collection of imagery has a texture to it which feels right for the period one is writing in."

Bowie is waxing poetic and making wisecracks at his own willing expense on an early Saturday evening in London as he describes his latest works: *The Buddha of Suburbia* (Arista/BMG International, out November 8 in England) and *Bowie: The Singles 1969 to 1993* (Rykodisc, due November 16).

The Buddha of Suburbia is a ten-track songs-and-setpieces score to the four-part TV series currently unfolding on BBC2, based on Hanif Kureishi's 1991 Whitbread Prize–winning novel about an Anglo-Indian teenager enjoying the punk frisson of late-seventies London. The latter release is a deluxe two-CD anthology yielding the brainiest selection ever of Bowie's U.K./U.S. chart bullets, with "Oh! You Pretty Things" (also a 1971 British hit for Peter Noone) cached alongside such overlooked hand-icraft as the 1986 *Absolute Beginners* movie theme and rarities like Bowie's yuletide 1977 "Peace on Earth/Little Drummer Boy" duet with Bing Crosby.

Those expecting a retro-punk exercise on *Buddha* will be pleasantly startled to find a lustrous, nonliteral evocation of reckless experience; the record contains some of his finest power ballads and funky, stream-of-mood club stompers (the heady title track, featuring Lenny Kravitz on lead guitar; "Sex and the Church"; "Strangers When We Meet") since the mid-seventies heights of "Young Americans." There are even some flexive strokes of acid jazz on "South Horizon" and "Untitled No. 1."

And while both albums sift the past in search of peak moments and prognostic meaning, each does a superior job of showing the acute originality at the core of Bowie's curious artistic composure.

"I just give thanks every day that I'm not a casualty," says the forty-six-year-old Bowie with a laugh, still smitten with the "new start" of his 1992 marriage to Somalian model Iman and the resultant *Black Tie White Noise* album formed from the music he wrote for their wedding ceremony. "It's wonderful that I've been so lucky to end up relatively sane, and with someone I love deeply. Life has just become much richer, fuller. I'm looking forward to this aging process, and I'm a two thousand percent happier man."

In which case it must be troubling to revisit, on *Buddha* and *Bowie: The Singles*, such unsettled private intervals as the seventies. Consider, for instance, the *Singles* album's "Be My Wife," which was done with

Brian Eno in Berlin in 1977 for the personally and professionally recuperative *Low* record.

"I was cleaning myself up, and the ingredients that went into that song was that I started to feel that I needed to learn how to conduct relationships," Bowie reasons. "'Cause when you get off drugs, the first thing that you notice is that you're not very good at making and keeping friends. I guess that, symbolically, 'Be My Wife' was just a general cry.

"All that stuff from that period was terribly personal," he adds. "By that time, I'd learned how to write from an inner perspective, rather than trying to kid myself that I was the stoic, objective, slightly distanced observer."

Not that earlier tracks amassed on *Bowie: The Singles* are without their chilling—and often prescient—merits. Bowie recalls that "the 'Diamond Dogs' song and the album as a whole were an attempt to stage *1984*, but the dear old second Mrs. [George] Orwell owned the copyright and she turned my musical down. So I blended it with [William] Burroughs-isms and fragmented it into these creatures called Diamond Dogs, this bunch of punked-out hooligans"—led by a charismatic scamp named Halloween Jack—"who lived on the tops of buildings." Bowie notes that he got the concept of the rooftop ruffians from his father, Haywood Jones, who worked for an orphanage originally founded in the 1800s by a doctor who'd discovered hundreds of homeless urchins living astride London's skyline.

"I put that image into the twenty-first century, after some raging, desperate ghetto war," Bowie says. "It's a bit scary now, in terms of how it feels in Los Angeles sometimes. Ironically enough, [director] Tim Burton has used a Halloween character called Jack in his new movie [*The Nightmare Before Christmas*], and I thought, '*Hel*-lo!' "

A more savory surprise was House of Pain's ("one of my favorite bands") request to sample "Fame" for its recent smash "Shamrocks & Shenanigans." Yet Bowie has been best at anticipating the equally fantastic transformations of his own psyche, as illustrated by the offhandedly harrowing 1977 British hit, "Heroes."

"That was something I was finding within myself," he affirms. "The story of this man and this woman in this song, the fact that they had developed a relationship, was for me at that time like an act of heroism. And I needed that deed in my life as well."

What he's accomplished in the decade since is summed up in the fresh credo of autonomy expressed on "Jump They Say," a song from *Black Tie* and the confident closing cut of *Bowie: The Singles;* more importantly, the song is a preface to his new life. "I'm very careful about doing solo work now," he admits, "because I had to find myself again. I think that *Buddha* moves on from *Black Tie* in a way I find very exciting." As a result, in addition to beginning his next solo studio record in January, Bowie is planning another venture with Hanif Kureishi, who also wrote the Oscar-nominated screenplay for *My Beautiful Laundrette.*

"It's got something to do with theater and music," Bowie says of the project, "and don't dare call it a musical! We're not sure what the animal is yet." Still, the composition simply feels right? "Exactly. When you put two pieces together that shouldn't be together, this third piece of information appears which is quite extraordinary. I've always found that fascinating. So I don't know where I'm going, but I'm really loving the ride."

SARAH McLACHLAN: IRONY AND *ECSTASY*

"WELL, I'M TWENTY-FIVE YEARS OLD," LAUGHS CANADA-born singer-songwriter Sarah McLachlan, "so what the fuck would I know about life?"

Yet what's so marvelous about *Fumbling Towards Ecstasy*, the much-praised McLachlan's fourth album (Arista/Nettwerk, due February 15), is the fact that she can write candidly about the things she can't always follow but aches to fathom.

McLachlan figures that her new record's fluent sense of searching might have been drawn from a disquieting trip to war-, poverty-, and AIDS (via prostitution)-torn Cambodia and Thailand with the World Vision charity organization; or possibly from her recent exposure to *Letters to a Young Poet*, German philosopher Rainer Maria Rilke's tracts on solitude and acceptance.

But when she admiringly mentions that her mother recently returned to school to gain a master's degree in English Literature —doing her thesis on *Clarissa*, English novelist Samuel Richardson's epic work of fiction—Sarah's careful description of that book's title character tells much about the

Sarah McLachlan

music Dorice McLachlan's emerging offspring creates: "All through her life she exerted her free will, and even though people did painful things to her, in the end she found ways to forgive them, because in her sheer determination she had kept her heart pure."

McLachlan began her career at nineteen, and acclaim for her debut album, *Touch* (1988), was immediate and sustained; local critics were hot to christen her as Canada's preeminent folk siren for the millennium. When American and British observers reinforced that high regard in 1992 following the studio sequel *Solace* and a live release, Sarah resolved to slow the pace of her widening reputation, lest it outdistance the seasoning of her talents.

Fumbling Towards Ecstasy opens with "Possession," a track inspired by a rapt fan whose misguided epistles to his heroine missed her true nature by a country mile.

"The ironic truth is that during the making of the first two albums, I was in a spiritually low place," says McLachlan—who adds that she's "not a particularly religious person. It just took me a long time to realize I should feel pride for what I do. That may show a big lack of confidence, but ultimately I was pleased I came to understand things on my own terms."

The question no mere fan could be informed enough to pose is explored in the octave-leaping monologues of other *Fumbling Towards Ecstasy* tracks like "Wait," "Plenty," "Ice," "Hold On," and especially "Elsewhere": "I believe/There is a distance I have wandered/To touch upon the years of reaching out and reaching in . . . /I believe this is heaven to no one but me."

Those presuming from such pensive-sounding excerpts and titles that McLachlan's work resides in a pat confessional mode will be surprised by the wit, literate grace, and unfussy intricacy of her material. As produced by Daniel Lanois protégé Pierre Marchand ("my friend and mentor," says McLachlan with undisguised gratitude), she establishes a consummate counterpoise of vocal fire and reportorial flow—each vibrant trill, insight, and instrumental touch too absorbing to remain in the realm of autobiography. No theme is worried, no image wasted.

"The things I saw and experienced in Southeast Asia made any troubles and problems I might have seem pretty trivial," she says. "These people have so little, yet they have a dignity and a kindness. I visited there after having been on the road in a cocoon for fourteen months after *Solace* was released, and it challenged me to be more responsive, discerning, and sensitive in my own life. For instance, 'Hold On,' on the

Fumbling album, came together in a matter of hours after I'd seen a documentary on the Arts and Entertainment channel, *A Promise Kept*, about
a woman whose fiancé was dying from AIDS. Since the album is already
out in Canada, I've heard from people who just take the song as being
about the loss of any intimate friend. I like that ambiguity, where listeners just perceive words of love as entities of faith."

Born January 28, 1968, in the Halifax, Nova Scotia, suburb of Bed-
ford, McLachlan was the third child of American marine biologist Jack
McLachlan and wife Dorice, a fellow Yank who shelved her own academic aspirations to support the education and professional wayfaring
of her husband. An often-lonesome Dorice McLachlan picked Sarah
over her spouse and older sons as her prime confidante, acquainting her
little girl with the isolation that regret places in the path of personal
fulfillment.

Invested by her firmly nurturing parents with a toddler-to-teenager
dose of classical training ("twelve years of guitar, six years of piano, five
years of voice"), and self-financed by years of dishwashing and counter
work in Halifax establishments like the Club Flamingo and the Second
Cup and Mother Tucker's restaurant chains, McLachlan was able to fuse
her mother's depth of pathos and her father's detached analysis into a
calm grasp of our culture's callous objectification of women.

"But it took me six years," she says, "to learn how not to edit myself,
to remain open in my music so that I touched greater levels of darkness
as well as some positive areas of escape."

The fruits of this unimpeded intuition are featured in "Good
Enough," "Fear," and the title track, on which McLachlan both grievously delves and bids goodbye to the emotional stasis her mother unconsciously tried to bequeath her.

"To know oneself is to find freedom," she says. "As a child, I was
never passionate about classical music, even though I put so much
energy into it. From the age of four, I preferred to improvise on the stuff I
was learning. And the moment I hit puberty, I got into popular music
instead and wrote my first song, 'Out of the Shadows,' in early 1987.
Now, whether I'm making decisions about the things I want to sing or
about the thirteen-member entourage that relies on me—actually, it's
twenty-four, because the Devlins will be opening for us [beginning February 26 in Las Vegas]—I know I have to do it for the right reasons."

With the pure curiosity of youthful intellect, and a musical proficiency rare in the popular idiom, McLachlan is now able to probe such

matters as if they were a still pool. "Living completely alone for the first time during the seven months I made the new album, I saw I could make myself happy, and that state gave me an incredible spiritual high," she says. "Since then, I'm in my first good relationship ever, and what he and I have doesn't fill some empty space. Love is meant to shine a light rather than fix a gap; that's the feeling I wanted to achieve."

McLachlan has made a record unlike any that one will hear this year, oddly ancient in its serene earthiness, utterly fresh in its patient inquiry. In exploring why we break each other's spirits, she posits an empathy accessible to us all.

"It's what honest music has always given me," she says, "and what I wanted to give back."

SAM PHILLIPS'S HYMN TO THE SILENCE

SINGER-SONGWRITER SAM PHILLIPS IS FARSIGHTED. ARTISTI-
cally, this trait translates into music that conveys a penetrating concern
for the fuzzy future. Optically, it means she "can't see up close, I can *only*
see things that are distant," a condition for which her art compensates,
helping her ascertain "what to leave out or include."

Martinis and Bikinis (due March 8), the third in a loose trilogy of
witty/wise Virgin albums by the East Hollywood–born Phillips, furthers
the uniquely humane vision of this
poet of impairment.

"Music gives shape to something that you can't express," says
Phillips, "and I feel that's always
been a key to what I've done."

Phillips's two previous records,
The Indescribable Wow (1988)
and *Cruel Inventions* (1991), won
strong praise for their ability to ex-
plicate the inexplicable. The trepi-
dant spell of tracks like "Holding
on to the Earth" and "Raised on
Promises" (both featured in the
acclaimed film *Ruby in Paradise*)
was lent pluck by the caustic,
lovely surety of Phillips's vocals,

Sam Phillips

her pitch hovering halfway between a bent clarinet and a contra-bassoon.

New songs by Phillips like "Same Rain," "Baby I Can't Please You," "Strawberry Road," and the fiercely beautiful "I Need Love" still use the familiar to help name the unknown, the artist employing chamber music elements (harpsichords, string quartets), plangent Beatles/Yardbirds tokens (treble guitars, backward-tape sequencings, sitars), and other testimonial touches to depict the personal gaps we must conquer in search of sufficiency.

"I'm a big reader of poetry and writing that has a profound side," says Phillips, "from Thomas Merton, Yeats, and Pablo Neruda to C. S. Lewis, who talks about this inconsolable longing that we all have, this feeling we try to describe as nostalgia or romance. That's what 'Strawberry Road' is about, and it takes its name from an old Iroquois Indian story that says the road to Heaven is paved with strawberries." Her throaty speaking tone teeters into a girlish giggle. "I don't like music that's either too into the head or too into the spirit—it should always have some sensual pull to it. *Martinis and Bikinis* is just a pseudonym—the real title of the new album is *I Need Love*. It's the plainest song on the record, and I love it for being so plain. It's an orphan, or something like that."

And so, in a purely emotional sense, was Phillips, the second of three children of transplanted Texan William Phillips and the former Peggy Smith, who met and fell in love at Los Angeles High School. Peggy became a medical secretary, and a disillusioned spouse as many of the qualities (athlete, painter) that attracted her to her husband quickly atrophied. Bill Phillips was an accountant by trade and a movie buff by inclination, sharing his film fixation with his daughter (christened Leslie but nicknamed Sam). "We would see these old movies, and he would take me to different places and say, 'This is where they filmed *Gone With the Wind*.' Movies were *his* family. It seemed magical to me when I was young."

But by her teens, her dad's behavior felt claustrophobic. "I began playing music at fourteen or fifteen as a cathartic thing, because I was having trouble with my parents—who are finally about to break up after letting it drag on too long—and the family was sort of cracked and lying on its side. One of the first songs that I wrote was called 'The Silence,' because my dad would go for weeks, months, sometimes years without speaking! He had an older brother who died when he was very young, and it really made his mother and father bitter, and they completely cut him off instead of embracing him, so my dad had damage that helped create the environment I was raised in: strange, unpleasant and very fragmented.

"So I put this into a song," she adds, "and he saw it on my piano and was shaken, because nobody had ever put that mirror up to him before. It started the process of the whole family looking at what was really going on. To me, that was a big moment."

And even though the precociousness of her prose also put her communication-starved mother on edge, Phillips pressed forward with the new outlet as the family moved from Hollywood to suburban Glendale. "I played my brother Bob's guitar, started investigating beyond top-forty music. We had a library in Glendale where you can check out records, and I found people like Randy Newman who wrote songs off the beaten path."

Phillips's talent and rejection of her chilly Protestant rearing led her to "the counterculture Christian movement in southern California; it was a reaction at that time to the hippie movement," and also precipitated a recording contract with A&M's gospel crossover label, Word Records. Her considerable reputation as contemporary Christian star Leslie Phillips concluded with *The Turning*, a postorthodox folk epiphany produced by Fort Worth, Texas, troubadour T Bone Burnett, late of Bob Dylan's midseventies Rolling Thunder Revue troupe.

The singer's studio mentor guided her to Virgin Records and secular rock'n'roll. ("I wanted to explore spirituality, not dispense God propaganda.") Phillips's decision to drop her ill-fitting identity as Leslie was a sincere impulse, done without knowledge of the legendary namesake who founded Sun Records in Memphis. (She later met and liked his son when Burnett worked on the soundtrack to the Jerry Lee Lewis/Myra Gale Brown biopic *Great Balls of Fire*.) Burnett and Phillips became a couple and wed, and he has produced her ever since, bringing out the brighter and bolder side of her Lone Star bloodlines.

"It's funny I ended up marrying a Texan," she says, "because my dad really wanted to get out of Amarillo as a boy because of its bleakness, and also the racial bigotry he saw black kids experience that turned his stomach. Nevertheless, I now know there are some great characters in the Phillipses' past Texas/Oklahoma ancestry like a great-grandfather who was on the Chautauqua theatrical circuit and an outlaw who made a sheriff dance on a bar at gunpoint!"

As important as the catalyst for any long journey is the quality of one's return. If the mark of truly accomplished artists is the full-circle acceptance of who they discover themselves to be, then Sam Phillips and the stunning trilogy she has completed with *Martinis and Bikinis* must be considered exceptional in every sense. As she bravely declares on "I Need Love": "I need love/Not some sentimental prison/I need God/Not the political church/I need fire/To melt the frozen sea inside me."

Generations onward, when others reflect on the hollows of our faithless age, the work of Phillips, like that of the poets she holds dear, will show that many still sought to improvise virtue after much common evidence of it had evaporated.

"I want to try to make a connection with all the strangers out there," says Phillips, "to be generous in that way and vulnerable, too. Music should be utilitarian but also inspire, helping you see things you can't, or to speak of what words can't say. Thomas Merton said that poetry is to point beyond all objects—into the silence."

ELVIS COSTELLO'S SWEET BIRD OF *YOUTH*

AH, YOUTH. THE COUPLE CLING TO EACH OTHER AS THEY
slip through the halo of the streetlamp at a remote corner of London's Holland Park, probably first-date lovers on an endless summer stroll. As they draw closer, the evening mist parts and the pair reveal themselves to be Elvis Costello and spouse Cait O'Riordan, taking the night air. London's like that: metropolis and village, vast haunt and intimate haven, a ceremonial city with the twilight ability to surprise. Some blithe spirit should write a song about it—and one just has.

The unexpectedly lovely "London's Brilliant Parade" appears on a forthcoming Costello album with the unlikely title of *Brutal Youth* (Warner Bros., due March 8), and it's a truly exultant ode to life's brief interludes of well-being: "Just look at me/I'm having the time of my life/Or something quite like it/When I'm walking out and about/In London's brilliant parade."

"I had just started the second period of recording for the new record when we met on the street that night," Costello recalls four months later with a bashful chuckle. "That song is probably as close as I'll ever get to writing

Elvis Costello

a sentimental song about the town I was born in [on August 25, 1954], even though I've never really regarded it as my hometown. But some places have a special personal significance for me." The lyrics mention precincts of Regent's Park, Camden Town, and the Hammersmith Palais, where father Ross MacManus sang from 1955 to 1969 with the Joe Loss Dance Orchestra. "If that's indulgent, then I don't really care. That's one of the extremities of this record."

Believe it or not, Costello has just turned eighteen as a recording artist, and he's obviously enjoying the last reckless years of his creative adolescence. Fans who fell for the scrawny singer-songwriter in 1977 because he could spout raw, flip-the-bird fury *and* fond laments will find the "Brilliant" track to be the "Alison" of this magnificent return to form. And further evidence of "Brutal Youth"'s broad range of mood swings is found on the first single "13 Steps Lead Down." A vicious satire on a twelve-step self-help program that goes a tiptoe too far, it has the same investigative wallop as "Watching the Detectives" or "Mystery Dance." And it heralds Costello's first indispensable album of the nineties.

It was late 1976 when petulant computer programmer Declan Mac-Manus (aka Costello) first entered Pathway Studios in Islington to begin cutting the pointed songs that would comprise his *My Aim Is True* album (reissued in 1993 with bonus tracks on Rykodisc's rousing four-CD boxed set, *Elvis Costello & The Attractions 2½ Years*).

Late in 1992, almost two decades after his gloriously pissed-off debut, Elvis returned to Pathway, a broom closet of a recording space tucked in an alleyway in a working-class suburb of London. Pete Thomas, drummer for Elvis' long-disbanded Attractions group, joined him on the demo sessions, which resulted in the uproariously rocking "Kinder Murder" and "20% Amnesia," both found on *Brutal Youth.* And there are dim bulbs and culprits galore in each of Costello's other gumshoe narratives of treachery, each paced by a snare drum that prods and pummels like a prosecuting attorney.

"To be honest," says Costello, "what sparked my going back to Pathway was just the desire to take a weekend off from my ongoing work with the Brodsky Quartet on *The Juliet Letters* record [1993]. I'd periodically pop back into Pathway to do experimental things, and in this case Wendy James [formerly of the pop band Transvision Vamp], who I'd never met, had run into Pete and said she would love me to write a song for her. I couldn't imagine writing *one* song, and thought I'd write a whole story based around a fictional character." That effort became James's 1993 solo album.

"Pete and I done all these songs from the Friday to the Sunday, and we decided we wanted to keep going. Because I found I actually liked recording there again, with the tiny room, the eight-track machine, the old perforated acoustic panels on the walls, the special drum sound . . ."

. . . And the irresistible urge once more to reduce his art to its trim, testy essentials, just as he had during the twenty-four hours of recording (at a cost of two thousand pounds) that yielded *My Aim Is True.*

"Once I got excited, and wrote some more songs," says Costello, "I realized that I needed a more solid kind of rhythmic base, so I needed"—he hesitates before wryly emphasizing—"a *band* again if Pete and I were going to get any kind of decent feel, rather than trying to do this piece by piece."

His notion of the evolving project was reflected in the tentative title he assigned it, *Idiophone,* which he says "is a word for an instrument derived from the substance of which it's made. A triangle would be an idiophone, whereas a drum, which is a skin head and a wooden shell, would not be. It was maybe a bit obscure," he chuckles, "but I was thinking of things that have a unique construction, like an individual singer's voice . . ."

. . . Or an irreplaceable musical alliance.

"[Attractions keyboardist] Steve [Nieve] joined Pete and me, and then I asked Nick Lowe to come in and play bass and contribute ideas," Costello continues, referring in the latter case to the man who piloted his debut record and also was his original stable mate on the Stiff label. "When Nick felt a few songs were not his speed, I brought in Mitchell Froom to help produce, and Mitchell had been working with [former Attractions bassist] Bruce Thomas," to whom Elvis had not spoken since a strained parting in the eighties. "Once we got to talking it seemed silly for us not to do it."

And now an Attractions tour is planned! Yet prior to his collaboration with the Brodsky classical chamber group, Costello had long skirted involvement with any one performing unit. The Attractions were absent on his celebrated *Spike* (1989) after having had studio and touring involvement in nearly every previous studio project from *This Year's Model* (1978) to *Blood & Chocolate* (1986). Meanwhile, Costello was enjoying home life in the Wicklow Mountains below Dublin with actress-musician O'Riordan, former bassist of the Pogues, whom he'd married in May 1986.

Always an eclectic, he played with the Royal London Philharmonic Orchestra, wrote songs with Paul McCartney and Ruben Blades, and even set poet W. B. Yeats's "A Drunken Man's Praise of Sobriety" to music for Britain's Yeats festival.

"And I find it amazing that I've managed to be making records for seventeen years!" says Costello. "But I have no desire to be seventeen again—I didn't particularly like it the first time. On the other hand, I think it's good to reflect upon the journey you might have taken from the time you were that age. My wife, Cait, knows that I've tried all these years to write one completely uplifting record about the positive side of life, but"—he bursts into laughter—"it seems it just doesn't exist! I also considered calling this record *Crank*, but you don't want to leave people without any hope for me. Let's say I'm suspicious of artificial optimism, although I quite enjoy the real thing."

LATIN PLAYBOYS
ROCK THE GONE AGE

ANCIENT TO THE EARS, YET TOO NEW FOR COMFORT, *THE LATIN*
Playboys (Slash/Warner, due March 8) is music a pop archaeologist might
discover after kicking over the console of a Mayan wireless. Random
melody amid the wreckage of a lost society, a relic recovered in a future
we may never reach, it is a telepathic overture of Latin America's chronicles as filtered through the static of an extinct transmitter.

Like the fevered historical narratives of Eduardo Galeano's *Memory of
Fire* trilogy (Pantheon Books, 1987), in which the march of Latino civilization is recreated in sequenced anthologies (entitled *Genesis, Faces &*
Masks, Century of the Wind) of brief ancestral vignettes, so *The Latin*
Playboys album is an intuitive exposition of a sacred heritage. Raw
and otherworldly in
its strangled horns,
fuzzbox *canciones*,
and storm-cellar per-
cussion, the Play-
boys have created a
masterpiece of found
composition and ex-
perimental roll, jam-
ming in short bursts
with the ghosts of
Montezuma, José
Marti, Perez Prado,

Latin Playboys

and the *norteño* and *conjunto* traditions that throw mad shadows on the walls of Latin rock.

The fact that most of the album was recorded on a Tascam four-track tape deck during late nights in the Whittier, California, living room of Los Lobos singer-guitarist David Hidalgo is central to the pathos and mystery of its overpowering spell.

"Coming out of [1992's] *Kiko*," says Hidalgo, "we were all really exhilarated by that creative process, and I hadn't dried up ideas-wise, so I kept putting my thoughts down as home demos, just following the feel. I was going for the innocence of early primitive folk recording, that humble setting where there's no pride involved and it's music for the sake of simple human celebration.

"For maybe six months," he adds, "I'd sit up a couple of evenings a week, after my kids went to sleep, and let my impulses take me on a ride. I'd have the mike of the tape deck up so loud that on a track like 'Lagoon' you can hear the TV audio from a Thailand beauty contest I was half watching. I'd go through the kitchen drawers, pulling out a plastic bag of barbeque skewers that I shook in my lap for a certain noise, while I used butter knives and spoons as slides for my guitar. Then I'd grab for something else and go on without stopping. I felt free of any expectations, and when I gave the tapes to [Los Lobos drummer] Louie Perez I left space for lyrics."

"What I heard," Perez recounts, "was all this 'chance music,' a lot of the stuff almost Zenlike in its use of available materials." At the time, Perez was listening to a lot of the post–hard-bop experimentalism of Rahsaan Roland Kirk, whose free playing incorporates woodwinds and quirky instruments, many of Kirk's own invention. Perez also was reading the poets of the Tang dynasty, whose work he perceived as "snapshots of something that's right in front of them, leaving no sense of an individual view."

And after twenty years of exploring Latin American music, Perez shared Hidalgo's quest for improvisations that would "tread on the turf of poets" without leaving footprints.

"The music David had done for what became 'Same Brown Earth' really grabbed me—it sounded like the story of Creation. Many people might wonder if this is the kind of music Chicano or Latin people should make—but we didn't want to fight the naturalness of it. I called [producer-keyboardist] Mitchell Froom, and he loved what he heard, but we knew it would be difficult for Dave to ever go back into a real studio to rerecord it.

So I put myself on a schedule each day at my place in Laguna Beach, writing lyrics to whatever the sounds suggested. Then I spent one evening transferring the four-track to multitrack tape. I showed up for final studio work with Mitchell carrying two cassettes of the demos and a stack of papers full of lyrics. Mitchell said he thought this could turn into a producer's nightmare, but we plunged in, with help from [engineer-bassist] Tchad Blake, and David and I did vocals.

"I'd attach words where they seemed to fit, and we'd run the tapes through outdoor bullhorn PAs or some junk amplifier. We used a Chamberlain [tape-loop device, akin to a mellotron], adding and subtracting whatever seemed right, during May and June of ninety-three. But still, we didn't formulate anything, saying 'this is where the "head" goes, this is where the "feet" belong.' "

Yet it was plain that the endeavor had become a project beyond even the artistically flexible frontiers of Los Lobos. "Other band members would say, 'What are you guys doing?' My honest answer always was, 'I'm not sure,' " Perez recalls with a laugh. "David and I never approached this project trying to stretch the limits of songwriting, but I think we did somehow."

Which is a modest way of announcing that *The Latin Playboys* is an enormously profound benchmark in modern rock for the Gone Age, helping define our equilibrium-starved decade with a heat matching Liz Phair's *Exile in Guyville,* Me'Shell NdegéOcello's *Plantation Lullabies,* and *Rage Against the Machine.*

Especially impressive is the range and tonal ring of the timpanilike effects Perez and Hidalgo brought to the tunes, the pongs and poundings upon bottles, tom-toms, and assorted surfaces lending a tinge of the familiar to a dark pageant only the imagination could attend. Received incantations from the East L.A. ether on "Ten Believers" and the ill-boding "If" are mestizo premonitions wherein Sgt. Pepper wears a Trout Mask Replica to a Cinco de Mayo festival. "New Zandu" and "Crayon Sun" are weirdly handsome rockers that crackle with the inky electricity of the Dia de Los Muertos holiday. And like the *canción ranchera* (peasant song) style that flourished in the luridly viril Mexican adventure films of the 1930s and 1940s, "Pink Steps" and "Manifold de Amour" are soundtracks to an ideal self-indulgence no modern urban *caballero* could ever find.

The Incas believed that history is a cycle of epochs divided by times of cataclysm called *pachakuti* or "overturning of the world." The sum impact of *The Latin Playboys* is disturbingly correspondent. We behold hymns to an equinox of bedlam, during which the lower world and the upper world reverse themselves. And while *The Latin Playboys* closes with the childlike charm of "Forever Night Shade Mary," a cradle serenade that speaks of "a moonbeam to light the way when the evening comes," even this piece seems to have lost its place in the order of things, offering a beginning where the end belongs. For it is the dread cacophony of opening song "Viva La Raza" that seems the fated destination.

"As we were making this record, we couldn't define or explain it," says Perez. "And at the end of each day, when Mitchell Froom would leave the studio, he'd say the world seemed upside down. The music has a definite groove, an Afro-Cuban/Latin American meter, but most of all it reminds me of the rhythm of breathing, and the beat of hearts. It's a response to the way we now live, tempered by what has come to surround us."

AFRO-PLANE AND THE POWER OF SURPRISE

ROCK'N'ROLL IS THE CREATIVE TROUBLE OF MAKING ART, AND the creative art of making trouble. Emerging in the aftermath of a world war that almost obliterated mortal decency, the best rock, R&B, and rap have agitated in the decades since for the fierce social convictions beyond failed social conventions, doggedly railing against the dimming of human dignity.

Forty years since the dawn of Roy Brown and Muddy Waters, the sounds that would be rock, blues, R&B, or rap wear many masks, copious costumes. But it's only those in the frank ranks that still dispense fact above fashion and truth without tidiness, courting no ritual, seeking no acolytes, respecting no demagogues, requiring no pimps.

Afro-Plane is four intense young men from Atlanta whose debut album, *Afro-Plane* (RCA/Kaper, due April 26), is one of the few debuts of 1994 that audaciously asserts its own sonic and narrative will, deeply gritty and often just as witty. In a period when many performers want all your attention but none of your scrutiny, Afro-Plane bluntly

Afro-Plane

invites listeners' closest appraisals, as on "Ghetto Blast," a sweetly rising
a cappella street riff that suddenly becomes a brutally unsparing parody
of a TV beer spot:

"Ghet-to Blast! Ghet-to Blast! . . . /'Hey, what's up? What's that in
yo' hand?'

" 'It's the ghetto to the B-L-A-S-T can!/When I get a thirst, I drink the
worst/Malt liquor in a cup, to get fucked up/A dollar forty-nine, yeah I
got mine . . . I walk with the can, I talk with the can/I *eat* with the can,
ya see I *sleep* with the can/I live with the can, I die with the can/See, they
don't understand, I'm the Ghetto Blast man!/So what you gonna do, you
and your group?/'Cause whoomp there it is, we like the Ghetto in you!'

"Ghetto Blast Malt liquor, the shit that's killing niggers by the ounce/
Get yours today, wherever fucked-up malt liquors are sold."

The raw sendup comes fast and cutting, flipped into the midst of an
amazingly broad brace of material, from the sultry acid jazz of "Shine"
and the gliding, old-school aesthetic of "Daisy's Mission" (a lament for a
co-ed prostitute) to "Tin Soldier," in which poetic meditations on the
allure of militia violence could be heard as antigang or anticareer GI.
Cool anger and sardonic heat make Afro-Plane a riveting hybrid with a
rich heritage.

As author Mel Watkins notes in *On the Real Side* (Simon and
Schuster), his excellent new study of the underground tradition of African-
American humor, "Since African-Americans have been inescapably
engaged with the absurdity of America's racial arrangements for centuries,
survival and sanity dictated that they adopt a comic view of society. . . .
And the comic vision assures that those who embrace it maintain vigi-
lance on themselves even as they satirize the hypocrisy and follies of
others."

Blues, aka Houston Bryan Perry III, the twenty-one-year-old leader of
Afro-Plane, expands on the point. "The element of surprise is a big part of
Afro-Plane, because we formed this group for the purpose of being totally
original, just trippin' out as we pleased on anything we felt. None of us
had been in groups before, so none of us had any idea of what we couldn't
do, couldn't play, couldn't say. For instance, the whole silly malt liquor
thing just whacks us out, so that song was our stick at that. When you're
watching another corny malt liquor commercial come on with some guy
trying to rap some fad for kids, it's so pitiful you gotta react."

Which returns us to the art of making "Trouble (Thought It Was
Love)," a conscience-scalding track on *Afro-Plane* in which a taut rhythm

bed of drums, conga, and chanted harmonies creates an aural trampoline for the group's electrifying testimony: "All this talk about leadership/Malcolm, as much as I love him, he's a legendary MTV Buzz Clip/And Martin, yes he's dead, too/And what did they do? They reduced him to a fantasizer, a dreamer who didn't exist in the real world . . . But as for other so-called leaders/They've turned us into bleeders . . . They are old, tired, burned-out, sold-out . . . spending their time trying to create illegitimate clout . . . Trouble thought it was love/And now we've lost the branch *and* the dove!"

Coming of age during the dozen years of the Reagan-Bush regimes, the members of Afro-Plane first intersected as two pairs of friends frequenting Atlanta's club scene. At the time, Nous (pronounced "know-us," the Egyptian word for reality), aka Rodney Trevon Oliver, was a student at Decatur High School; Blues was a political science major at Clark Atlanta University; Moon, aka Khalil Sharif McIntosh, was enrolled at Cheyney University; and "Brother Soggi," or Christopher Lehman Turner, attended Georgia State.

"We all began hanging in late ninety-two," says Blues, second child of car dealer Houston Perry Jr. and the former Doris Oliver, an accountant. "And we listened to house music and acid jazz and did homemade demos that included songs on the album like 'Flower Child,' 'Afro-Desiac,' 'Dig Deep,' and 'Shine,' which was our attempt at a pop song with a poetic message.

"We all write together, Moon being into the U.K. club vibe of Stereo MC's, Soggi liking heavy jazz like Coltrane and Thelonious Monk, Nous digging old-school hip-hop, and me influenced by Hendrix, Sly and the Family Stone, and the Doors. So it's a big pot of influences," laughs Blues, "that we call 'psychedialectichypnofunk.' "

Afro-Plane's demo got the group signed to BMG's Kaper subsidiary, and the finished album was co-produced in Los Angeles with Atlanta-based engineer David Pensado, who'd worked with Mother's Finest and Bell Biv DeVoe. "We recorded live with session players and no samples whatsoever," stresses Blues, who notes that a new Afro-Plane support band of bass, drums, guitar, percussion, and two backing singers has just begun rehearsing for a tour later this year.

Arriving at a time when rap is outgrowing the adolescent gullibility of the gangsta pose, Afro-Plane exudes the grace under oppression and the eloquence of spiritual word and political deed that have characterized African-American activism. Last week marked the ninety-ninth anniversary of the passing of Frederick Douglass, the nineteenth-century orator-writer who enriched our literature with tales of his triumphs over slavery. Both Blues and Soggi visited Douglass's home-turned-museum as teenagers, and were moved by the sight of his library of works and his gift, in Blues's words, for "self-contained accomplishment," which is also an Afro-Plane aim. Maybe next year, on the centennial of Douglass's death, someone will make "Trouble" a tribute to all the brands of it that deserve to endure.

"Afro-Plane," Blues concludes, "is made up of black men who have reached twenty-one—a thing that's not supposed to happen these days. And we're from the ghetto and the projects and the neighborhood, but we still got ourselves to college. And there's no bandwagon for us but the fact that we're coming up and *boom*—we are gonna get over."

THE AUTEURS: SINS OF THE NEW VICTORIANS

JUST AS NEWSPRINT CONTAINS THE SHORTHAND OF THIS century's social history, so popular music has sketched the essence of its shifting moods. When the moment comes to recapture the frayed spirits of cosmopolitan London in the mid-1990s—that frustrated time when rock stardom seemed an enviable white-collar profession amid the crumbling class system—one suspects that Auteurs records will supply the keenest echoes of an era in which feckless knaves and decent folk were equally apt to risk anything for a vestige of fashion.

As chronicled by the rising British band on *Now I'm a Cowboy,* its lucid, electrifying second album (Hut Recordings, due in the U.K. May 9), social mobility is an iffy proposition with an ugly undertow, leaving slummers and strivers in states of dismay as they grasp for the trappings of who they're not, regardless of caste. To borrow an ambiguous trope from the scathing new record, each thwarted accomplice is "a thief with style."

Luke Haines of The Auteurs

England has come a long way from the abusive Victorian stratification Charles Dickens described in such nineteenth-century novels as
Nicholas Nickleby and *Dombey and Son*. The distances between class
lines have dwindled along with the difficulties in crossing them. Stripped
of the ability to disappear into new spheres or echelons, most dilettantes
must reluctantly address unfinished issues of personal identity. On "Chi-
nese Bakery" (the current U.K. single), a woman who "comes from
uptown" is "going downtown, 'cos she's a poet . . . and she says she's
gonna show me around." The self-involved narrator of "New French
Girlfriend" views his hollow relationship and summarizes, "That's the
price of success/Want a girl to hold my hand/When the plane lands." In
"The Upper Classes," an erstwhile confidant resurfaces to gauge the
depth of his former associate's supposed transfiguration: "Some of the
clothes you stole from your lover's house/Are better than the clothes we
stole from the shops."

"I want to make music that shatters and changes someone's life," says
the Auteurs' Luke Haines, the twenty-six-year-old singer-songwriter who
leads the poetic and effortlessly elegant four-piece (which also includes
bassist Alice Readman, cellist James Banbury, and new drummer Barney
Rockford). Haines's vow could be misread as callow boast or arrogant
cant, but exposure to the Auteurs' *Now I'm a Cowboy* reveals such statements as the hopeful sound of experience.

"That's exactly what certain music did for me—shattering my perceptions in my teens and forcing me to push forward beyond what I knew
up until then," Haines explains. "I still remember the first time I heard
my parents playing the Parlophone single of the Beatles' 'She Loves You'
in a semidetached house we lived in at Walton, Surrey. But it was Scottish singles I bought at fourteen or fifteen by Orange Juice, Josef K, and
the Go-Betweens on the Postcard label that had the biggest effect. They
were cheap-sounding, but to someone who believed nothing ever
changed in the dull, bleak world of suburban or urban Britain outside
London, they were a hormonal affirmation that would take on a greater
meaning."

The obscure early-eighties releases Haines mentions were issued by a
short-lived but beloved U.K. indie label whose Motown-derived slogan
("The Sound of Young Scotland") bespoke its bold drive to redirect a lost
generation's rigid destiny. For Haines, that inspiring pride of purpose
found personal expression in songs on the Auteurs' 1993 debut, *New
Wave,* a poignant manifesto short listed for the prestigious Mercury

Prize, on which the resigned tone of singles like "Show Girl" ("I took a showgirl for my bride/ . . . Took her bowling, got her high") said as much about the letdowns of empty attainment as any social parable by Dickens.

The Auteurs' drawing-room delicacy and decisive rock accentuation continually invest story-songs like "Lenny Valentino" and "I'm a Rich Man's Toy" with disquieting clarity. The latter track might be the lament of a kept lover or a stalled pop idol, yet in either case, demimonde dependency in unemployment-plagued England is no less claustrophobic than the idleness that preceded it.

"The dole has been the mainstay of so many many bands in Britain in the last ten years—at least you had something to do with your time," says Haines, whose pre-rock applications for jobs delivering sandwiches or driving an ice cream truck were undercut by his lack of a bicycle or a driver's license.

Born October 7, 1967, the only child of naval engineer Michael "Mick" Haines ("he designed missiles," his son says) and wife Joy, a secondary school English teacher, Luke grew up in Hampshire's coastal city of Portsmouth, home of a major naval base and the historic site of what one scholar called fierce local attacks on "a shabby mongrel aristocracy" during the Victorian age. Luke's childhood was punctuated by piano lessons ("they taught me about chord structure") that he commenced at nine, studying Chopin, Bartok, and Albeniz. After a year at Portsmouth College of Art and Design, he transferred to the London College of Music ("where Brahms and Haydn were *it*, and Stravinsky was considered too avant garde; for three years I did just enough not to get kicked out.")

Having no siblings, his isolation was further augmented by frequent family relocation to such North London points as Camden Town, each locale reinforcing Haines's general impression that "nothing ever changes in the English countryside, except to get worse. There's this myth that this was different, say, in the swinging sixties, but that scene never touched anywhere outside of London. And that's not meant to sound depressing or even wrong—it's just a reality."

Besides the nudge into music, Haines says he's indebted to his mother for the value she placed on literacy. "She encouraged me to read, which was very important. But I was never one for writing, though, when I was younger. I never dabbled in prose, or tried songwriting with my first band, the Servants, because I was more into becoming a better guitar player. The first song I'd admit writing was 'Bailed Out,' on our *New Wave* record. I composed the melody at sixteen, but the words were about finally starting out on my own." The refrain: "Bailed out/This skin is shed/Bailed out/This thing is dead."

Despite Luke Haines's resolve to "escape" the milieu of his formative years ("Now, I only like London and parts of Scotland"), his lyrical gift for social critique has ample antecedent in the lore of his itinerant upbringing. Charles Dickens lived as a boy in Camden Town, describing its dust heaps and "blighted country" in *Dombey and Son*, and Dickens traveled to Portsmouth in 1838 to gather local color for *Nicholas Nickleby*. Perhaps we cannot escape becoming all we've beheld.

"Well," chuckles Haines, "I've always felt that good art of any sort should be completely accessible, and beyond fashion. And any good record, even if it's not particularly happy, should have the power to make you feel less isolated."

O'YABA: SOUTH AFRICA'S NEW FOUNDATION

"WE DECIDED IN 1989 THAT IF WE WERE GOING TO BE SOLDIERS of peace, the name of our group must coordinate with that," says Tshidiso Alexis Faku, lead vocalist and chief songwriter for rhapsodic eight-man South African reggae harmony group O'Yaba. "So Benrobert Mopeli, our keyboard player, told us about *o'yaba,* a Swahili word which means 'peace song of Africa.' "

During the year of O'Yaba's for-mation, the task of finding polit-ical and racial concord in the band's apartheid-torn homeland fell to centrist reformer F. W. de Klerk, an Afrikaner lawyer who won the 1989 white general elec-tion by a clear majority over rad-ical opponents on the left and the right. In 1990, as O'Yaba issued its debut *Tomorrow Nation* album on the local Gallo label, de Klerk unconditionally released Nelson Mandela, head of the antiapart-heid African National Congress, who had served twenty-seven years in jail. Amidst a groundswell of political progressivism and vio-lent public impatience with an

O'Yaba

official racist doctrine dating to 1948, the album's title track proclaimed the peril and promise of the moment: "Time goes by/Flowers start to bloom/With a beauty and a madness."

By 1992, when O'Yaba's first two Gallo albums (the second being *Caught Up*) were distilled into an acclaimed collection issued in America as *The Game Is Not Over,* de Klerk and Mandela had embarked on a multiparty negotiating forum dubbed the Convention for a Democratic South Africa to draft a new constitution. Meanwhile, the reggae-gospel uplift of *The Game Is Not Over* seemed a millennial merger of the seminal Zulu choral sound of Solomon Linda & the Evening Birds (Linda's "Mbube" composition was covered in the fifties as "Wimoweh" or "The Lion Sleeps Tonight") and the portentous Bob Marley–inspired spirituality of Zulu reggae stylist Lucky Dube.

Which brings us to O'Yaba's new U.S. release, *One Foundation* (Shanachie, due April 25), which reaches stores the day before the start of three days of elections ending white rule in South Africa. It would be hard to devise a finer memento to this historic defeat of tyranny and drive for enfranchisement.

On the opening track, "Armageddon," lovely, churchified piano passages and the murmur of Faku's dusky tenor preface the lush vocal quaking of what seems a packed choir loft. The sacred aura is suddenly rent by a crackling reggae one-drop, the stomping bass drum pattern and swelling organ figure whipping the proudly cadent tempo toward a cascade of exultant harmonies. Set against a dawning of ballot-box liberation that many considered implausible in our lifetime, the wrenched ode of reconciliation will trigger a deep emotional response in even the most detached listener as Faku intones: "People spirit is still ruling/Together we stand up strong."

A committed infantryman in the artistic campaign in support of suffrage and the pan-racial olive branch, Faku is nonetheless awed that South Africa has brought itself to this epic threshold. *One Foundation* reflects his political pragmatism as well as a personal quest for music as richly devotional as the dream of his people.

"What I'm saying on this whole album," Faku explains, "is that we've been struggling so long that the habit of fighting for freedom could become the evil of killing our own brothers and sisters, black and white. 'Armageddon,' 'Merry Go Round,' 'One Foundation' all deal with the situation in South Africa from the day *after* elections onward. If we can stay together in the unity of what our votes decide, then we are really going to win; but if we *don't* accept one another in our combined ethnic character, then we only fought for the right to go from being puppets to being fools.

"Which is why I composed a party song on the album called 'Ho-lala,' which means 'happy song,' a little song that can become a big song—everybody's song—when it's sung in Sotho, Zulu, Xhosa, or English." Indeed, it's this practical response to difficult realities that characterized proletarian music under state segregation, as black South Africans forced to coexist under the common pressures of ghetto, work camp, and *shebeen* (illegal saloon) culture sublimated their tribal differences and spawned marvelous new vocal and instrumental forms like *marabi, kwela, mbube, mbaqanga,* and "township jive/jazz." This past instinct for accommodation will be the same indispensable element for securing South Africa's future stability—and it's a trait inseparable from Tshidiso Faku's own tale.

One of nine children of Sotho descent, he was born June 19, 1970, to Paul Faku and wife Mammamesi in Welkom, an Orange Free State town built as a model development for the thousands of mining employees drawn by the discovery of gold in the area in 1947. "My father, who's a baritone, and mother, who sang the harmony parts, met in the choir of the Old Roman Church in Welkom," says Faku, whose own secular musical education occurred while "secretly listening to my father's gramophone records of the a cappella King Messengers singers." His tastes soon turned to Boney M, Jimmy Cliff, and Michael Jackson's *Thriller* album. Faku's moon-walking mimicry of Jackson's "Billie Jean" dance routine led to participation in Shell Oil's Road to Fame talent contests and stints as backing vocalist in two groups, Impact and Sabela.

Former Sabela manager and longtime mentor Johannes Mokhera proffered Faku a fifty-dollar dare to write his first song overnight, "about South African youth," and Tshidiso copped the cash prize with "Tomorrow Nation." When family tragedy intervened, Faku dropped out of Photagauta Secondary School to support his parents' household by writing and performing his own material.

"What happened," he recalls somberly, "was that my older brother Constanous was crushed to death in 1986 by a car while riding his bicycle. In court, despite witnesses, they blamed my brother for the accident. The shock of the injustice made my father lose his memory, so he could no longer work. I took over my brother's job at a water-pump factory, and then did music full time when members of Sabela and a group called Comedy formed O'Yaba."

Encouraged by Mokhera, Faku wrote rapturous reggae hymns that fused aspects, as he shyly asserts, of "Marley, Burning Spear, and James Ingram," and sent a demo tape to Eric Gallo's pioneering label/studio enterprise in Johannesburg.

From that tentative step came a new realm of promise, and a loyal following for O'Yaba. On April 27, when Faku enters the polling booth at Philip Smith Hall in Welkom ("named for a former white mayor, it was the blacks-only version of the town hall"), he will help lay the foundation of an even wider world of possibilities.

"Nelson Mandela, after all those years in prison, still had the faith to get us this far," Faku muses. "The guy's got guts, you know? He taught us to keep the past for history, and begin again. So when I listen to *One Foundation*, I remember what my friend Johannes Mokhera told me when I had to quit school to survive. He said, 'Now it's time to get along with your dreams.' "

DAVID BYRNE:
SONGS OF A
SELF-MADE MAN

IT IS THE WAY OF ALL FLESH TO FEAR ONE'S FLAWS, DISGUISE one's gaps, deny one's losses. Yet it is only in the public course of acceptance and compensation that we discover the power of our sufficiency.

"As a child, a teenager, and a young adult, I was much more shy and withdrawn than I am now," says David Byrne, talking quietly in his loft home in Lower Manhattan's Soho district as he considers the long prelude to *David Byrne* (Luaka Bop/Sire/Warner Bros., due May 24), his first self-titled record. "I was born May 14, 1952, in Dumbarton, Scotland, coming to this country with my parents when I was two years old, and I had a Scottish accent until I was in the second grade. I had to lose it because my classmates couldn't understand me. And we moved around a lot, to places like Ontario, Canada, and Baltimore, because of my father, who worked as an electrical engineer for Westinghouse. I always had to find whole new groups of friends, yet I was able to remake myself every time I made those new friends, so I wasn't saddled with their knowledge or awareness of the person I was before. I learned self-reliance.

"As for my music," he confides, "to complete my personality I *had*

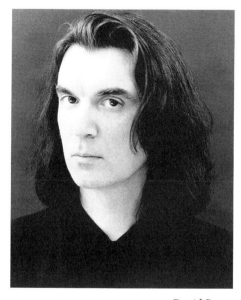

David Byrne

to jump onstage. It became a way for me to introduce myself, to meet and talk to people. Now, I'm hooked."

But no less needy?

"Right," he laughs. "In fact, just before my last East Coast club tour in September and October of ninety-three, when my new band [drummer Todd Turkisher, bassist Paul Socolow, and vibes-marimba player Mauro Refosco] helped me break in the new songs on *David Byrne,* I'd been listening to music like Patsy Cline and Thelonious Monk, with very direct emotional qualities. And I thought, 'Hey, maybe some of that's missing in what I try to do.' "

And in the act of responding to that protracted artistic imbalance, Byrne has fashioned the kind of record even his most loyal votaries could not have anticipated: a frank, confessional work of frail simplicity and forceful compassion. Whether reviewing past aspects of his professional and personal schema in "A Long Time Ago" ("I kept my feelings to myself/Until the perfect moment comes") or assaying their outcome in "Angels" ("I can barely touch my own self/How could I touch someone else?/I'm just an advertisement/For a version of myself"), Byrne mixes wit and wistfulness with the calm will of someone who has bypassed any crisis of self in order to embrace the enigma. By the time he arrives at "A Self-Made Man," he's gently mocking the hectic vocal hook of Talking Heads' seminal "Psycho Killer"—the first song he ever wrote and performed.

Byrne recalls his boyhood as a period of seldom-interrupted self-absorption, father Thomas Byrne and wife Emma encouraging any artistic drives on the part of David and younger sister Celia. "I liked to draw as a kid," he says, "and I would sketch pictures of rockets, or scenes from James Bond or *The Man from U.N.C.L.E.*" Music (Scottish and American folk) was heard often in the Byrne household, as were the tolerant philosophies of his mother's Quaker faith. In his midteens, Byrne took up the guitar, violin, and accordion, later attempting to write "fake Bob Dylan songs."

"When I first got into pop music, I was a sophomore in a suburban Baltimore high school called Arbutus," he says. "My father helped me rig up a Norelco reel-to-reel tape recorder so I could do overdubs." Time spent at the Rhode Island School of Design and Maryland Institute College of Art helped him cultivate a social circle that led to involvement in groups with names like Bizadi and the Artistics (also known as the Autistics). In 1975, the latter combo became the basis of Talking Heads, the Byrne-led group taking its name from a passage in an issue of *TV Guide.*

Talking Heads did its first shows at CBGB in June 1975. Eighteen years later, Byrne jumped back onstage at the venerable Bowery club to complete the "prerecording road test" of *David Byrne*.

"I put my name on this project because it seemed like a beginning," he notes. "Like when I started performing." As co-produced by Arto Lindsay, Susan Rogers, and Byrne, the new album is a purgative potpourri of unpremeditated melodies and inspired miscellany, its orderly twelve-track structure belying the messy substance and blessed accidents that ultimately evoke the gift of emotional engagement. What triggered such candor in the customarily cautious Byrne?

"It began," he says, "with 'Buck Naked,' a song I wrote in January 1992 when Tina Chow, the sister of my wife, Bonny, was dying of AIDS. I was singing it to my little daughter Malu, who liked to run around the house without clothes. Events like the loss of a family member help catalyze your deeper feelings. And for me it led to things like the record's first single, 'Angel,' with that sense of soaring above the world, detached, but also intense physicality, accepting the funk and sweat as part of the beauty of life."

The album is not without a tinge of the incorporeal, its traces of mysticism and spirituality perhaps linked to the Scottish heritage Byrne has explored since his youth. "My relatives all live around Glasgow," he says, "and my family would go back every couple of years to visit. I'd hitchhike up into the Highlands, to Edinburgh, or out to the Isle of Skye. My last trip was a little over a year ago, and since then I've started reading about Scottish mythology and fairies, which seem to be a remnant of pre-Christian Druid society. A lot of it is taken by the people to be fact, like ancient tales of UFO sightings and abductions. I definitely feel a kinship with the beauty and mystery of the culture, and with their music, too, which swings in a way that shows its affinity for R&B. Like most things, an appreciation of it depends on acceptance of its unique differences."

Meanwhile, avid fans will have to get accustomed to David Byrne works with the vulnerable abandon of "Back in the Box," "Lillies of the Valley," and "You and Eye," as well as material ("A Self-Made Man," "Sad Song," "My Love Is You") that is touching enough to move listeners to the verge of tears.

Having progressed as an artist to the point where he could return, without guile or apology, to the purest underpinnings of his talent and its hunger for human attachment, Byrne has rendered the best album of his entire, restless career. One cannot mourn what one has not loved, and in that depth of pity is the most sincere gesture of respect and cherishment. As Byrne summarizes in "Sad Song": "There are those who are happy/ There are those who are wise/But it's the truly sad people/Who get the most out of life."

"Real sadness is such an all-encompassing, intense thing that it takes you out of your humdrum existence," Byrne says softly. "If you can still function, you want to savor it while it's peaking. So when people tell you to cheer up, it's not always the best thing. Like your conscience, sadness is a natural and beautiful impulse that gives you moral guidance. These things are the foundations of most religions. And in their humanity, they're just like music."

LOGAN MENDS BROKEN SPIRITS IN *BULK*

JACK LOGAN WRITES SONGS THE WAY HE FIXES ELECTRIC motors: with offhand proficiency, in the company of chums, and at a frightening clip.

"The next few months are gonna be *very* busy," he assures, before pausing to assist a patron who's just ambled into the Doraville Electric Motor Service. One assumes that Logan, a Mississippi-born, Georgia-based rock bard of considerable underground reputation, is referring to the impending release of *Bulk* (Medium Cool-Twin/Tone Records, due June 14), his two-CD, forty-two-track debut album culled from a stash of more than six hundred unissued demos.

But, no. "Repairing motors is a business with intense seasonal cycles," he continues, "and I'm gonna be working almost nonstop on swimming pool pumps until the end of the summer. With luck, the boss'll give me time off for this stuff." Meaning his music, which the thirty-five-year-old Logan regards as a fond but "dodgy" hobby. To illustrate, he ponders the fine points of his album's opening tune, a remarkably kindly ballad titled "Fuck Everything."

"I just get in these writing moods where I'm *not* nice," Logan explains in his cordial drawl. "It's usually due to a funk induced by my brain chemistry. But that song is not

Jack Logan

really about being pissed off so much as seeing the cycles of life in the long run. I stand by it," he chuckles, "although I hope I can explain it to my Methodist mother better than I am to you."

Born February 8, 1959, in Greenville, Mississippi, to Midwestern Gas Transmission supervisor Jack Richard Logan and the former Polly Taylor, the singer-songwriter is descended from Scottish and English immigrants whose offspring included sharecroppers near Isola, Mississippi. The Logans moved to Illinois, near the Kentucky border, when Jack was a child. He and younger brother Mark grew up to the stirring rumble of the first LPs Jack purchased: Jimi Hendrix's *Rainbow Bridge* and Creedence Clearwater Revival's *Cosmo's Factory*.

Logan has worked at Ron Hazelrig's Doraville Electric outside Atlanta for the last seven years, along with Kelly Keneipp, who's been Logan's closest cohort since they attended Lawrenceville Township High School in Southern Illinois. After college, both men stole below the Mason-Dixon line, settling in the Atlanta area in 1984 and forming a band with old pals Jeb and Greg Baldwin called Lava Treatment. The group's 1986 indie album, "Lake Eerie," is a coveted alternative collectible.

Jack's employer was the Athens, Georgia, Kmart when local musician Todd McBride caught a Lava Treatment gig. McBride coaxed Logan and Kelly to take their unhurried sound to a more aggressive plateau in a new combo they formed together called Liquor Cabinet, which played at the migratory 40 Watt Club made famous by house regulars R.E.M. By this time, Liquor Cabinet's extended musical tribe included Indiana farmboys Terry and Jamie Rouch, who introduced their footloose associates to the lo-fi immortality of home taping. Guitarists David Phillips and Mike Gibson, drummer John Crist, and multi-instrumental whiz Rob Veal completed the ragged clan of garage-rock compeers—some of whom started a collateral band called the Dashboard Saviors, which got signed to Peter Jesperson's Medium Cool label in Minneapolis.

As the Saviors' fortunes expanded, so did the folklore surrounding the all-hours taping sessions of the moonlighting electricians. Droll devils and absurd saints; comic mayhem and religion gone awry; sudden death and hasty resurrection; drinking blood and eating "awful meatloaf"— such themes are prosaic grist for their music. Camped out with a Fostex eight-track in the kitchen of Logan's Winder, Georgia, home, the guys kill weekends constructing songs much as Jack and Kelly rebuild burnt-out rotors: by harnessing the energy of raw magnetism until it raises enough current to run a dynamo.

Logan emphasizes his sundry sound is collaborative, with him handling "mostly lyrics and vocal melodies" on tracks that trace every rustic idiom from country folk and gospel blues to the crustiest rock. But it's his singing, with its fierce weariness and flutelike nasal waver, that imparts the harsh beauty of the haunted soul.

"The songs're done in a distinct style I'd call *unfocused*," Logan quips. "We're just willing to try anything. We'll write five or six songs at a time, never starting them before we sit down to record. In a college town like Athens, your audience tends to graduate and move away, so you only have a few years to make your point. Meanwhile, the Saviors told Peter Jesperson about our tapes and he asked for samples. Hell, I was willing to send two ninety-minute cassettes to the man who discovered the Replacements."

As Jesperson now knows, there's nary a tepid track in the entire two hours and seventeen minutes of music on *Bulk*. The grossly observant grip of "Shrunken Head" and "Female Jesus" ("About young women who live the hipster student life"), or the gothic backroads grandeur of "15 Years in Indiana," "Farsighted," and "Drunken Arms," recall the grimly ironic southern fiction of Flannery O'Connor (*Wise Blood*, "A Good Man Is Hard to Find"), wherein wrong turns and misplaced faith can transform a scenic drive into mass murder of the most homespun, existential sort.

"I get giddy when I think of the writing of Flannery O'Connor," says Logan, confessing his awe with the prim-looking Bible-Belt writer (1925–64) whose terrifying but never gratuitous tales of human misadventure depict the force of universal charity and its unique southern detours. As with O'Connor, Logan's songs are populated with the drifters and misfits just beyond civility's reach, each having a savage desire for epiphanies and a paucity of spiritual pride.

How else to account for the woman in the "little black slip" with a dozen-plus cadavers stashed in her boudoir in "Underneath Your Bed," or the stud with his anesthetic-soaked hanky crooning "don't resist the sandman" in "Chloroform"? And then there's Logan's carol in praise of a woman who dreads the evil insights her TV seemingly delivers in "Weatherman": "His seeded clouds piss on the grass/She drowns like ants inside a water glass."

Like Flannery O'Connor, Jack Logan reveals the dangers and distortions of a myopic spirituality, yet he moves us to the marrow with the honest illusions his characters inhabit. There is gentleness in Logan's unassuming instinct, literature in its agility, and thunder in his grasp of grace among the grotesque. Marking the full-blown arrival of an exceptional comiserator, *Bulk* will stand with the most substantial rock'n'roll of this decade.

"It's an American dream to make a living at your hobby," Logan notes as he returns to his duties tending engines. "I think music is an enriching but also an inexplicable thing, and like anything that's capable of good, it can also be a source of the worst in us. I try my very best to get at an indescribable something in each memorable moment, and to look down on no one. It's wisest for writers or musicians to just share what they've seen or learned, and not make too many judgments. What we all want to deal in is revelation."

PAULA COLE'S HOPEFUL *HARBINGER*

IN AN ERA SO LACKING IN LEADERSHIP AND UPLIFT, SELF-reliance often assumes the intensity of religion. If it's hard for some to accept the fact of psychic solitude, it's inspiring to hear others describe the feeling.

"A lot of my music is on the darker, sadder, or more serious side," says singer-songwriter Paula Cole, "so I find that when I'm doing it I get very internal and dark. The first time I sang 'Bethlehem' at New York's Café Sin-é in October of ninety-two, I broke into tears at the gig, which is not good, not professional, but I just hadn't performed it live before."

The tale of a New England nativity too dreary and disheartening to draw the barest notice, "Bethlehem" is a provocative high point of Cole's *Harbinger* (Imago/BMG, due July 19), an album whose small-town apologues of spiritual emptiness and personal doubt resound as both autobiography and analysis of a foundering society.

Such risky, self-exposing music tends to a draw a strong, unpremeditated response. In the audi-

Paula Cole

ence on that October evening, watching Cole come undone, was Imago Records president Terry Ellis, who approached her after her set and asked her to sign with his label. "He told me he didn't want to change anything about me or my songs," says Cole, chuckling bashfully. "He said I should continue to do whatever feels right."

As far as her debut album is concerned, Cole has succeeded on the basis of her instincts, creating a collection of songs that examine the crucible of self-esteem in a culture that no longer serves as an apparatus for great expectations. The twenty-six-year-old composer also shares her experiences as the offspring of sixties children, growing up amid the sometimes selfish/self-righteous residue of its improvident idealism. Raising a family was often the last ambition on an endless wish list for late-sixties bohemians intent on doing their own thing. Yet the purest test of one's heart remains the quality of one's parenthood. The affection Cole shows for her background does not blind her to its flaws.

"I called the record *Harbinger*," she explains, "because the word means a symbol of something to come. The first flower can be a harbinger of spring, and a bird falling dead can be a harbinger of plague. It's a wonderful word, suggesting a blossoming and a speaking out—but also the outcome when you can't or don't."

Born April 5, 1968, the second daughter of longtime Salem State College biology professor Jim Cole and the former Stephanie Cannon, Paula and sister Irene matured in a financially and emotionally strained household in Rockport, Massachusetts, a picturesque but desultory summer resort village whose townies suffer from dead-end cynicism and claustrophobia: "Quarry miners, fishermen/In my town of Bethlehem/Picket fences, church at 10/No star above my Bethlehem . . . Everybody's talking about Becky's bust/The boys on the basketball team just fuck the same 10 girls."

Cole's upbringing in this Yankee outpost was the end result of a sudden romance between her dad, who left a full scholarship at Boston University to hitchhike around the country, and her mom, who was studying at the California Institute of Arts and Crafts in Oakland when Jim Cole wandered back into her life. Songs of Paula's like "Happy Home" and "Watch the Woman's Hands" examine the midcourse adjustments necessitated by Stephanie Cole's sudden pregnancy and marriage, the nineteen-year-old boho giving up her dreams of a career in art while her new husband struggled to complete his schooling.

Cole's folks had known each other during their formative years in the mill town of Manchester, Connecticut, where Jim was descended from Irish, Polish, and Italian immigrants and Stephanie's heritage included *Mayflower*-borne settlers as well as Massasoit, famed chief of the Wampanoag Indians. If Massasoit's people hadn't befriended the starving Pilgrims, teaching them to plant corn and beans, they would have perished. And if the white colonists hadn't brought their strange diseases and warring prejudices to the New World, their Native-American hosts wouldn't be all but eradicated from the Massachusetts that bears their tribal name.

On "Our Revenge," "Chiaroscuro," and other tracks from *Harbinger*, Cole delves into these historic ironies as well as her own, since without these mercies and transgressions we also would not have the unsettled hybrid that is Paula Cole, a dark-eyed beauty whose features seem an angular aggregate of her distant Polish and Wampanoag ancestries.

Ever the reluctant outsider, the adolescent Cole accumulated her share of Rockport scorn and disappointment while aiming for the sort of regard that only amplified her isolation. "My music is full of memories of my family needing money, of no heat in our house, of things that started out sad but ended up funny," she says. "Out of sheer, pointless determination I was class president at Rockport High, but nobody cared, and I became junior prom queen but still couldn't get a date!" she adds, her laughter rising. "And when I also didn't get a date for the senior prom— where I was supposed to hand my crown over to the next queen—I didn't go, tossing the crown in some closet."

Cole went on to attend the Berklee College of Music in Boston, where she studied jazz improvisation, sang at Cambridge jazz clubs like Ryles, waitressed at the MIT Faculty Club, and rejected a label deal from GRP Records as her tastes shifted to the rock of Kate Bush and Peter Gabriel. Paula discovered her stunningly visceral vocal style, with its smoky treble and trumpetlike head tones, while in Berklee's gospel choir. After two postgraduate years in San Francisco working in the Tassajara bakery and writing the material for *Harbinger*, Cole moved to New York. There, through guitarist David Rhodes, she auditioned for—and got—the role as Peter Gabriel's duet partner on his *US* tour when Sinéad O'Connor dropped out.

Paula will spend the summer interspersing her own "coffeehouse" shows with Gabriel's WOMAD concerts and some opening spots for

Counting Crows. Such unforeseen turns of fortune seem apt for an artist whose music is so sensitive to surprise denouements and the dangerous business of taking anyone lightly.

Like the rest of the *Harbinger* album, first single "I Am So Ordinary" and likely followup "Saturn Girl" are vigorous, vehement coming-of-age narratives, their splintery passion suited to the present alternative scene but showing a plainspoken openness rarely heard in popular music since the late-sixties rise of the great singer-songwriters. Filled with an inky frisson of youthful betrayal, first brushes with deep sensuality, and faltering retrieval of personal faith, *Harbinger* burns with the honest fire that won the confidence of Terry Ellis and Peter Gabriel. If there is a future to be salvaged from our squandered past, perhaps new artists like Paula Cole will point us to it.

"For me," Cole reflects, "music is a vehicle to bring our pain to the surface, getting it back to that humble and tender spot where, with luck, it can lose its anger and become compassion again."

TRUTH, LIES, AND THE GETTING OF WISDOM

CAN A RECORD BE EXCELLENT IF, AT ITS ESSENCE, ITS MOTIVES do not excel? If music matters, then the answer is no.

From the start, this column was intended to celebrate the intrinsic properties of forthcoming albums that were truly surpassing in content and spirit. Given the many, many releases of any calendar year, the aim herein has always been to offer special recognition to artists whose latest projects exceed accepted limits and standards, bettering their own previous efforts as well as those of their contemporaries with work of uncommon merit.

The opportunity to provide this kind of endorsement, in a publication read with confidence each week in 107 countries, is both a great joy and a grave responsibility. No one is allowed to pitch an act or project for this space, and the most renowned performer is on an equal footing with the most obscure. The column is meant to be an expression of a professional assessment, enthusiastic in its advisory, unequivocal in its endorse-

Afro-Plane

ment. And when that endorsement must be withdrawn, it is with grievous regret.

Earlier this year a "Music to My Ears" installment was devoted to the debut album by RCA/Kaper act Afro-Plane ("Afro-Plane and the Power of Surprise," *Billboard*, March 5). At the time, I admired the rap group for its ability to transcend the adolescent gullibility of gangster rap with inventive music whose political and social commentary seemed to succeed at "courting no ritual, seeking no acolytes, respecting no demagogues, requiring no pimps."

But I was mistaken.

Sadly, as writer Jon Pareles stated in a recent *New York Times* article ("Can Good Guys Challenge Gangster Rap?" Sunday, June 12), "Afro-Plane . . . has no such tolerance for gay people." Pareles discerned a heatedly spoken passage within the dense wordplay of a track called "Trouble (Thought It Was Love)" that I had missed, one in which Afro-Plane rejects any human rights or civil rights parallels between racism and bigotry toward homosexuals, further advising gays and their allies that "sooner or later you'll have to do some repenting."

Going back after reading the *Times* piece and listening more closely to "Trouble," any personal perception of the song's essential sagacity and uplift was both clarified and spoiled. Whatever the Afro-Plane record's other commendable attributes, that buried dictum in "Trouble" was bigoted malice to my ears. And this column was not intended to support records that contain such hateful attitudes.

Moreover, it's increasingly hard to understand why our industry should accommodate, without sustained censure, any such music. To offer an artistic and social parallel, back in 1988 Guns N' Roses issued a collection of material called *GN'R Lies* (Geffen), which included a song called "One in a Million." Notwithstanding the musical strengths of the record, the song in question contained the following lyrical outburst: "Police and niggers, that's right/Get out of my way/ . . . Immigrants and faggots/They make no sense to me/They come to our country/And think they'll do as they please/ . . . Or spread some disease/They talk so many goddamned ways/It's all Greek to me."

Then, as now, one of the most difficult things to accept about the *GN'R* track was the skill that obviously went into crafting, and therefore excusing, the song at every step en route to its commercial realization. An adult had to sit down with some presence of mind and compose the stanzas, working out the rhyme scheme, deliberating over the choice of words. A fragment of melody had to be fleshed out to enhance the theme, and then a band had to be taught the basic composition. Studio time had to be booked, and the musicians had to conceive the full-bore arrangement, with assorted percussion and several guitars added as effective accompaniment. The track had to be engineered, with attentive technicians manning the board, such personnel likely conferring about the overall brightness of the acoustic guitar or the vocal levels on the lead singer's mike as he launched into his "Police and niggers . . . immigrants and faggots" soliloquy. The finished tune, which was carefully produced, had to be mixed at one location and mastered at another, its presence on the album sequenced in relation to the other selections. And then the final product had to be handed to marketing and promotional people to begin packaging, publicizing, and selling it. Thus, at each stage of the process, many thoughtful people were apparently willing and able to proceed with the enterprise.

And while "One in a Million" drew its share of denunciations at the time, the song is still on the *GN'R Lies* record, still available for purchase, still making money for the artists who recorded it, with domestic sales in excess of four million units. And it is still a piece of racist, gay-bashing garbage, a brainless screed affronting any humane person who believes in art's mandate to articulate the truth.

As a consequence of our industry's role in this culture's inability to shame Guns N' Roses into voluntarily withdrawing "One in a Million" and making constructive restitution for the social harm it inflicted, we all share some blame.

With these matters in mind, this column closes with an open letter sent on June 14 to Afro-Plane:

"As you know, I'm a big supporter of your music, particularly its powerful critiques of the politics of self-delusion. Nonetheless, the *New York Times* recently singled out a textual assertion in 'Trouble (Thought It Was Love)' that deserved very serious scrutiny as well as additional reflection on your part, namely the passage (which I missed on the album) in which you state: 'Faggots take us in sayin' I'm your friend, me and you black man, we got the same Zen . . . I don't dig that . . . you need to do some repenting.'

"People who are being oppressed hardly are in competition with one another, although oppressors tend to love the supposed pecking orders that destroy the powerless by pitting them against each other in turf battles.

"Bigotry is wrong not because of any particular sort of humanity being oppressed, but because *all* bigotry is wrong. Period.

"People can no more repent for being gay than they can for being heterosexual. One can repent for the bigotry one inflicts on another, but one cannot repent for being the way God made him or her.

"If God put us here for anything, I suspect God put us here to learn: to celebrate our differences, love our similarities, and conquer the fears that divide us.

"I remember a conversation I had with Bob Marley in Kingston in 1975 about the irony of the vast white audience he'd initially gained outside his core Caribbean constituency. He looked me straight in the eyes and said: 'To me, them have no difference. Wherever, we are friends. Jah give you the wisdom to understand it.' So true, but how often do we use that wisdom?"

JUAN LUIS GUERRA'S FRENETIC *FOGARATÉ*

IN THE REALM OF THE SURREAL, ONE SPEAKS OF A GOOD TIME by using the wry language of a grim act. Thus, an evening spent tempting delirium in Santo Domingo—mixing Presidente Beer with shots of Barcelo Gold rum, while joining the city's young *movida* in a ballroom booming with the 2/4 tempo of merengue—is commonly termed "ripping the parrot."

Imagine a fierce cloud of feathers amid a pounding sensual din, and you're getting close to the sensation of *perico ripiado.* But it helps to know that *perico* is slang for prostitute, as well as a near-extinct plumed bird indigenous to the Dominican Republic, and that *ripiado* also refers to this Caribbean country's rural poor. Lastly, *perico ripiado* is local musical lingo for the frenetic folk merengue that originated in the Dominican Republic's northern Cibao Valley, where Christopher Columbus landed at Hispaniola—the island the Spanish-speaking Dominican Republic shares with French-tongued Haiti.

If all these overlapping concepts seem linked in a cleverly earthy sensibility, than you've

Juan Luis Guerra

grasped the allure of Latino superstar Juan Luis Guerra and his group 440, the spectacular ensemble whose latest album, *Fogaraté* (Karen Records, due July 19), is one more racy piece of the puzzle.

"The word *fogaraté* is the name of an acidic plant in the Dominican Republic," laughs the lanky, bearded Guerra, "so, like everything else in my country and my music, it has a double meaning. If the leaf of this plant rubs against your skin, it's gonna hurt you a lot, and you'll jump up and run around. So when a woman or a man's got fogaraté, they're pretty hot and can't stand it!

"My biggest influence," he says, "is the surreal world I grew up seeing in Santo Domingo, during the time of the dictatorship of [Rafael] Trujillo and the political troubles after that. It was a time of the very rich next to the very poor, and a lot of extremes—the kind of world you read about in books by Gabriel García Márquez [like *The Autumn of the Patriarch*," based in part on the brutal last days before Trujillo's assassination in 1961]. And so I put local folk sayings and surreal metaphors by Márquez, or poets like Federico García Lorca, into the lyrics of my music."

Arguably the most literate and inventive artist in Latino music today, Guerra became a sensation in 1989 when he released *Ojalá Que Llueva Cafe* (Let's Hope It Rains Coffee), a boldly creative collection featuring such tracks as "La Galleria," a meld of gospel and merengue unlike anything in the annals of Hispanic pop. The next record, 1990's *Bachata Rosa*, combined the uniquely fast-paced Dominican merengue with rock, jazz, Cuban *son*, and bolero to reap sales of more than five million units and win a best tropical album Grammy for Guerra and his three-member vocal *grupo* 440 (the number refers to the frequency standard of perfect pitch: A above middle C at 440 cycles per second).

Guerra's 1992 *Areito* album (named for the social gatherings of the Dominican Republic's pre-Columbian Taínos tribe) further strengthened his reputation as the "Tropical Mixmaster," incorporating elements of merengue, Haitian compas, Zairean soukous, and *bachata* (an austere country idiom with simple guitar and *güira* gourd scraper) to make powerful statements about economic inequality in the Caribbean, as well as the legacy of colonial genocide and exploitation accented by the five hundredth anniversary of Columbus's arrival in the Americas.

Now, with *Fogaraté*, Guerra seems likely to complete his steady progression from native phenomenon to Latino sensation to singular international performer, able to sell out New York's Radio City Music Hall on recent successive nights. And the new album boasts his most novel mélange thus far, featuring a *bachata* treatment of a song by soukous star Papa Wemba, two tracks reuniting Guerra with noted Zairean guitarist Diblo Dibala (who played on *Areíto*), and the central presence of guest artist Francisco Ulloa, the virtuoso accordionist whose sound virtually defines the rustic, squeeze box–propelled passion of *perico ripiado.*

"We recorded the new album in New York," says Guerra, "and to have someone so incredible as Francisco agree to come all the way from the northern town of Santiago with his band just to play with us was amazing. He's a perfectionist, and his playing is so quick on the first single, 'La Cosquillita (The Little Tickle)'! The *perico ripiado* is so Dominican—it makes me happy to bring such a common sound to a bigger audience. It's like discovering a new music. Sometimes what's greatest about ourselves is what's closest: our roots."

Born June 7, 1957, the youngest of three sons by respected Dominican basketball player Gilberto Guerra and his attorney wife Olga, Juan Luis grew up in the Gascue, the old-town precinct of the capital city of Santo Domingo, located across from the famous Parque de la Independencia, the point of the country from which all highway distance markers are said to be calculated. By day, Juan Luis played basketball in the streets, "pretending to be Wilt Chamberlain," and in the evenings his brothers played Beatles LPs on the family Victrola while he picked out the melodies on his Taya Spanish acoustic guitar.

"The Gascue was a magic place to be a boy," Guerra says. "It was filled with people talking, and vendors, and the big park on the sea." He smiles. "As I said: just like in a book by [García] Márquez."

To quote, then, from a stream-of-consciousness passage in *The Autumn of the Patriarch:* ". . . The Babelic labyrinth of the commercial district, the pushcarts with cane juice, the strings of iguana eggs, the Turks and their sun-faded bargains, the fearsome tapestry of the woman who had been changed into a scorpion for having disobeyed her parents . . . and suddenly there it was, the waterfront . . . the dock and its spongy planks."

And beyond the waterfront was Boston's Berklee College of Music, where Guerra studied guitar in 1980–81. "But there were so many good guitar players, like Pat Metheny and John Scofield," he says with a shrug. "I learned a lot, and I had good teachers, and when I came home, I was ready to experiment with 440 [Adalgisa Pantaleón, Roger Zayas, and Marco Hernández], who are fine singers. At first we tried to be like a Latin Manhattan Transfer. But we kept growing, learning, mixing instead of imitating, and adding our Dominican roots. At twenty-seven I wrote my first good song, 'Si Tú Te Vas' [If You Leave], and it was a merengue. I had remembered a party back in Boston where I tried to imitate Wes Montgomery and Pat Metheny—until I impressed people by playing merengue!"

Fogaraté, which even has a lovely English-language *bachata* bolero called "July 19th," is Juan Luis Guerra y 440's most impressive work yet.

"I'm touched by merengue because it's the music I have in my heart," he confides, "and I'm touched by surrealism because it's a belief in a perfect, impossible world."

IVAN NEVILLE GIVES
THANKS FOR
VOODOO

HE PLAYS ROCK'N'ROLL THE WAY IT WAS MEANT TO BE:
lowdown and swampy, with a snarling edge and an unceremonious sense
of dread and delight, kindled by a voice as undeniable as a nagging conscience. The sound of Ivan Neville on his new *Thanks* album (Canyon
International, Japanese import) and the arresting earlier *If My Ancestors
Could See Me Now* (Polydor, 1988) shows nothing less than the sure maturation of a roaring young lion.

"I'm a black man who's into rock-
'n'roll that's ratty and funky and hopefully inspiring, too, the way Sly and the
Family Stone, the *Hard Day's Night* Beatles, and Larry Williams's *Bad Boy* were
for me as a kid," says the outspoken
Neville, son of renowned singer Aaron
Neville. "It pisses me off sometimes that
there's prejudice and typecasting, even
among black people, about the kind of
music we're supposed to be playing and
who we're supposed to do it with. I mean,
Sly had a white drummer back then, and
I thought that was *bad!* That's why I feel
there's a bond that people like Corey
Glover of Living Colour and Lenny
Kravitz and I have in terms of the rock-
'n'roll thing. Our message is that we're

Ivan Neville

all born and we're all gonna die, and the rest is just icing, so we've gotta get past what doesn't matter and express the deeper truth."

What that means in terms of Neville himself is a dedication to the underlying "creative ambition" in everything he plays, the ability to "take your own part in any song or group and reap the rewards of helping make it into something bigger for everybody else."

As the son of one of the most acclaimed singers ever to emerge from New Orleans, Ivan Neville was taught from the start to be a team player. He served a seven-year apprenticeship alongside his dad in the Neville Brothers band, leaving in 1981 to become a member of (the post–Chaka Khan) Rufus before embarking on the years of session work that seasoned his first solo album, *If My Ancestors Could See Me Now.* One of the most distinctive and foreshadowing rock records of the last decade, *Ancestors* was produced by Danny Kortchmar and featured the personnel (drummer Steve Jordan, guitarist Waddy Wachtel) who joined Ivan that same year as the X-Pensive Winos on Keith Richards's *Talk Is Cheap* album.

Ancestors had a top-thirty hit in "Not Just Another Girl," and also charted via Neville's duet with Bonnie Raitt on the entrancing "Falling Out of Love," but it was the dramatic, percussive ferocity of tracks like "Primitive Man" and "Money Talks" that left a lasting impression on Ivan's peers and the man himself.

"I was in debt when I wrote 'Money Talks,' " he says with a laugh, "and I'm proud I could bring something good out of that time. I love the angry lyrics ['Wake up all you dead presidents/If you were here you'd know what you represent']. But, ironically, the *Ancestors* album was written about things I witnessed yet hadn't really lived myself. A year or two after the record was done, I stopped being an observer and wound up in the middle of those songs about heartbreak and pain. I didn't realize how open and sensitive I'd been to what was coming; I was surprised I was capable of feeling it. It's crazy, but I listened back to my own record and said, 'Damn, I should heed my words!' "

At that point, Neville had been touring with Bonnie Raitt after helping her cut her *Nine Lives* album (on which she recorded a Neville song, "All Day, All Night"), which coincided with Raitt's being dropped from Warner Bros. and undergoing the personal and artistic transformation that preceded her stunning current success.

"Bonnie was always like a surrogate mother to me," he says, "and I also saw my own father turn around in that same 1989 to 90 period and get his own shit together, literally changing his life and career. They were amazing lessons for me." As a result, Neville shelved a 1991 album he'd been working on and decided to start fresh with *Thanks.*

"The title of the new record describes how happy I felt that the last project didn't come out," he confides. "It was computerized, slick, and machinelike. *Thanks* has more of the spirit of *Ancestors,* the humanity and the humility."

Born August 19, 1959, in New Orleans, the first of three sons and a daughter by his famous father and the former Joel Roux, Ivan was christened Aaron Jr., but his name was changed when he was six months old. "My family realized," says Neville, "that it was a blessing and curse to be named after my father, with all the honor and pressure it would bring." Growing up on Valence Street in the Crescent City's Thirteenth Ward, Ivan played football in the Pontchartrain Park league and attended Aaron's alma mater, Walter L. Cohen Senior High. He considered pro ball as a vocation "'til I heard James Booker on piano—I said, 'Shit, that's for me!' "

He bought his first Fender Rhodes keyboards with money earned washing dishes and working as an orderly in the Stanton Manor old folks' home on St. Charles Avenue. After winning a citywide talent contest in 1976, he formed his initial group, Ivan Neville and Renegade, and gigged frequently at the legendary 501 Club, known since as Tipitina's.

Now married with a three-year-old daughter, Neville continues as a member of the X-Pensive Winos, and also appears as keyboard player and/or backing vocalist on eight of the fifteen tracks on the Rolling Stones' new *Voodoo Lounge* album. "Keith phoned me up as the Stones were recording in L.A. and said, 'Man, we want to get you in on this.' Standing in the studio singing with Mick, Keith, and Bernard Fowler was the most fun I've ever had, and I just love 'Brand New Car' and 'Baby Break It Down.' "

But Neville rightly believes his own best efforts consolidate the unselfish vigor of his session contributions with the tingling vulnerability of his solo work. Anyone obtaining a copy of *If My Ancestors Could See Me Now* would be astounded that a record so spellbinding in its pre-Seal storytelling could possibly have been overlooked (although it sold a respectable 175,000 units).

Thanks is just as revelatory—and cries out for release in this country —with tracks like "Same Old World," "Don't Cry Now" (with Bonnie Raitt), "Meet Up with You," and "Hell to Tell" framing the swinging lilt of Neville's rhythmic sense as well as the almost frightening intensity of his razory tenor. Friends Richards, Glover, and Branford Marsalis, and his dad, Aaron, also lend support to the latest stunning installment in an emerging lion's "lesson in how to live my music."

"These new songs," says Ivan Neville, "are about learning the difference between happiness and pleasure, and understanding the hope people get from seeing somebody play for more than just himself. Music isn't about me, it's about *us*."

LIVING UNDER THE SPELL OF JANN ARDEN

JANN ARDEN WAS A TWENTY-YEAR-OLD STREET MUSICIAN living in Vancouver, British Columbia, when she experienced her first stunning hit.

"It was around seven P.M. on a warm October evening in 1983, and I had been singing for about half an hour in the old Gastown shopping district when I was suddenly drilled—*boom*—right between the eyes," she says. "I woke up a few moments later, lying on the cobblestones, clutching my guitar, and the four dollars in my open guitar case had been cleaned out. I had two black eyes, and the force of the blow also broke the blood vessels in my eyeballs, so they were all red. I felt sick from disorientation, and it happened so quickly—I remember catching a quick, sidelong glimpse of a man in a red-checked lumberjack coat before I blacked out—that it's probable that passersby didn't see the guy hit me in the face.

"No one helped me, and since I had no money left, I had to sneak onto the ferry back to North Vancouver. I felt so humiliated that I

Jann Arden

quit being a street musician and took a job as a deck hand on a salmon boat, gutting six hundred to seven hundred fish a day. It all was very painful—but at least I got a fishing license out of it!"

During the dozen years Arden was absorbing her hard knocks in the music business, she worked as a ball cleaner at a golf course and as a singing waitress at Orlando's Bistro in Calgary, Alberta (where the neck of her beleaguered Washburn guitar was broken during a brawl between patrons). She also cut what she calls a "hilarious" 1980 indie single, "Never Love a Sailor," as Jann Richards (Arden is her middle name).

If Arden's luck changed at the start of 1994, as her debut album, *Time for Mercy,* achieved Canadian gold sales status and helped her earn two Juno Awards (the Canadian equivalent of a Grammy), the good news is that the fundamentals of her atypical musical talespinning have not. Each song on the forthcoming *Living Under June* (A&M Canada, due August 10) carries the deft impact of a Jann Arden reminiscence, its droll but strangely affecting facets always culminating in unexpected punchlines.

"The June in the record's title," explains the singer-songwriter, "is a sixty-year-old divorced English landlady in a three-story brick apartment building on Twenty-third Avenue in Calgary. For years, I lived below June in the basement apartment of that place"—pictured on the album cover—"and I could hear every conversation and occurrence on any floor through the air vents. So I was an involuntary voyeur until I learned to tune out everything I overheard. The title song is accurate but also humorously exaggerated in its reactions ['Can't believe the things I hear/Falling from the atmosphere/Sexual atrocities are happening right over me/And I can't see!'] because I'm trying to capture ordinary people's responses to extraordinary things."

It's this sympathetic but astute gift for observation, etched with a thrillingly subtle and full-throated vocal vigor, that makes *Living Under June* such an extraordinary listening adventure. Good songwriting triggers an admiration for the potency of a narrative perspective. But great songwriting activates an appetite for notions unimagined, the artist's expressive clarity moving us to consider aspects of our own secret selves that no music could describe.

Arden's much-admired first album showed the emergent force of a young writer learning, in her phrase, "to let words fall from the heart." But the growth shown on darkly exquisite *Living Under June* tracks such as "Could I Be Your Girl," "Demolition Love," "Looking for It (Finding

Heaven]," and "Gasoline" is so startling it could be the output of a different person.

"In a way, I guess I am," Arden says with a laugh. "For instance, just a month ago, I finally moved above ground after five years [i.e., out of June's basement]. And though this album has some of the sweetness and introspection of the last record, it's much more plainspoken."

As with *Time for Mercy, June* was produced with Ed Cherney (Eric Clapton, Bonnie Raitt) in Jackson Browne's Groove Masters studio in Santa Monica, California, with keyboardist Jeffrey "C. J." Vanston once again assisting on arrangements. "We tracked the whole album in six days, doing most of it live," says Arden. And by the time the team cut the album-summarizing "Good Mother," its gliding sweep came as close to a pure, undiluted path of thought as the recording craft allows.

" 'Good Mother' is the most autobiographical piece," Arden says, "and it's such a simple sentiment I didn't believe I could call it a song. When I sing 'I've got money in my pockets,' I had exactly $20. And I *do* have 'a good mother.' I've learned I don't need much to make me feel well."

Jann Arden Richards was born March 27, 1962, in Calgary, the daughter of construction contractor Derrel Richards and the former Joan Bentley, a retired dental assistant. "My father is a nonpracticing Welsh Mormon whose family came from Utah to Canada in a covered wagon," she says. "My mother is one of two children of English-Swedish-Prussian descent, and her mom grew up in a house with a dirt floor in a logging camp on the Peace River in Northern Alberta. My grandfather was a hard-drinking, brutal man, but fortunately grandma remarried."

Arden and older brothers Duray and Patrick grew up in the foothills of the Rocky Mountains. Arden's first guitar was an eighty-dollar Yamaha acoustic hand-me-down from her mom (who had given up on lessons she received from the local preacher); Arden used it to compose material for her graduation ceremony at Springbank Community High School.

"My parents are very quiet, shy people who support me totally yet have never commented on my music," Arden says. "My mother has difficulty coming to my shows, because she gets so scared for me that her heart races and my dad has to take her outside to calm her. They talk so little about themselves that I only just learned my father once sang in a choir. And my mom recently disclosed that she and dad would lie in bed at night wondering what I'd do with my life; a statement as basic as that was enlightening new information."

And it hearkens back to a mideighties period in which Arden's habit of excessive drinking on the bar circuit led her to a critical crossroads. "I was twenty-six and dysfunctional and struggling hard," Arden reflects. "I've been sober ever since, though I still struggle with my fears of life and death."

And the value of every fended ambush and quiet fight is evident in the radiant power of *Living Under June*.

"All my parents ever asked of their children was honesty," says Arden, alluding to her rendition of Ann Loree's "Insensitive" on the new album. "In a world as desensitized as ours, genuine emotion is, to me, a victory. Never be afraid of what you feel. Be proud of it."

JONI MITCHELL'S MANY SHADES OF *INDIGO*

A WOMAN DRIVING THROUGH THE BRENTWOOD SECTION OF Los Angeles on the last day of the city's 1992 riots pulled up behind a long, white luxury car paused at a stop signal. The pale automobile's license plate read "JUST ICE." And the woman, who happened to be one of the world's finest songwriters, couldn't help wondering if justice really *was* merely the means to be cold.

"I still believe in the power of the word, that words inspire," says Joni Mitchell, and in considering the proposition that chance and a traffic sign had placed before her, she later turned to Plato's *Republic,* a philosophical discussion of moral ideals written and dramatized four centuries before Christ. "I also believe in the idea that the performing arts, including songs and plays, are capable of slowing people down and touching their souls in order to generate thoughtfulness. The premise of Plato's 'play' is the presentation of the argument that the strong do what they can, and the weak suffer what they must, debating if that's both true and fair."

In the act of exploring these and other related notions, Mitchell would create an inspiring, ten-song

Joni Mitchell

series of musical dialogues and playlets that comprise this autumn's *Turbulent Indigo* (Reprise, due October 25), one of the most commanding statements of a peerless, seventeen-album career that has itself questioned most accepted precepts in popular music. "The arts are an important part of cultural justice," says Mitchell, "and truth and beauty are the essence of their greatness, so artists have a big responsibility in every era to probe the rules by which we live, inquiring whether they serve us well."

By means of *Turbulent Indigo* material like "Magdalene Laundries" (named for the Irish work convents to which alleged disreputable women were given life sentences), "Not to Blame" (a pre–O. J. Simpson parable of battered spouses), and "The Sire of Sorrow (Job's Sad Song)," (based on the Old Testament tale showing that suffering need not be associated with sin), Mitchell asks why the current quality of mercy is so strained, and why daily evidence of fairness is so elusive. And if pain in its many forms is the teacher that turns arrogance into humility and selfishness into sharing, how does one avoid the bitterness that short-circuits such lessons?

Each of these questions is at least as old as the Book of Job, and at a time when many insist that success and self-fulfillment should be standard rewards, such issues boil down to modern society's single most resounding demand: justice. We want it from our friends and enemies, from shopkeepers and public officials and the Supreme Court. And yet, since biblical times, the original and ultimate definition of justice was not institutional but personal.

Justice as displayed in Plato's *Republic* is the restraint of one's own selfish aims when they conflict with the well-being of others. Thus, until the day that each citizen is willing to do good while expecting absolutely nothing in return, there shall be no justice.

In musical spirit and emotional hue, *Tubulent Indigo* most closely resembles Mitchell's landmark 1971 *Blue* album—a timely, stylistic irony, since the new record is her first in twenty-three years for Reprise, the label she left shortly after *Blue.* And the resplendent pop motets that rank with "All I Want" and "A Case of You" for sheer unshakability are Joni's elevating cover of James Brown's 1986 "How Do You Stop" and "Sex Kills," with its shattering chorus regarding callous desire: "Sex sells everything/And sex kills."

"For the second time in recent historic memory, we have a sexually transmitted plague," says Mitchell. "Before the discovery [in 1928] of penicillin, the earlier scourge was syphilis, and the cultural response during Queen Victoria's reign [1837–1901] was a prudish conservatism that made open pregnancy indiscreet and put long skirts on everything, including piano legs! Meantime, I'm told the London whorehouses were never so popular. Back then, the fearfulness created some public courtesies, but these days the family structure is rocking and nihilism is rampant among the young.

"But I don't like using scary or tragic chords in heavy material like 'Sex Kills.' Music provides the emotional skeleton for a lyrical plot, and songs need to be more direct than poetry because the hybrid of pretty sounds and serious images creates pathos. So I try to lighten up melodically to open the listener's heart."

A native of Alberta, Canada, Mitchell was born Roberta Joan Anderson November 7, 1943, her adult surname being the result of a brief midsixties marriage to fellow folksinger Chuck Mitchell. At age nine, Joni contracted polio in an epidemic that swept her country, "and it was predicted I might never walk again." Like Job, she resisted the temptation to curse the Almighty for her ill fortune, though she does recall screaming out Christmas carols in her hospital ward as a gesture of secular defiance. Regaining her health, she devoted herself to artistic modes of self-improvement, principally dancing, painting, and music. In 1967, she was signed by Reprise and recorded her first album with the guidance of longtime friend David Crosby, with whom she co-wrote the song "Yvette in English" on *Turbulent Indigo.*

"The title song of the new record comes from a conference of the Canadian Council of the Arts that I spoke at in the early nineties," she explains. "The name of the conference was 'Making van Goghs,' and they said they wanted to focus on indigenous peoples, ethnic groups, and women. I opened my talk by saying you cannot make van Goghs, and that artists can be encouraged or even groomed but not manufactured. Art is the result of experience, and van Gogh's despair and suicide are not what you'd want to duplicate." As Joni laments in the lyrics: "You wanna make van Goghs/Raise 'em up like sheep/ . . . You see him with his shotgun there/Bloodied in the wheat/Oh what do you know about/Living in turbulent indigo?"

In other words, the pursuit of art, like the presence of justice, is a personal responsibility. Mitchell's latest acoustic guitar–entwined tour de force was coproduced with her estranged second husband, bassist Larry Klein, and includes guest appearances by Seal and textural/timbral jazz sax colorist Wayne Shorter. But its triumph of mood-cum-message—a brave blend of romantic faith and fervid realism—is her most devoutly individual discourse in a decade.

"I've never been a feminist, because I believe in male-female relationships without apartheid," she summarizes. "And I've never been a nihilist, because I continue to feel the heart is the healer."

CLAPTON'S *CRADLE:* A TRIUMPH OF BLUES POWER

LIKE THE BLUES, THE HEART HAS ITS OWN HERITAGE.

Eric Clapton's *From the Cradle* (Reprise, due September 13) is the legendary performer's long-awaited homage to the music whose "instant physical feeling of excitement and fear was my original impulse to be a musician."

Indeed, since Eric Patrick Clapton first forged his recording reputation in the sixties with the Yardbirds and John Mayall's Blues Breakers, he vowed to one day create the pure blues testament his rapt affection for the form had always betokened. But if this sixteen-track live studio session of songs by blues greats like Leroy Carr, Eddie Boyd, Lowell Fulson, Willie Dixon, Freddy King, Elmore James, and Muddy Waters was simply a seasoned gesture of artistic reverence, it would not deserve its undeniable status as the British guitar giant's supereminent solo recording. What makes the darksome *From the Cradle* so bottomlessly beautiful is the fact that, in its desire to resume the studious engrossments of a comforting adolescent obsession, it also updates the endless searching of an injured and incomplete spirit.

Eric Clapton

"There's anger and love and fear on this record," confides Clapton, "because I was deep into something which was exposing me this way. It's to do with the relationship that I was involved in, with a very beautiful woman, which started and ended over the same time as the record was made. We'd broken up in January or February of this year, and I went downstairs one night and I wrote that rhyme from which the record is named ['All along this path I tread/My heart betrays my weary head/With nothing but my love to save/From the cradle to the grave'].

"I just keep falling into this cycle or trap of not being able to make a relationship work—this latest one being the first really important one I've had for many years—and it tied in with loving this music from the cradle to the grave, and my attempt to finally make a clear statement about it. I've been *raw* doing this, exploring myself inside, finding out who I am in a social and domestic way as much as a musical way."

Clapton sighs heavily and continues: "The front cover artwork of the album is a picture of the inside of my gate at my home in London, and it's like me living behind this gate all the time. And at the bottom of this gate is this little streak of light, which is where I'd see her feet when she walked up to ring the bell. My life is that way: as if I've been waiting behind this gate to get out and finally say what I want to say, be what I want to be, love what I want to love. And so it really runs through the whole project."

As for the order of the broad brace of rustic and urban laments on *From the Cradle*, Clapton says, "Each one of them spoke about a certain element of the blues that I wanted to convey, but after agonizing over it I had to call [coproducer] Russ [Titelman] in. I let him find a meaningful sequence from his own intuition, and it worked straight away for me."

The album commences with Carr's "Blues Before Sunrise," followed by Boyd and Dixon's "Third Degree," Fulson's "Reconsider Baby," and Waters's boastful 1954 single of lust and black magic, "Hoochie Coochie Man." By the time Clapton passes the midpoint of his blues transit with James's "It Hurts Me Too" and King's "Someday After a While," the listener has been immersed in one of the most diversely textured emotional excursions the form could evoke.

"I identify with all of these blues in different stages," Clapton says with a sad laugh. "They were all part of this thing I was going through in my personal life. 'Reconsider Baby' would be talking about the breakup, or 'Someday After a While' is saying you'll be sorry when you realize what a good man you lost. A lot of it is in terms of growing up, and some of it is quite childish in a way, but it's about expressing that instant emotion of anger or self-pity.

"All of these songs are the hardest I was able to pick out of the blues catalog, because they've all got a very intense character of their own; they're not jamming, but instead have distinct melodies and structures. Some of them, like 'Hoochie Coochie,' are ones I thought about in the past as being untouchable, but I thought it was important not to hide or duck or hedge the challenge."

In the act of trodding this pained path of self-examination and rediscovery, Clapton also paralleled the probative meditations of the musical heroes he holds dear. His choice of "How Long Blues," for instance, shows a sympathetic ear for the same ode to flight from one's dreary beginnings that city-bound dirt farmer Muddy Waters said was the first piece he learned as a boy. As with "Blues before Sunrise," it was penned by Nashville-born, Indianapolis-bred pianist-singer Carr, whose alcohol- and despair-steeped Vocalion sides of 1928–35 were a fierce influence on Robert Johnson. The traditional "Motherless Child" was another compassionate and self-exposing selection by Clapton, who was born out of wedlock on March 30, 1945, and was largely reared, like the orphaned Waters, by a kindly grandmother.

As with its *Unplugged* predecessor, *From the Cradle* is sufficiently fresh in its explorations that veteran fans might not recognize the full-throttle vocal thrust on "Blues after Sunrise" and "It Hurts Me Too" as Clapton's. Similarly, Eric's guitar attack is so loyal to the ethos of each ensemble piece that he has finally found the freedom to solo and/or weave a support fabric on material like "Blues Leave Me Alone," the dobro-directed "Driftin'," and initial album rock focus track "I'm Tore Down," yielding a sound so much in sync with the finest contemporary roots roll that many listeners may never peg *From the Cradle* as a blues treatise.

Those fortunate enough to have heard the searing May 2 concert debut of the album at the now-famous "Eric Clapton Live At Lincoln Center" benefit for the T. J. Martell Foundation know that Clapton's experience inside the blues crucible is revealed not as a dead-end condition, but rather as a triumphant quest.

"I've finally come back to where I was supposed to be with John Mayall," Clapton says. "The fountainhead of my spirit was strongest before I got disillusioned by the business, by the trappings, the personalities, the showbiz, the women, the drugs, and the bullshit. I'm back to the innocence I had in the first place; sometimes I was singing so hard I didn't even recognize myself! This was about feel and the message, rather than selling myself."

Yet it's also the most personal record he has ever released.

"Because it's the thing I've loved from day one, the most exciting and satisfying thing I've known. That's what *From the Cradle* means."

J.B.'S, BYRD, AND
ALL THAT ACID JAZZ

TO RIFF ON AN OLD ZEN PROVERB, WHEN THE STUDENTS ARE ready, the masters will appear. Such seems to be the case for the England-Germany axis of acid jazz, the get-down aggregate of traditional jazz, sixties-seventies funk and the cutting nineties edge of the house/hip-hop dance pendulum. Hot acts like US3, the Young Disciples, the Sandals, the Brand New Heavies, Galliano, and Carleen Anderson have helped intensify fans' appetites for the exploding scene's parent sounds, and you can't hardly get closer ancestry wise than the J. B. Horns featuring Fred Wesley, Pee Wee Ellis, and Maceo Parker, or the full-bore bluster of Bobby Byrd and band.

As a result, no self-respecting acid jazz DJ in London, Hamburg, or Tokyo dares face a packed dance floor these days without a turntable-ready copy of Byrd's "I Know You Got Soul" (King Records, 1971) or Fred Wesley and the J.B.s' "Doing It to Death" (People Records, 1973).

"It all goes back to when the 'rare groove' thing was first happening in London around eighty-eight to eighty-nine," says Crispin Taylor, Galliano's drummer extraordinaire and a favored fusilier on the acid jazz session scene. "People in the

Bobby Byrd

clubs were crazy for every choice of obscure American funk and Blue Note seven-inch single from the seventies, especially B sides. That's why it was called 'rare groove.' The punctuation and the soul of those records was mysterious and mesmerizing, and the breaks in hip-hop were getting people back into that early funk fusion by Byrd and the J.B.s.

"Unfortunately," adds Crispin, "the musicians themselves were left out of the club scene in the eighties, because live music was never important in dance the way it was in rock. But now, the live band feel that was pioneered by James Brown's top players is back in a big way."

And luckily, the battle-tested lieutenants of Brown's original soul garrison are alive and swell on Byrd's *On the Move* and the J. B. Horns' *I Like It Like That* (Instinct Records), two inspired new installments of the Manhattan-based label's ongoing "This Is Acid Jazz" series. To be blunt: There can't be a new-bohemian club anywhere that wouldn't be content to alternate the two albums for an entire evening, since nothing so beautifully biting as Byrd's "Never Get Enough" or the title track of the J.B.s' record (which features Taylor) could possibly put a crimp in any dancer's cool.

Instinct Records, founded in 1988 by journalist Jared Hoffman, licensed these latest acid jazz jewels from Germany's kindred Soulciety label, which sponsored the London-Hamburg-Nashville studio dates that resulted in the exhilarating releases. For Galliano's Taylor (whose group recently wowed a crowd at New York's Supper Club with a set from their new Talkin' Loud/Mercury record, *The Plot Thickens*), the chance to play with Fred, Maceo, and Pee Wee "was an unbelievable honor."

"I grew up in North London listening to their old James Brown tunes with those R&B and jazz horns against that loud, acoustic snare drum," explains Taylor. "So when the Young Disciples helped get Byrd and the J.B.s to come over to England to play in the late eighties, it was amazing. The chords of their new music still do summon up a mood that's deeper emotionally than the usual pop."

Bobby Byrd concurs as he speaks from his own experience on the British-German acid jazz circuit. "I hadn't heard the term 'acid jazz' until a few years back, when my band and I were playing a show in Kassel, Germany," Byrd recalls with a raspy laugh. "This young man came up after the show, asking me about my days singing with James [Brown] in the Famous Flames. And he said, 'Your stuff has got pop, jazz, rhythm and blues, and funk in it, just like this record'—and he showed me an EP that said 'acid jazz' on the cover. I said, 'Well, if those are the ingredients, that must be us too!' "

The welcoming aspects of the multigenerational acid jazz world were further crystallized for Byrd during a 1989 gig with the J. B. All-Stars at London's Town and Country venue, during which his wife and vocalist, Vicki Anderson, coaxed their daughter Carleen onstage at the start of Vicki's featured singing spot.

"Basically, I turned my solo slot over to her," says Vicki, "'cause I wanted people to hear what her daddy and I had been hearing at home. Afterward, Fred Wesley came over to me and said, 'Only a mama would do what you just did!' but it paid off, 'cause my baby just slaughtered them, killed them." Indeed, such rites of passage paved the way for Carleen's 1991 performance on the Young Disciples' smash international single "Apparently Nothing."

While awaiting the stateside release of her acclaimed *True Spirit* U.K. solo album (due October 18 on Virgin), Carleen Anderson contributed guest backing vocals beside her mom and sister Keisha for "On The Move," a rollicking family affair that also boasts a rhythm section composed of Byrd's four sons and a horn phalanx that includes three uncles.

As with the J.B.s' "I Like It Like That" (one of the finest acid jazz sides since US3's *Cantaloop*), which finds vocalist Jaye Ellen Ruth, formerly of the Brand New Heavies, lending lovely support, Byrd's album also shows a blend of the schooled expertise and youthful exuberance that are the crux of the acid jazz experience. There will always be a place in the funk canon for pulse-halting eruptions like Byrd's "Try It Again," a sweat-drenched close-order drill no dancehall should be without. Similarly, no matter how often one hears the impeccably persistent honk of Maceo and Pee Wee's saxes or the elastic purr of Fred's trombone on "Evening in New York" and "Bop U" from the *I Like It Like That* album, they remain forever fresh.

"You really gotta have hope for the international future of this kind of music," says Byrd, "when you think that I got signed to record for Soulciety by two *German* guys while I was on tour in *Paris*. Then the next thing I know I'm doing a *London* show and I look down and see every kid in the audience knows the words to the tunes!

"And now," adds Byrd, "the same week *On the Move* comes out in America, my phone starts ringing off the hook! The song on the album that says it all for me is 'Try It Again,' which I wrote way back in seventy-three in Houston, Texas. I was very frustrated at the time and I got advice from a preacher that when things you believe in don't always go your way, try 'em again. If what you're shooting for really is a part of who you are, you don't have a choice but to keep yourself pointed towards it."

Or, to quote another bit of Zen wisdom, "Fundamentally, the marksman aims at himself."

FLACO JIMÉNEZ'S
TEX-MEX TRIUMPH

THE TALE OF SAN ANTONIO, TEXAS, IS A DRAMA OF SHIFTING power, with nine different flags having flown over the so-called Alamo City since Spain seized the sunny river town from the Coahuilecan Indians in the 1690s. Its musical legacy is just as contentious, with German and Czech polkas and waltzes vying for primacy over topical Mexican *corrido* story-songs in a territory where Mexico's struggles (1810–1821) for independence from Spain soon overlapped with European settlers' Texas statehood–spawning revolt against the dictatorship of Mexico's General Santa Anna.

Although Davy Crockett, Jim Bowie, and 186-odd others perished defending the Alamo mission in 1836, the crossbred traditions fused in the aftermath of the bloody Tex-Mex siege still resound in local cantinas—and the current names behind them are no less legendary.

"My dad used to say that blood speaks for itself," says accordionist Leonardo "Flaco" Jiménez, whose heart-pounding new *Flaco Jiménez* (Arista Texas, due October 25) is a pancultural transfusion of the first rockin' rank. While the San Antonio–bred musician is describ-

Flaco Jiménez

ing skills derived from his famed pedigree, he's also acknowledging the complex ancestry of the high-spirited *conjunto* sound that is his lineal endowment. "My grandfather Patricio used to go to the dances that the Germans had who settled around the San Antonio area. He went just to check it out, but he loved it and picked up the diatonic accordion—he always used the Hohner-brand instrument, made in Germany—and my dad learn to play from *him*."

Jiménez's father, Santiago, was the original "El Flaco" (the skinny one). He was also a pioneer—along with fellow accordionists Pedro Ayala and Narciso Martinez, and the band Los Alegres de Teran—in the late-1930s evolution of *conjunto* (ensemble) music from a polite string-laced parquetry of European dance idioms and northern Mexican *norteño* folk styles into a feisty honky-tonk party form.

Recording numerous 78s for the Decca, Globe, Imperial, Mercury, and RCA labels, Santiago scored regional hits with songs like "Viva Seguin" (in praise of that Texas hamlet) that wedded the rhythmic articulation of an alto sax, a small-combo drum kit, and a *bajo sexto* (massive, bass-toned twelve-string guitar) with the newly amplified staccato incursions of the diatonic squeeze box. This was a sound capable of filling a *plataformas* (open-air ballroom) or sizable saloon, and Santiago's group became the house attraction from the midforties to the midfifties at the El Gaucho Garden on the corner of Navidad and El Paso Streets, packing the place with frisky polka outbursts that earned a Latin America–wide reputation.

"Before my dad, this kind of music was mostly for dancing, and it was a lot of instrumentals," says Jiménez. "But when he started recording, he started adding lyrics to the songs." And in 1953, Santiago also began adding his young son to his El Gaucho sets, asking him to sit in on the *bajo sexto* for featured numbers.

"He let me play two or three polkas the first night, and then the guy on upright bass took an empty beer cup and walked through the crowd as they dropped in quarters, nickels, and dimes until they reached to the brim. Then he gave it to *me*. I said, 'Man oh man, I'm gonna keep on playing, 'cause I like this!' "

Roughly a year later, Jiménez cut his first single with his parent, a 78 for Corona Records called "Alma De Texas." In 1955, he switched from *bajo sexto* to accordion and gathered a group of his own, Los Caporales (later expanded and recast as Los Caminantes), cutting sides for Rio, Falcon, and other small local labels.

"My father expanded the sound of *conjunto*," says the slender Jiménez, who was bequeathed the "Flaco" nickname when his papa retired. "But I wanted to expand the limits of my instrument. The diatonic accordion is very difficult because unlike the keyboard accordion, it's a different note when you push in and pull out, like a harmonica. In 1955 I began jazzing it up, putting in the dynamics and critical notes of blues, country, and more progressive things."

The turning point, in 1957, was the Tipico Records single "Hasta La Vista"/"Pobre Bohemio," an authoritative instrumental backed by the fable of a poor troubadour. The energy in the music amazed listeners and even earned some local airplay. Over the next two decades, Jiménez's determined virtuosity led to sessions with Doug Sahm and the Sir Douglas Quintet, Willie Nelson, and Ry Cooder (on the matchless Reprise albums *Chicken Skin Music*, [1976] and *Showtime* [1977]), catapulting contemporary Tex-Mex music far beyond its core Chicano following.

"I always give credit to Ry," says Flaco, "because he really was the one who opened the doors for me to record for a major label and expose my solo stuff." But it was Flaco's rippling, high-treble artistry, a fluctuant Tex-Mex permutation of Astor Piazzolla, Charlie Christian, Chet Atkins, and Freddie King, that transformed his fortunes and those of younger performers he influenced. It also typified the outlook of the Grammy-winning Texas Tornados tour band he formed in 1990 with Sahm, Freddy Fender, and Augie Meyers. What's more, the no-borders Latin-country-rock meld of rising acts like the Mavericks would have been unlikely without the prior explorations of Jiménez, so it's perfect that the college-album alternative format–steered radio single from *Flaco Jiménez* is "Seguro Que Hell Yes," a horns- and guitar-fired duet with Mavericks lead singer Raul Malo.

"The word *seguro* means 'sure, why not,' with a lot of gusto," says Jiménez, chuckling. "So the song is the 'live it up' combination of country and *conjunto* that I've dreamed of since I was a boy."

Born March 11, 1939, to the senior Jiménez and the former Luisa Mena, Leonardo was one of seven children growing up on unpaved Pastores Street near Brackenridge Park in the limestone-rich terrain known locally as the "Rock Quarry." "It was just a railroad street, but lined with a lot of pecan trees," he recalls wistfully. "As kids, we made homemade kites with newspapers and sticks, gluing them together with flour paste. Then we would go to a nearby polo field to watch the matches. In the evening, my mother would cook vegetable stew with beef, and lemon pies—the best in the world."

One hopes the sweet genius of Jiménez's San Antonio–like truce between the trials of the past and the present will someday gain him a place in the Rock and Roll Hall of Fame. For now, the tender invention of *Flaco Jiménez* tracks like "Jealous Heart" (with Radney Foster) and "Carolina" (with Oscar Tellez) are distinction enough. "The sound is modern," Flaco says, "but with the atmosphere of the old-time barrio."

HENLEY: FAREWELL TO A GOOD DAY IN *HELL*

HELL FREEZES OVER (GEFFEN), THE EAGLES' FIRST ALBUM OF new recordings in fourteen years, entered stores this week with a flourish amply justified by its fifteen thoughtfully burnished and often bittersweet tracks. But for Don Henley, who has just moved back to his native Texas, this is the end of the iterance.

"I feel pretty good about the record," says Henley, who recently relocated from Los Angeles to Dallas with his fiancée and plans to marry next May. "But I doubt, in all candor, that there'll be another one. I think [first single] 'Get Over It' is good, and I really like 'Learn to Be Still.' I also like the way we broke down the live things [from the April 1994 MTV concert sessions] on arrangements like 'Hotel California,' 'cause I don't think people ever realized that song is a reggae song, with Spanish influences, about the state of America. Talk about multicultural—it really was.

"But I think that after this tour [set to resume in January after an abrupt hiatus occasioned by Eagle Glenn Frey's emergency stomach surgery], that'll be it. At times, it's been very satisfying," Henley notes with a heavy sigh. "And there's been pain involved, as there always is in any endeavor of this magnitude. Some of the things that broke us apart years ago have not gone away, evidently. I thought maybe they had.

Eagles

But somebody said to me the other night, 'You know, all that stuff is still there; just 'cause fourteen years went by doesn't mean it's gone.' "

Henley chooses his words with care, sounding older and wiser than the only child who exited the piney woods of East Texas in 1970 in search of musical self-definition in the wilds of Los Angeles. Leaving home in his late adolescence with a combo called Shiloh, and achieving success two years later with a new group that first coalesced over beers at the Troubadour as Linda Ronstadt's backing band, the literate Henley helped the Eagles create a crisp rock compound of regional roots music that perfectly embodied the mood of displacement in the twilight of the American Century.

Pulling away from an enervating past, hurrying toward a receding horizon, the Eagles' commanding music was the often-aggrieved oratorio of a generation gulled by instant gratification and thus immune to greater contentment. The crackling tension and acute yearning in the band's songs was a direct consequence of the personalities intent on creating them. As with the original versions, the emotional coloration of new live limnings of "Take It Easy," "Tequila Sunrise," "Life in the Fast Lane," "In the City" (with its droll coda of the Beatles' "Day Tripper"), and the *cante flamenco*–overtured "Hotel California" each displays in anxious strokes the essence of a cruel dilemma. And the new songs on "Hell Freezes Over," including "Love Will Keep Us Alive," "The Girl From Yesterday," and the seemingly auspicious "Learn to Be Still," all update/delineate the Eagles' problematic outlook with stunning grace. Yet no description, however unerring, can ever be as satisfying as a solution.

"I think that's the history of a lot of bands," says Henley, whose last solo album was *The End of the Innocence* (1989). "Everything is a matter of timing, and that was our time in the seventies. But I had a really rough time when the Eagles got successful; I got really confused for a while. I always go back to that song by Paul Simon called 'Fakin' It.' Everybody in the rock'n'roll business or the movies has that fear of being found out. Deep down inside, they think or know they're not really as good as everybody thinks they are, because there's no logic to the starmaking machinery in this country; even when you get a body of work, it's not as respected as it might have been once.

"Songs like 'Get Over It' and 'Learn to Be Still' are opposite sides of the same coin," he says. "One is talking about the whiners who have an overblown sense of entitlement—and, of course, we realize there are people who are genuinely victimized in the world—while 'Learn to Be Still' is about those who aren't introspective enough. Sometimes, in order to see yourself as a part of something, you need to go into the wilderness alone.

"As for the Eagles"—whose reconstituted ranks also include Don Felder, Joe Walsh, and Timothy B. Schmit—"we've grown in different directions now, as people should, and so we'll finish our obligations and go our separate ways again. And frankly," he says, chuckling, "I'm looking forward to that. It's been very difficult, especially for me, to develop a sense of self-worth that is not attached to one's career, because we're taught we *are* what we do. But it must be done at some point, and it generally comes later in life. My dad was a role model for me, but he suffered from the same malady: all his life was tied up in his work."

Born July 22, 1947, in Gilmer, Texas, and reared forty miles to the northeast in the Cass County hamlet of Linden, Donald Hugh Henley was the solitary son of NAPA auto parts dealer Con Junell Henley and the former Hughlene McWhorter. "My dad—who hated his name; just plain C.J. was fine with him—sold parts out of his shop from World War II until 1968, six days a week, six in the morning until six at night. But you have to see it through his eyes: He grew up during the depression in a town called Como, where his father was a farmer, growing cotton, corn, and various other vegetables. My dad had to quit school in the eighth grade and go to work in the fields with his brother and sister to support the family. It was very hard for him to take a break, give it a rest.

"I started a song about him once," Henley says. "But I never finished it, and I'll give you two lines: 'He took the orders and he tried to fill 'em/Daddy had a little business and the customers killed him.' "

Henley says he is enjoying life in Dallas, the East Texas hub that is a hilly vector nearly equidistant from Shreveport, Louisiana, and the fabled border town of Texarkana. However, his curiosity about these southwestern crossroads is more than casual.

"Two great black artists were born in my hometown of Linden: [blues guitar great] T-Bone Walker and [seminal ragtime composer] Scott Joplin. Texarkana and a lot of places in the area are claiming Joplin, but old-timers tell me he was born just outside my town. And Shreveport is where Huddie Ledbetter [aka Leadbelly] was born.

"There's great history in Dallas in the Deep Ellum area, too; I'm not the first person in Texas who's interested in the blues, but I'm gonna record down here, with the songs tied musically, at least, to my explorations. Thematically, I don't know where they're going."

After his fast-lane redux, it sounds like Henley is, well, eager to get over it and learn to be still. "That's what I've always wished for fervently," he says, laughing. "Now I'll finally see what happens."

BETTIE SERVEERT'S BRAVE *LAMPREY*

THE BRAVE BUT EMOTIONALLY EMBATTLED MUSIC OF DUTCH band Bettie Serveert has the probative code of a traders' guild that has banded together for mutual protection. It searches everywhere for new alliances, but it reckons solely on its inner resources. "I can't trust the things I see/I can only trust in me/And if the whole world should drop dead/I'll build my own inside my head," sings Canada-born, Netherlands-reared lead singer–songwriter Carol van Dijk on "D. Feathers," one of the adamant yet imploring tracks on the group's glorious second album, *Lamprey* (Matador/Atlantic), due January 24.

Those beguiled by the moody, postpsychedelic wiles of Bettie Serveert's previous and much-praised *Palomine* album will be more than pleased with the folk-rock austerity and snarling sonic warnings of the group's new collection. The jangle 'n' hum of Peter Visser's guitar has grown in its exploratory melodicism, and the obstreperous rhythmic bite of Herman Bunskoeke's bass and drummer Berend Dubbe's unruly patterns has deepened. The most dramatic expansion, however, is in the portentous tilt of van Dijk's beautiful

Bettie Serveert

tonal verse, which discloses one of the most novel emergent voices in rock.

She describes "Ray Ray Rain," the new record's forlorn first single, as having been inspired by "the cadence of a car engine on a rainy night" during a recent Holland road trip in which she sat huddled before a streaked windshield. As recounted in the stanzas, the minds of driver and passenger were both "occupied by memories," and each lonesome passage resounds from within a personal sphere of tentative trust and improvised security.

As it happens, such intimate truces with uncertainty were also the historic building blocks of Dutch society, as well as its modern rock manifestations—including the backgrounds of Bettie Serveert's membership en route to their current association.

Born April 22, 1962, to photographer Henk van Dijk and wife Carolien, Carol van Dijk spent the first seven years of her life in Vancouver before her family returned to Holland and took up residence in the ancient country town of Deventer, in the province of Overijssel. Located on the Ijssel River, Deventer was an important trading center as early as the sixth century. By the thirteenth century it was a member of the pirates-foreign competition–fighting 150-city Hanseatic League of medieval Flemish-German mercantilism.

The rise of the merchant class in Flemish towns signaled a new freedom from the feudal power of local royalty, whose writs frequently did not extend to such economically independent new communities. Serfs could even gain their freedom in some towns if they lived in them for a year and a day. "The air of the town makes for free," an old Dutch folk saying goes, and so town dwellers (i.e., burghers) in progressive, postfeudal seats of commerce and learning, like Deventer, became living symbols of a previously undreamt-of independence.

"Deventer was very picturesque, full of lovely buildings hundreds of years old," says van Dijk, who lived in the handsome bourg of 65,000 inhabitants until she was twenty-one, spending her initial years after high school graduation managing one of the Leonidas chain's luxury Belgian chocolate shops. "For visitors, Deventer is a great place, but very boring for the young, because it's so conservative and interested in preserving itself for tourists."

Since Deventer was the former home of twelfth-century thinker Gerrit Groot and Renaissance theologian Erasmus, any music heard there besides the classics was expected to emanate from the forty-seven-bell carillon of the towering St. Lebuinus Church that remains its focal point. "My teachers didn't know about pop music, or ignored it," says van Dijk, who studied flute and guitar. "But my influences became the lyrics of Elvis Costello and also of Joni Mitchell—she makes music seem so clean and tidy, but she wrote great songs."

Van Dijk's initial songwriting attempt at sixteen, titled "White Tales," was dismissed by friends as—she laughs—"a Velvet Underground rip-off," although she had no knowledge of that group. The desire for exposure to rock's more impressionistic heritage led her to move to the larger city of Arnhem (population 128,000), where she fell in with a clique of rock-loving Arnhem Art Academy students and was hired as the live-sound mixer for de Artsen (the Doctors), a celebrated underground band that released two locally respected albums. Visser and Bunskoeke were in de Artsen, Dubbe was their roadie, and a musical side project in which all four friends participated became Bettie Serveert. (The group's name stems from the random phrase "service to Bettie," taken from an instructional book by Dutch tennis star and 1977 Wimbledon finalist Betty Stöve.)

Dissolved after only one 1986 gig, Bettie Serveert reunited in Amsterdam in 1990, where Dubbe was attending the Rietveld Academy. "A number of famous Dutch bands came from this academy," the drummer notes proudly—and those acts included the Talking Heads–inspired Blue Murder, singer-audiovisual artist Fay Lovski, and the fabled Nits, a somewhat Beatlesque band on Holland's CBS/Columbia affiliates that defined "Dutch Beat" in the early seventies and continues to excel at surrealist, contrapuntal pop, and even some quasi-symphonic works.

If Bettie Serveert possesses pop credentials similar to those of Holland's earlier avant garde, the group also seems stung by the same clashing intersections of art and commerce, theology and technology. Abroad in a sea of suspicious wayfarers, eager for contact but wary of connection, Bettie Serveert is moving nervously through a world without sure emotional or moral moorings.

The band collaborates on its music, but its lyrics are by van Dijk, and Dubbe professes strong admiration for her visceral but visionary viewpoint. "Her words have the feeling of someone who's looking from high up at something happening to someone else below, but not judging."

Simultaneously electrifying and languorous, Bettie Serveert's songs crest and subside on the nuances of van Dijk's asthmatic-belcanto cries, powered by a band attuned to every change in her inner and outer weather. *Lamprey* is named for an eel-like marine animal, usually considered a parasite or pest; the album itself is characterized by sudden squalls and exquisite still points of the sort that confuse any needy creature swimming against the current.

Van Dijk says the anthemic "Crutches" encapsulates Bettie Serveert's very Dutch perspective on how to craft trade-offs or tread water in a world adrift. "I guess the song is saying that everyone uses emotional crutches sometimes, but that's OK. Be strong when you can, but you shouldn't feel bad if you sometimes want to let yourself float or slide. Just trust your moods."

RELISH: OSBORNE'S LIVES OF SAINTS

EVERY ARTIST LONGS TO SEE TOO MUCH, INTENT ON UNVEILING all the essential traits of the era through which he or she struggles. Yet if they come close to divining the crucible of humanity's common experience, the vision offered is often too poignant in its inward and outward clarity to be perceived as artistry. Despite the sound and fury of the effort, such work's profound merit resides in the terrible simplicity of its truth telling.

"I'm very interested in gospel music and religious music from different cultures," says Kentucky singer-songwriter Joan Osborne, whose stunning major-label album debut, *Relish* (Mercury, due March 7), manifests an almost mystical grasp of a culture in spiritual disarray. "It's a shame religion has become such a huge institution with all its political and authoritarian power, as opposed to something that can release you—which obviously was its original intention. When I'm singing, it's a very moving experience for me because it has this very expressive nature that you feel in a

Joan Osborne

lot of religious music: the extreme tests you go through with anything that requires faith."

Subcelestial relationships can also demand a trust that borders on the sacred, and the earthy sensuality of Osborne's robust vocals intensifies her revelatory musical testament.

Matters of the spirit and the flesh coalesce on *Relish* as if culled from a forbidden codex; the peculiar motifs in songs such as "Right Hand Man," "Pensacola," "Dracula Moon," and "Lumina" show an alarming overlap between a bold seeker of the sanctified and a blind sybarite. The bedevilment reaches a breaking point on the remarkable "St. Teresa," a mandolin-impelled slice of alterna-pop in which damnation vies with innate venerability on a city street corner.

"I live on First Avenue in the East Village," Osborne says, "and when you look out the window there's a bunch of women—not much more than girls—who are selling drugs all night while they stand with their little kids next to them in strollers. I wanted to explore the 'little crime' and the complete innocence that were together in that scene. When I was a kid, we went to Catholic Church, and I was into the whole ritual and the beauty and mystery of the stained-glass windows, so the religious imagery of St. Teresa came from that kind of background.

"Later, after I wrote the song, I looked up the historical woman, who was a nun from Spain in the 1500s; she started having these visions and seizures where she saw these incredible things that frightened her. The priests of the Spanish Inquisition asked her to write down her experiences in great detail, and they're incredible manuscripts. I had no idea of this at the time, but certain things in the lyrics correspond to that. It's interesting that you can write a song thinking of one particular thing, and suddenly it branches out to other connotations."

Mother Teresa of Avila (1515–1582), who founded a rigorous form of the monastic Carmelite Convent, was not just a leading religious figure of the sixteenth century but also a revered writer, whose 1565 autobiography was widely discussed in royal and ecclesiastical circles. Living in the midst of Spain's so-called Golden Age (the cultural heyday of Cervantes, El Greco, Titian, and the imperial might of the Spanish Armada), she captured the country's material splendor as well as its divided soul. To this day, *The Life of Saint Teresa of Jesus* is one of the most engrossing esoteric tracts ever published, partly due to the glimpse God purportedly permitted her of the precincts of Hell.

As generations of readers have discovered, Teresa's passages on the topic, which shun customary depictions of an underworld fireforest, do not easily fade from memory; offered in the canoness's calm, first-person style ("In that pestilential spot, where I was quite powerless to hope for comfort"), they are subtly troubling upon first perusal but assume their greatest impact as afterthoughts, stealing back to dislodge any peace of mind as they adapt to one's inmost definition of personal horror.

Happily, Osborne's songwriting is closer to joyous conviction than Hadean despair, yet she makes the latter condition seem convincingly harrowing for those who cannot appreciate the latent meaning of life's small moments.

As conveyed in the hilariously offhanded "One of Us," written by guitarist Eric Bazilian (who contributes to most of the tracks on *Relish*), Osborne's central message is the nearness of self-redemption. "That song's message is very interesting," she notes, "because you see yourself sitting on a bus, looking around at the people and thinking, 'What if God—and I don't mean that it has to be Christ or whoever—*were* "just a slob like one of us," ' as the lyric says. I hear a lot of music these days that's expressing a lot of anger and self-hatred—and it's legitimate to express anything you want—but I feel there's a certain sense missing of just being happy to be around."

Joan Osborne was born on July 8, 1962, in Anchorage, Kentucky, near Louisville; one of six children born to building contractor Jerry Osborne and the former Ruth Yunker. Getting her first acoustic guitar from a boyfriend while a senior at Mamie Sweet Waggener High School, she initially used it only for postgraduate puttering while studying filmmaking at New York University. Between jobs as a Fotomat clerk and a singing telegram messenger ("they made me wear a gorilla suit in July"), she sauntered onstage during an open-mike night in a tavern to sing a Billie Holiday tune and was asked back for the bar's weekly blues jams.

Either touring or recording for the last four years, Joan also issued the *Soul Show* CD (1991) and an EP called *Blue Million Miles* (1993) on her own Womanly Hips Music label, while accumulating an array of rave reviews for concerts that layer bantering ease and broiling intensity.

Splicing gospel onto the grittiest saloon soul, Osborne's sets have an unpredictable air of outreach and insight. These traits recur on *Relish* with the spellbinding strangeness of "Ladder" and "Spider Web," two infernal fables fit for St. Teresa herself in which a lover cracks the "little code" of her vanished mate and Ray Charles regains his sight but loses his voice.

"The one promise I made to myself when I went into the process of making this record was to be as open as possible to the ideas around me," Osborne confides. " 'Ladder' is about self-doubts, while still wanting to believe. And I love the surreal imagery of Ray Charles taking his glasses off, and when you look inside his head there's a thunderstorm."

DAR WILLIAMS'S NEW ENGLAND HONESTY

IF ONE HEARS MELODY IN THE DAILY ROAR ON MAIN STREET, then traditional folk music would be the back-alley stillness paralleling that steady rocking ferment. Always seeking a conscious remove from the madding crowd, folk music shows the virtues of modest audibility in a clamor-beset culture.

In the latest issue of the Cambridge, Massachusetts–based *New England Folk Almanac,* living legend Pete Seeger views traditional forms as "music you make for yourself and not music you listen to," but advises that "this is a functional definition, not a structural definition."

The seventy-five-year-old Seeger's comments came in a symposium-like survey piece headlined "Why Is Folk Music So Popular in New England?" in which folkies as diverse as Chris Smither and Scottish singer Jean Redpath also considered the question—Smither citing the area's college-intensive "willingness to exercise introspection," Redpath attributing it to the music-loving region's "ancestral memory," and Seeger positing, "Why

Dar Williams

are there more coffeehouses in New England than other places? I'd say New England has a great tradition of small organizations, and now that they're no longer going to churches as much, they go to coffeehouses instead."

Which brings us to Dar Williams, the twenty-seven-year-old auburn-haired composer who is the hottest young performer on the New England folk horizon as well as a favorite in the Internet's Folk Music chat zone. The reasons for her success are evident on her self-produced album called *The Honesty Room* (Razor & Tie Music, due February 21), which is topically penetrating but has unapologetically pretty music that neither aims for alternative status nor longs to be an acoustic offshoot of modern rock. Williams has no qualms about being a stylistic descendant of what she terms "the nonsteroid version of America that includes the Shakers, hammered dulcimers, Pete Seeger, and the handicraft side of our society's history."

The Honesty Room opens with "When I Was a Boy," a witty guitar-and-voice oratorio based on a famous children's fantasy ("I won't forget when Peter Pan came to my house, took my hand/I said I was a boy, I'm glad he didn't check"). The song's insights on preadolescent androgyny and its emotional liberty reflect the provocative pre-Disney impropriety of Scottish novelist Sir James Matthew Barrie's central character and Peter's six "lost boy" confederates. But the somber edge in Williams's vocals evokes not the girlishly smitten Wendy of the tale who is abducted by the menacing Peter, but rather the luckless tone of Slightly, Peter's troubadour sidekick. Stranded in Neverland, the waifish Slightly "cuts whistles out of trees," as Barrie wrote in 1904, "and dances ecstatically to his own tunes. . . . He thinks he remembers the days before he was lost, with their manners and customs." As the song affirms, to be lost is sometimes less a matter of unfamiliar surroundings than a lack of self-fulfillment.

"It's not surprising that the original Peter Pan character had some menace in him," says Williams. "In the story, Wendy wanted to be just like Peter and also in love with him—but somebody like Peter, who won't grow up, would be terrible in *any* real-life relationship."

The youngest of three daughters by Yale-educated medical writer-editor Gray Williams and the former Marian Ferry, a Vassar graduate who does fund raising for Planned Parenthood, Dorothy Snowden "Dar" Williams was born April 19, 1967, in Mount Kisco, New York, and came of age in neighboring Chappaqua. A student of the guitar since the age of nine, Williams wrote a "maudlin" ditty titled "I Should Be Happy Where I Am" at camp during her eleventh summer. Indelicate critiques stopped her from writing for another six years. While attending Wesleyan College in Connecticut, she resumed her tune spinning, but the "turning point" came in late 1992 to early 1993 in Boston when a deep depression over professional impasses and the breakup of a relationship found her again considering a halt to performing in favor of pursuing a graduate degree in "theater, speech therapy, or psychology."

Her struggles with that quandary eventually resulted in "You're Aging Well" and "I Love, I Love (Travelling II)," two far-sighted ballads whose spiraling bursts of free association and soprano trills merge the complexities of the Celtic air and the medieval motet. Free of pop compromises, they are handsome folk plaints of an almost classical stripe, yet contemporary enough to compel the patronage of prudent college or alternative-music programmers. "The point of those songs," says Williams, "is that I'm looking forward to aging, affirming the ancient but currently unpopular idea that getting older can make you wiser and physically and emotionally stronger."

Deciding to depart Beantown while completing the new material, she moved to Northampton, Massachusetts, the college-dominated (U. Mass., Smith, Amherst, Hampshire, Mount Holyoke) town that is also the home of Dinosaur Jr, whose sometime engineer, Mark Alan Miller, worked on *The Honesty Room*.

"There's a rhythm to where I live that helps my music," says Williams. "And it includes the mountains, high snows to constantly dig yourself out of, and geese clucking along the shoulder of the main road into town."

Williams mingles easily with the eccentric local rock community, but prefers the folk circumambience celebrated in the *New England Folk Almanac* with its ads for arts festivals, handmade mandolins, and the folk broadcasting orbit of FM outlets, including KOPN Columbia, Missouri, and WUMB Boston, which cater to an unbounded community with few protocols.

"If you have a guitar," says Dar, "and earn about two hundred dollars a year getting a room's worth of people to pay attention while you sing a bunch of songs that includes at least three originals, you can rightfully call yourself a folk singer."

Still, any genre extending such a tolerant entry-level welcome is apt to tempt the insipidity of too many atonal strummers. "Well, you can just imagine all the levels of performance in a music scene that includes everything"—Williams's laughter spills out—"from your crazy aunt leading an after-dinner sing to Boston's huge undercurrent of small cafés and Unitarian church concerts. But it's generally thought that you work yourself up through the ranks. I didn't mind cutting my teeth in rough bars, but it's difficult to be developing in an environment that doesn't readily remove the big question mark hanging above your head. Only the folk audience can take it away, and even then it requires a long, patient process."

Does Dar Williams have the stamina to stay the course?

"I'm excited but realistic," she says, "because in songs like 'Boy' and 'I Love,' you hear me following my mind and not my heart. What *The Honesty Room* is saying is that I like the artistic freedom I have inside my head. Still, folk music in New England is audience defined rather than industry defined.

"And unlike a lot of pop or rock, folk music is about a high level of very, very intimate communication; it's the art of reaching individuals rather than a huge group. On a night when a show goes really well, the great paradox of the folk audience is that the people don't feel the singer has been heard, they each feel that *they've* been heard."

GOO GOO DOLLS'
BLUE-COLLAR GUTS

"THESE ARE PEOPLE OF INCREDIBLE CONVICTION—THEY WILL not budge," says Buffalo, New York–born guitarist-singer Johnny Rzeznik of the Polish heritage that underlies the gallant roar of his band, the Goo Goo Dolls. "My ancestors were peasants from around Kraków who came to the East Side of Buffalo in 1913, right before the outbreak of World War I. From what I understand about Polish history, tanks would roll over these people, and they'd still live on, stubbornly praying the rosary. I admire that level of guts."

And it shows, grittily and gloriously, in every concussive facet of the Goo Goo's chronicles, as exemplified by the megapop band's incomparable fifth album, *A Boy Named Goo* (Metal Blade/Warner Bros.), due March 14. Masters of the hard-spanking melody line and other grand, aggressive gestures, this passionate power trio (chief songwriter Rzeznik, bassist Robby Takac, departing drummer George Tutuska, and tour replacement Mike Malinin) hails from the western extremity of the Niagara frontier, and the members' creative isolation feeds a combative tunefulness at the mighty end of the modern rock spectrum.

Slackerdom only occasionally is accused of generating anthemic uplift, yet at least half of *A Boy Named Goo* has the tense invigoration of the headiest video twitch game,

Goo Goo Dolls

plus enough thumping human tenacity to urge the alienated back onto the streets. Fight songs like the band-composed "Eyes Wide Open" or the Rzeznik-penned first single "Only One"—and his "Ain't That Unusual," "Long Way Down," and "Flat Top" (with its somber quip that "conscience keeps us quiet while the crooked love to speak")—are each exceptional in their undogmatic demands for restoration of a common dignity.

"What makes rock'n'roll worthwhile for me these days," says the affable Rzeznik, "is the real feeling that there's a musical movement right now that's part of an organic social movement. I notice all the kids have their bullshit detectors turned on, and that's a positive sign. Let's just hope the fucking marketing people leave us all alone."

In the case of the Goo Goo Dolls, they have so far been spared any commercial conditioning beyond a gradual upgrade in the sonic level of their releases. Their primitive *Goo Goo Dolls* debut on the Mercenary label was picked up in 1987 by Celluloid Records. Next came the *Jed* album on Death/Enigma (1989), which led to major-label visibility with *Hold Me Up* (1990) for Metal Blade/Warner Bros., a move coinciding with the stylistic enrichment of their punishing pop vision.

"Our influences are the Sex Pistols, the Damned, Devo, and the Plasmatics," says Rzeznik (the first *z* is silent), "and we wanted to do something with the same energy, but just a little more melodic."

By 1993's *Superstar Car Wash* record for Metal Blade/Warner Bros., the band's gleeful wall-of-gall approach to high-volume mellifluousness had attained a drenching new dither on tracks like "Fallin' Down" and "Already There." Here was a beautiful noise capable of resounding beyond the confines of the Great Lakes region.

But the Goo Goos still scrambled for rent money. Rzeznik was fresh off the road grind and "fooling with open tunings" in his East Side apartment a year ago, when he began plinking what would prove the apex of *A Boy Named Goo.* A distressed acoustic rocker called "Name" is "about the difference between being fifteen and twenty-eight" in a youth culture that sacrificed its sense of purpose: "You grew up way too fast/And now there's nothing to believe/And reruns all become our history."

Like so much of *A Boy Named Goo,* "Name" describes a generation suspended between the Old World and the Lost World. "I was fifteen years old and majoring in plumbing at McKinley Vocational High School in Buffalo, when I started writing songs with titles like 'I'm Not Gonna

Run,' " Rzeznik recalls with a soft laugh. "I didn't want to do dog work for the rest of my life, but I lived in an ethnic, working-class place that was a real throwback. Still, my grandfather was the kinda guy who had actually helped arrange—not entirely legally—for people to get their passports to America. So the challenge is to find a way to dig deeper inside yourself for a new direction."

Born December 5, 1965, to postal clerk Joseph Rzeznik and the former Edith Pomeroy, Rzeznik grew up with four older sisters on Clark Street near the corner of Kent Street. ("We called it the Superman corner.")

"My family opened a bar on the East Side when they first got here," says Rzeznik, "so I was used to being around self-employed merchants, which is how I decided to be a plumber. The year I turned fifteen was rough because that's also when both my parents died; my father was a bad alcoholic who died from drinking, and my mom was gone six months later 'cause she was so lonely. If it hadn't been for my sisters, I wouldn't have made it." And if it hadn't been for rock'n'roll, Rzeznik wouldn't have had a reason to try.

New York state's second-largest city (pop. 357,900), Buffalo began as a key Erie Canal port whose post–Civil War trade boom attracted hordes of immigrants and industrialists. The tough, frequently snowbound blue-collar outpost was plagued in recent decades by unemployment, but lately has regained its former boom status due to a tariff-lifting 1989 trade pact with Canada; Buffalo remains a sports- and tavern-loving party town whose 4 A.M. bar closings often prompt 5 A.M. traffic jams on the bridges back to Ontario.

"Frankly," says Rzeznik, "I was nineteen and drunk the night we started the Goo Goo Dolls. I'd worked as an assistant plumber for only one day, when I quit and enrolled at Buffalo State U.; I was playing in the Beaumonts, a hardcore group named for [actor] Hugh Beaumont [the father in TV's *Leave It to Beaver*] when I met Robby [Takac], who was in my cousin's metal band. We jammed and drank and named our new group after this spooky toy we saw in *True Detective* magazine, a baby's rubber head you moved with your fingers."

And *A Boy Named Goo* shows how far such game impulses can take gutsy young citizens of the Blizzard City.

"No matter where you're from, you've still gotta learn to keep your perspective," says Rzeznik. "When I wrote 'Only One,' some people thought it was about Kurt Cobain's death, but it was inspired by a Buffalo

rock star who got into bad stuff. Fact is, that kinda thing happens to anybody who gets high on their own fumes.

"Our music is saying that it's best to keep yourself more process oriented than outcome oriented," he adds with unbudgeable surety. "If you
can somehow do things from the bottom of your soul, but *not* get hung
up dwelling on them, then that's a good, unselfish feeling."

MORISSETTE'S *JAGGED* SELF-HEALING

AS ANY FORMER CHILD ACTOR WILL TELL YOU, AN EARLY DOSE of adult reality is a dangerous thing.

"To be blunt, whenever you're on stage doing anything that isn't one hundred percent yourself, then you're only acting," says Ottawa-born singer-songwriter Alanis Morissette, whose spellbindingly frank U.S. debut album, *Jagged Little Pill* (Maverick/Reprise), due June 13, is likely to fascinate listeners on both sides of the Canadian border. However, adds the twenty-year-old performer, "When you're doing work that is a completely truthful side of yourself, each time you express it you can get back to the creative place you were when you initially discovered it, and I love it there"—as *Jagged Little Pill* makes disconcertingly plain.

Unlike many recent efforts by even the most gifted new female artists on the modern rock horizon, Morissette's often severe writing voice has the crackling certitude of someone who's long past tentative vulnerability or impulsive confessionalism. Nobody taking a first stab at self-scrutiny could fake the indubitable thrust of the album's first single, "You Oughta Know," in which a teenage girl dumped by

Alanis Morissette

her beau for a more mature woman ponders the bumpy transition for all parties. In a tone too peeved to be mistaken for coy sarcasm, she dares pop the questions that define the grimly visceral relationship: "An older version of me/Is she perverted like me/Would she go down on you in a theater? . . . I hate to bug you in the middle of dinner/It was a slap in the face how quickly I was replaced/Are you thinking of me when you fuck her?"

Lyrics that appear roguishly uncouth when read off the page are piteous when heard leaving Morissette's lips. Because she dares to stand naked in her remembrances, the narrator allows herself no comfort zone for self-righteousness, and as she builds steam in her incantatory checklist of public indignities and private indiscretions, the singer's wounded outrage mingles with a gathering courage that gives the listener a giddy desire to cheer her on. Keyed to the quaking drift of a discordant rock rhythm section, "You Oughta Know" makes disturbing, yet conciliatory points about a culture that exploits innocence in the pursuit of selfish emotional adventure.

Like the rest of *Jagged Little Pill*, the song succeeds because the singer is so charitable in her perspective and generous with her personal insights. Whether considering the spiritual confusions of a Catholic upbringing in "Forgiven" or detailing the psychic injuries of juvenile overachievement in "Perfect," "Hand in My Pocket," and the contagiously funky "You Learn," Morissette's album is the jarred journal of somebody who's been there.

Alanis Nadine Morissette was born on June 1, 1974, one of three children (she has an older brother, Chad, and a twin brother, Wade) by former high school principal Alan Morissette and his teacher-wife, Georgia Feuerstein, who fled to Canada from Hungary in 1956 during the anti-communist revolt.

"My parents are outgoing, worldly, direct people who are very cute together," says their darkly beautiful daughter. "For instance, my father went up to my mother in an Ottawa schoolyard when he was twelve and told her, 'I'm gonna marry *you*.' "

Morissette herself has been a precocious and outspoken figure in both the American and Canadian entertainment industries since she was ten. Although she's played the piano since she was six and began writing songs at nine, Morissette's initial exposure in the mideighties came as a semiregular actress on Nickelodeon's *You Can't Do That on Television* cable program. While the general assumption was that she would continue acting, her ambitions lay elsewhere.

"At ten, I took all the money I earned on the TV program," she says, "and I financed the making of a record which I did with keyboardist Lindsay Morgan, who produced it, and guitarist Rich Dodson of the Canadian band the Stampeders" (who notched a number-eight hit in 1971 with "Sweet City Woman").

Morissette pressed up two thousand copies of the homemade single "Fate Stay with Me," her fledgling attempt at songwriting ("Fate stay with me/I want to be free/What did you think I'd be doing now?/When you left me I was thinking aloud!") and a thematic foretaste of her unequivocal style. Issued on her own Lamor label, the record got Alanis signed with MCA Publishing in Toronto at the tender age of fourteen. She went on to cut two popular dance-rooted albums for MCA/Canada, *Alanis* (1991), which earned her a Juno Award as most promising female artist, and *Now Is the Time* (1992).

Along with these early career peaks came periodic personal valleys.

"When I was growing up, I was always around people much older than me," says Morissette, who lived in the former West Germany from age three to six, when her parents taught the children of U.S. military forces. "My early sense of independence enabled me to accomplish a lot professionally and to appear confident on the surface. But I had no real self-esteem because of being in an industry so immersed in what others thought I should be."

The dilemma also created a "chronic incompatibility" in her romantic relationships. "I'd date older men so I could talk to them and then get my sexual fix with younger guys. What I gained in intellectual stimulation I lost in youthful exuberance."

The private climax of these developmental incongruities arrived four years ago, when Alanis "freaked out" in her parents' living room as they were departing on a business trip. "I'd taken too much on myself," she says, "and for once I dropped my façade of total assurance." Alarmed, her folks canceled their plans and stayed home to help their daughter sort out her tangled dreams. The limits and laurels of such bittersweet experience are embraced on the scintillating *Jagged Little Pill*, with most of the thirteen songs (including an unlisted "Your House") cut live at producer-collaborator Glen Ballard's studio in Encino, California. "All the vocals are one take," she says, "and we threw out anything that felt too inhibited."

As Morissette embarks on a round of showcase gigs with her new four-piece band, she admits with a chuckle that "people are surprised I'm not angry like my music, but there's nothing festering in me—I release it all.

"It's OK to have sad and bleak sides," she counsels, "but our society doesn't much encourage that fact outside music or the arts. I say things in my songs that I wouldn't say in normal conversation or even the most serious talk. Music helps you find the truths you must bring into the rest of your life."

MOZART REVISITED— GARDINER'S WAY

WHO MEASURES WHAT IS RIGHTEOUS IN A WORLD DEVOTED TO reckless individualism? What is goodness worth to a pliant civilization where low guile equals high style and the physics of greed grip the popular imagination? And of what possible use is the portent of spiritual doom to people who deny the judgment of a watchful divinity?

These are the dilemmas facing a young musician in a period of profound philosophical ferment and class upheaval, when science has forever altered humanity's outlook on the earth and its relation to the universe, and religious conservatism among the economically fortunate has put them on a social collision course with common citizens supporting human rights. We're describing the end of the eighteenth century, of course, as revolutions in America and France threw all of Europe into a moral debate. Music would soon heighten the seething argument, and the composer with the courage to inject political and ethical issues into his art was one Wolfgang Amadeus Mozart, working feverishly in Prague with librettist Lorenzo da Ponte in October 1787 to create what many consider the greatest opera of all time: *Don Giovanni.*

Mozart

Two centuries later, this chilling operatic account of a remorseless rascal-rapist and his satanic reward (subtitled *The Rake Punished*) has been given its greatest modern rendition by the Monteverdi Choir and the English Baroque Soloists under the baton of John Eliot Gardiner (Archiv Produktion/Deutsche Grammophon/Poly-Gram Classics, due July 18). Playing on period instruments as they did for the five previous installments in Gardiner's series of recordings of the seven great Mozart operas (*Abduction from the Seraglio, La Clemenza di Tito, Così Fan Tutte,* the Grammy-winning *Idomeneo, Le Nozze di Figaro;* and, arriving in 1996, *Die Zauberflöte*), the orchestra adheres to Gardiner's thrilling mandate of "playing at full stretch," as he calls it with a chortle. "I wanted them to perform to the absolute limits of the authentic instruments' power."

It would be difficult to envision a more unrelenting and transformational production of this towering work—or a more mind-flexing version with which to introduce anyone into the realm of opera at its Mozartian pinnacle. Truly, as author Maynard Solomon asserts in his superlative new biography, *Mozart: A Life* (HarperCollins), this music confirms that "Mozart is one of those rare creative beings who comes to disturb the sleep of the world." And Salzburg's prolific boy genius has finally found his ideal contemporary interpreter in the uncompromising maestro Gardiner.

Prior to Gardiner's ambitious series, the preferred period-instrument recordings of such major Mozart operas as *Figaro* and *Don Giovanni* had been those by Swedish conductor Arnold Ostman, whose small-scale warmth brought listeners nearer to the ambient orchestral interlace of a performance in Mozart's day than previously thought possible. Gardiner's further achievement with both works lies in his capacity for recapturing the human vitality of the themes behind the musical constructions. The hard-driving force Gardiner elicits from the musicians is so intimate and dialoguelike in feel that one either expects the vintage instruments to disintegrate in their sympathetic grasp or be seized by the principal singers to be employed as apt weapons in the onstage action.

"Underneath Mozart's elegant, graceful patterns and highly rhetorical side there was a very turbulent aspect to his nature," says the British Gardiner, noting, "Not all my colleagues would agree with my approach, saying that you don't *need* to interpret Mozart. But I believe there's an aggression and violence in some of his music that's often overlooked. Mozart was equivalent only to Shakespeare in his ability to identify with and be compassionate toward even his most despicable characters, showing you their fragileness and thereby making them totally convincing."

The son of frustrated court composer Leopold Mozart, Wolfgang was a *Wunderkind* by turns nurtured and manipulated by his possessive father, but Solomon's prodigious research in his book reveals the "zones of freedom" (music, eroticism, surrogate families) accorded the savant who was reared as a mythic "eternal child"—thus bringing new insight into the wellsprings of Mozart's empathy as well as the redirection of his inner rages.

As for Gardiner, he was born April 20, 1943, in Dorset, England, the son of gentleman farmer–forester Rolf Gardiner and wife Marabel, who were dedicated amateur classical singers. Gardiner "took to music very happily," studying violin and piano from the age of six, and intended after graduation from Cambridge to be a professional farmer like his ecology-minded dad—until an inherited love of choral singing led to formal classical study with musicologist Thurston Dart in London and composer Nadia Boulanger in Paris.

Gardiner calls singing "a fundamental response to human needs, communicating things that cannot be conveyed by normal language." His intense affinity for the voices of people and instruments is plain in the charged musicality he summons between soloists baritone Rodney Gilfry as Don Giovanni and bass singer Andrea Silvestrelli as Il Commendatore, the slain parent of one of Giovanni's illicit lovers. When the stony ghost of the Commendatore confronts the Don in the opera's frightening finale, Gardiner has the cast's vocal chorus form a human chain (supplemented by spectators) that reaches into the audience as the imposing Commendatore appears from the back of the theater, supported by a troupe of trombonists, to demand Giovanni's repentance.

"When Don Giovianni refused," Gardiner says, "the Commendatore threw him over his massive shoulder like a sack and carried him out through the chain of people and down into Hell. At that point in the production, the complicity between the audience and the company and the musicians was so complete that when it was all over I felt bereft; I was grieving."

But veteran Mozart fans and novices can rejoice in Gardiner's recordings as well as the Solomon book, which serves as a complementary companion. Gardiner's years-long immersion in Mozart's operas concludes this summer with performances of *Die Zauberflöte* in London. What moved him to undertake such a vast project?

"To subvert people's expectations of what Mozart was doing and bring them closer to his time and intentions," he explains. "Frankly, I'm an irregular churchgoer, but I believe, like Mozart did, that in our troubled world it's music that is proof of a divine order and a superhuman pattern we're all a part of. I think it's impossible to be a serious musician and not believe that. I'm religious *because* of music."

OSTROUSHKO'S AMERICAN HEARTSTRINGS

"MUSIC IS THE BEST POLITICIAN IN THE WORLD TODAY," muses instrumentalist-composer Peter Ostroushko, "because the similarity in all music is much greater than the differences." The Minneapolis-born mandolin and violin virtuoso laughs at the simplicity of his insight as he bounces his young daughter, Anna Kim, on his lap, but the logic of the statement resounds through an impressive recording career that commenced in 1974 with uncredited mandolin accompaniment on Bob Dylan's *Blood on the Tracks* collection and has reached a pungent new high point with the appearance of his latest, just-issued album, *Heart of the Heartland* (Red House Records).

Fans familiar with the extensive session work Ostroushko (pronounced Oh-strew-shko) has logged with Emmylou Harris, Willie Nelson, Chet Atkins, Norman & Nancy Blake, Taj Mahal, the St. Paul Chamber Orchestra, the Minnesota Symphony, and radio's *A Prairie Home Companion* (serving as music director until 1986) will know him as a player of miraculous

Peter Ostroushko

adaptability. But those aware of Ostroushko's own half-dozen eclectic albums on Rounder and Red House (including 1989's acclaimed *Blue Mesa* and the 1992 *Duo* collaboration with guitarist Dean Magraw) will be pleasantly shocked by the enchanting coalescence of the ten pieces on the new release. The suitelike sequence of compositions is so transfixing in its depictive power many listeners may initially fail to focus on the fact that the music is wordless.

"It's strange that you say that," confesses Ostroushko, "because my father, who was a shoemaker born in the Ukraine, was an incredible storyteller. People went to his shop in our Ukrainian neighborhood on the northeast side of Minneapolis not just to get their shoes fixed, but also to be in his presence. Being a musician—he played mandolin, too—he was methodical in his conversational approach, and he could take you on a wave of descriptive experience so otherworldly that two hours later you wouldn't know where the time went, and you couldn't believe you never left the same room you stepped into when he first began to speak."

One of four siblings, Peter Vasilyovitch Ostroushko entered the world of his father on August 12, 1953, just a year after William Ostroushko and the former Katerina Evtushok had emigrated from the Ukrainian Soviet Socialist Republic. Peter inherited his dad's theatricality, as well as his family's facility for stringed instruments, initially "fooling around" at age ten on his parent's mandolin and an older sister's "thirty-five-buck plywood Harmony guitar, studying the Bob Dylan and Joan Baez song books she brought home from college." Subsequent boyhood trips to the music section of the Minneapolis Public Library on Nicollet Avenue exposed Peter to Folkways' Appalachian field recordings of Roscoe Holcomb, Hobart Smith, and Wade Mainer.

Peter passed through assorted rock and blues bands at Minneapolis's Sheridan Junior High and Edison High School, while also acquiring a taste for classical music ("especially baroque") and modern jazz. But he ultimately determined after some training in acting and drama that his prime nonperformance métier was composing for the theater. Thus began long professional associations with the Children's Theater Company in Minneapolis, the Actors Theater Company of St. Paul, and ACT Theater in Seattle. As with the title track, many of the pieces on *Heart of the Heartland*, like "Prairie Sunrise" and "Dakota Themes," derive from commissions from these organizations or from original scores written for documentaries sponsored by Twin Cities PBS outlet KTCA-TV.

Anyone attempting to summarize the spacious grace and emotional delicacy of Ostroushko's sound on *Heartland* would be sorely remiss in not mentioning the late, great composer Aaron Copland (1900–1990), for whom Peter would have been an ideal featured player. Often referred to as the first American composer to make a living at his craft, Copland was gifted at blending ethnic and popular styles like Appalachian and southwestern folk, jazz, and traditional Mexican into a comprehensible "American sound." Whether writing ballets ("Billy the Kid," 1938; "Rodeo," 1942; "Appalachian Spring," 1944), film scores (*Of Mice and Men*, 1938, and *The Heiress* and *The Red Pony*, both 1949), operas (*The Tender Land*, 1954), or his neoclassical orchestral (*El Salon Mexico*, 1936) and later atonal serial works, Copland was always a risk taker and never a snob, finding nobility in the everyday scheme and reinterpreting with astute innocence the exuberant spectrum of our nation's antecedent song forms.

Ostroushko laughs shyly at the mention of the late master's name. "Dean Magraw and I recently did 'Hoe-down' from Copland's *Rodeo* in a concert with the St. Paul Chamber Orchestra," he explains, "Dean and I jumping in and out of what Copland wrote to suit our fancies. I'm definitely a fan of his music, so I'd like to think or at least hope he would have liked what we did." And the Brooklyn, New York–bred Copland, whose own vision of America was filtered through a prideful Lithuanian-Jewish perspective, would have felt a strong affinity for the melancholy yearning in Ostroushko's *Heart of the Heartland*. Both men were reared at pivotal twentieth-century still points between the blaze of this country's optimism and the shadow of its immigrant struggles. To bid farewell to a heritage of sacrifice in order to grasp the hugeness of the Promised Land's flawed liberties may be the hardest single goodbye in the American parable.

William Ostroushko died shortly before Christmas 1991, just as his now-married son was nearing a transition in his artistic maturity and popular acceptance. And despite delving deeper into the classical idiom (he recently performed an eighteenth-century mandolin concerto by Giovanni Paisiello), Peter still prefers to stay in the undefined compositional realm he currently inhabits. "Even though, for people who write nonclassical instrumental music," he chuckles, "the popular lifespan of a piece is about six months before it disappears for another seven to eight years."

Yet anyone who's harkened to Copland's "Old American Songs" (1950–1952) or "The Promise of Living" finale of *The Tender Land,* with their blatant relish for life and its mixed benedictions, will love such like-spirited *Heart of the Heartland* melodies by Ostroushko and his nine-piece ensemble as "Seattle (The Fantasy Reel)," "Virginia Reel from Hell Medley," and "(Twilight on) The Sangre de Cristos."

In its finest and surest aspects, American music acknowledges by distillation all the distinctions among us, caressing the exotic traits in our midst because they epitomize the alien traces of our past. Having made a nation out of *all* nationalities, we daily mold a culture from its culminations. And by showing fondness for our contrasts, we each find our own initiation into the American experience.

"With the world's attention span supposedly getting shorter," says Ostroushko, "nobody wants to be brought gradually into the occurrence of a good story, yet all good stories happen gradually! Historically, music has kept the generational lines open, helping teach everything from pagan rites to family lore to community identities. It allows a true understanding of other people's heartbeats. But all of us just have to make the commitment to really *listen.*"

SUDDENLY, TAMMY!
WILL *GET THERE*

"LIFE IS FRAGILE," SAYS BETH SORRENTINO, PIANIST-VOCALIST- songwriter for the group known as Suddenly, Tammy!, "and so our music is protective overall of that quality."

Like a brief cloudburst that cleanses a muggy morning, or the accidental poetry in a child's exclamation, the uncluttered clarity of this Lancaster, Pennsylvania, union of piano/vocals, bass, and drums has a natural rightness as calm and penetrating as the modest moments the trio's music portrays. There is a term, *mimesis,* for the innate skill of description in literature or the arts, and the poignant force of Suddenly, Tammy!'s appreciative power can make one lament all the little things in life that get overlooked.

Despite a silken proficiency at mimesis and a steadily building college fan base, Suddenly, Tammy! is itself in peril of being neglected by an inattentive public. Following two EPs and a self-titled 1993 album on Manhattan's independent spinART label, the group's major-label debut, *(We Get There When We Do),* was issued by Warner Bros. last March. Unfortunately, the new album's expected chart success has thus far proved elusive.

After two national tours and considerable critical acclaim, Suddenly, Tammy!'s popular clout is best en-

Suddenly, Tammy!

capsulated by a recent late-night gig at the tiny but taste-setting Sin-é club in Manhattan's East Village. Known for surprise sets by the likes of Bono or Sarah McLachlan, the hip, no-frills downtown café was literally swollen to the rafters with a youthful cross-section of pilgrims from campuses up and down the Eastern Seaboard, each spectator able to silently mouth the lyrics to even the most obscure, unrecorded portions of the live Tammy! repertoire.

The compact but avid crowd also embraced the band's placidly potty sense of levity, wherein bass player Ken Heitmueller (a ringer for the Jeff Spicoli character in *Fast Times at Ridgemont High*) trades the sort of eccentric banter with Sorrentino and her drummer brother Jay that yielded the act's title (taken from the cosmetics-disdaining Beth's put-down of Tammy Faye Bakker's daily war paint).

"We take a few simple things and keep rearranging them in our music and our performances," explains Beth slyly, "just like you would with the eyes, nose, ears, and hat on a Mr. Potato Head. We're the Mr. Potato Head of music."

"It's our own brand of free association, something extra for the audience's entertainment dollar," sniggers Heitmueller, onetime resident sound engineer at Lancaster's legendary Chameleon Club, the breeding ground for the Ocean Blue, Live, Innocence Mission, and other notable Pennsylvania groups. Born to a local printer and his social worker wife on March 20, 1971, Ken is the second Heitmueller to make his mark on the region's thriving music scene (older brother Karl manages BBC Records on North Queen Street, another Lancaster landmark). It was in the younger Heitmueller's basement CatBox Studio ("The name comes from the five cats and their kitty litter boxes that were scattered around Kenny's four-track," confides Beth) where the band, all graduates of Hempfield High School, began rehearsals in 1989.

The two five-song EPs emerging from the CatBox, *Spokesmodel* (1991) and *El Presidente* (1992), contained many of the tracks that became scarcely embellished highlights of the spinART record and *(We Get There When We Do)*, among them "Long Way Down," "Mark of Man," and the first piece Beth wrote for the band, "No Respect Girl."

The latter song's story concerns "a charismatic girl," in Beth's words, "who rolled through town like a hurricane," at a point after Beth returned to Lancaster from a two-year stint (1986–88) studying musical theater at the Boston Conservatory of Music, Dance, and Theater. "I was amused and amazed," she reflects, "by the effect a strong, remorseless personality can have on others. The line that begins the song, 'It can go either way,' sums up the observant but unjudging perspective." The tune also serves as a précis for the crisply pruned tonality of Suddenly, Tammy!'s sound, which drummer Sorrentino sees as "alternative in the truest sense. Since we don't have electric guitar, we emphasize melody and subtlety, and we don't really emulate any current styles.

"My dad was a jazz drummer, and Beth and I grew up hearing Ray Charles, Broadway show tunes, the Beatles, Edgar Winter, and Donovan. I was a snare drummer in the Hempfield Black Knights marching band and also learned percussion in the school jazz band, so our stuff is rock-'n'roll with slightly skewed dynamics."

Jay Sorrentino (born December 29, 1966) and his sister (who arrived on March 23, 1968) are two of three offspring—twenty-four-year-old Martha sang backup on *(We Get There . . .)*—by attorney James Sorrentino and the former Linda Hills, who were divorced in the early seventies. Like her mom, who now works in adult rehabilitation at the Hershey Medical Center, Beth has a propensity for special education and care giving. "I used to teach at the Montessori Academy of Lancaster," says Beth, "and in nineteen ninety-three to ninety-four they asked me to develop a twice-a-week Music and Movement program for the day care classes, which gave me a lot of insights into children and how they're treated in our society."

The experience led to a track co-written with her brother on the new album. Titled "Not That Dumb," it will be serviced to triple-A radio late this summer. "The title phrase," says Beth, "comes from something I saw a parent yell when scolding a child in a mall: 'Quit doing and saying that all the time! You're not that dumb!' Another line in the song, 'I had a gun, I'm gonna use it,' isn't meant literally but refers to the close-minded attitudes of people determined to do anything they have the power to do, regardless of how it mistreats others."

Beth grows increasingly serious discussing other formative influences on her songwriting sensibilities, which range from the lingering pain of her parents' breakup to the early deaths of friends in elementary school—which found metaphorical expression in the requiem "River, Run," an ode to the late actor River Phoenix, "who became any river, any flowing thing that could have been saved."

For Beth Sorrentino, whose delicate yet declarative piano technique was culled "from studying Carole King's 1971 *Tapestry* album since the age of six," Suddenly, Tammy!'s outlook is "elemental in its joy or sadness."

"I hide my feelings in our songs," she adds, "by describing images that can speak for themselves. That way I don't have to say exactly what I mean. The music goes so deep for me and Jay and Ken that we protect ourselves by playing it publicly. Otherwise, we'd have to put our fingers on it alone."

JOYFUL BEDLAM:
LIFE WITH BOGMEN

"I'D LIKE OUR MUSIC TO BE HEARD AS UPLIFTING," SAYS lead vocalist Bill Campion of the jubilant bedlam that is the sound of the Bogmen, but he admits that the point of "The Big Burn," the first single from the band's inaugural album, *Life Begins at 40 Million*, (Arista, due August 29) is "having fun treating the apocalypse as a picnic."

Hedonism, like nihilism, is sometimes a romantic bid to wreak havoc on sham and recapture hope, with adherents believing that anything left standing after such passionate punishment could prove the basis for a new beginning. "I think that sounds about right," Campion agrees with a guffaw, "and the sense of humor in our music is intended to make the dark stuff in it go down easier."

Envision a military parade drill by a renegade cadre of shellshocked vets, the close-order march disintegrating into spit-and-polish pandemonium, and you'll grasp the alarmingly unbalanced fife-and-drum brio that is the Bogmen's portrayal of our national discord. Witnessed live during a dangerously packed gig last May at the Mercury Lounge on Manhattan's Lower East Side, such songs as "The Big Burn" are august in their wacky precision but most affecting for the loco oratory Campion imposes on the proceedings, as if

The Bogmen

the grand marshal of a stately occasion had suddenly flipped his illustrious lid.

"Button your lip, you're talking out of turn!" he barks in a caterwaul. "Another cell out of your brain, another marble from the urn! Certain things you can't replace! Once you're a raisin, you can never be a grape!"

Granted, such gaga glibness may never overshadow the Gettysburg Address, but it stokes the grinning Mercury Lounge throng into an almost metaphysical boil.

"When I originally heard the ranting licks our guitarist Bill Ryan came up with at rehearsals," explains Campion, "it suggested something destructive, and I blammered out these stream-of-consciousness ideas— which is how I get a lot of the surprising words."

But what is equally uncontemplated is that the lyrical outcries come off as spiritual.

"Well, if I really tried to be prophetic," he says, "I'd be a laughing stock, but there is something within myself and the world that I'm searching for. Sometimes it's just the hangover delirium of feeling sick of myself, but other times I start firing off synapses and seem to get moved by the spirit."

On June 2, 1992, the Bogmen coalesced into their current six-man membership (Campion notes, "Our name stems from the fact that we all worked on clam barges in the bogs off Long Island [New York]"). Since then, the group has been causing a healthy stir on the club circuit between New England and the Mid-Atlantic states, regularly attracting sellout crowds of 1,500 or more to such halls as New York's Irving Plaza and Tramps. "They rapidly drew an extremely faithful college audience from D.C. to Boston," says Steven R. Martin, senior VP of the Agency Group Ltd. U.S.A., which eagerly handles the band's concert bookings. "But what made these guys so unusual was the fact that though they may have sold or circulated a few homemade demos, there was no real independent record or CD to help build their following. The huge interest was pure concert word-of-mouth, based on the spontaneity of their shows, Billy's charisma, and the fact that you're never sure what's gonna happen whenever they play. Arista immediately saw this band's potential, believing like we do that they can go all the way."

Thankfully, producer Jerry Harrison, former Talking Heads keyboardist, was able to harness the crazed exuberance of the Bogmen in the studio; with *Life Begins at 40 Million* (the album's title and cover-art spoof evolution and the recent rash of midlife crisis books), he allowed the band to set a live tone without sacrificing its flair for the incongruous flourish.

"Jerry did a good job," says Campion. "He did things like change the arrangement of 'The Big Burn' drastically, and he came up with the bass-line for the song 'Englewood.' We clashed in a fun way, because I didn't want him to be in the control room for my vocal tracks, and he agreed to just back off and let me fly."

Born February 21, 1971, in Huntington (New York) Hospital, Campion is the youngest of the six kids of computer marketer Robert Campion and the former Patricia McCann. Billy is Irish on both sides of the family: "My dad's name was originally Norman, and his people are from County Antrim and Cavan, while my mom's relatives are from Limerick and Armagh." He concedes an interest in his Irish roots, including the musical ones, but spent more time in his teens learning the music of Violent Femmes, the Replacements, and the Kingston Trio—"We did a weird version of 'Scotch and Soda' "—for high school cover bands Dead Fleas, Bad Hair, and the Plumbers.

Once the present Bogmen (Campion, Bill Ryan, keyboardist Brendan Ryan, bassist Mark Wike, percussionist–backup singer P. J. O'Connor, and drummer Clive Tucker) had graduated from or dropped out of assorted eastern schools (Boston College, Hofstra, Providence College, Berklee College of Music), they took refuge in a rented house in Lynbrook, New York.

"We called the place Disgraceland," he says, "and all we did was write, jam, and drink cases of beer from the 7-Eleven across the street. Living next door were two strippers and their pimp, who ran a business called Body Talk Ltd., and when things were slow, we made eighty dollars a night driving them to bachelor parties in the area."

A regional fan system seeded by stints playing the Bayou in D.C., the Paradise in Boston, Mother McGee's in Huntington, and diverse bars in Queens, New York, enabled the Bogmen to dub small batches of their demos, selling them for five bucks apiece. The most notable were titled *You'll Shoot Your Eye Out* (1993) and *Glow-in-the-Dark Balls* (1994), the latter yielding larval renditions of three killer cuts on *Life Begins at 40 Million*: "What's Behind Your Coat?," "The Doubter's Glass," and "Dr. Jerome (Love Tub, Doctor)."

Crackling drums, carefree melodies, and the AWOL exuberance of Campion's lounge-crawling schtick build upon each other on the new album, as they do at the Bogmen's drolly militant concerts, rousing to a certified frenzy a widening retinue of what Campion affectionately calls "confused, postgraduate drifters." There may be other 1995 debuts as fine as *Life Begins at 40 Million,* but few will be as free of formulas and, yes, uplifting.

"Concepts like nationalism may be dead for many young people," says Campion, "but the honesty of rock'n'roll as a social barometer and rallying point is not. With the Bogmen, I'd like to appeal to the loneliest people with the least self-confidence, restoring their faith in others and in what's coming next."

GARCIA: A LEGACY
BUILT TO LAST

IT WAS HIGH NOON ON A SUNNY SEPTEMBER IN 1989 AT LE Clube Front in San Rafael, California, the warehouse–rehearsal hall headquarters of the Grateful Dead, and husky forty-seven-year-old Jerry Garcia was just starting his day as members of the Dead strummed "Death Don't Have No Mercy" behind him.

"It's nice to be here!" Garcia giggled to this writer, alluding with a wink to the strains of the Reverend Gary Davis blues dirge he'd just been singing. "Nice to have you here, but it's also nice to be here, too."

The eighties had been a dicey decade for the Dead, with former keyboardist Keith Godchaux perishing after a car accident in July 1980 and Garcia battling substance abuse from 1982 until 1985, when he was busted in his car and put into a treatment program. The still-fragile guitarist lapsed into a five-day diabetic coma in July 1986, and his recovery coincided in 1987 with the release of *In the Dark,* the million-selling album with the

Jerry Garcia

single "Touch Of Grey," which would be the first top-ten hit in the Dead's history.

On this gorgeous day, the Grateful Dead were poised to release their follow-up album, *Built to Last* (which quickly went gold) and had been practicing new material for their October 1989–April 1990 shows, which would later be mixed at Le Clube Front for a live album.

"Come on Bob, get yourself a chair," beckoned Garcia to Dead guitarist-singer-songwriter Bob Weir, while Dead pianist Brent Mydland formed the opening chords of a ballad of adieu from *Built to Last* called "Standing on the Moon."

Weir and Garcia fell into a discussion of "Moon" and how close it came to the model that was in Garcia's head when he composed the song with Dead lyricist Robert Hunter, Garcia fretting about "the Grateful Dead energy that we've always had such a hard time getting on record— the combination of control and clarity and discipline."

Within ten months of Garcia's remarks, Mydland would die from a drug overdose, and 1990's gold, two-CD *Without a Net* concert collection, the band's first live package in nine years, would prove to be the last formal Grateful Dead album before Jerry Garcia himself left the planet.

Control, clarity, and discipline were qualities Garcia managed to bring to his music, but in his private life they posed a more daunting challenge. Watching Garcia chat so unguardedly with buddy Bob Weir during that day in Marin County, expressing the simple wisdom that shone in their best work, it was plain that the bond they shared stemmed from a mutual desire to have music seal the fissures in their fractured personal backgrounds.

Weir volunteered the unfamiliar fact that he was adopted, and Garcia mentioned that, when he was nine, his musician dad had drowned in a fishing accident. Garcia later told how he saved his own stepdaughter, Sunshine, from drowning—"The ultimate horror trip," as he put it—by using the mouth-to-mouth resuscitation procedure he learned as a Boy Scout.

"Hey, I was in the Cub Scouts!" Weir rejoined, adding that his mom was his pack's den mother. "But they kicked me out, shortly after my mother got fed up and abdicated, because I wasn't a real good kid or serious scout. I was seriously into fucking around."

"Absolutely!" Garcia ruled, slapping Weir on the back in gleeful solidarity with the grave degree of juvenile delinquency they shared. "*I* stopped doing homework at seventeen, because I thought it was a waste of time."

Yet Garcia never stopped looking for extended family or the public rites of communion that could salve his deficient sense of self. As Joel Selvin recounts in his excellent *Summer of Love* book about the blossoming of San Francisco's bohemia in 1965–71, Garcia and Weir found an enduring sense of belonging in the Haight-Ashbury hipster mise en scène that the Dead came to dominate.

Do the times make the band, or vice versa? "Well, the times provide the context," said Garcia. "It's probably serendipity or synchronicity. Something that seems so appropriate to the moment may have no actual relationship to it at all. But if it seems to universally apply—it's *art* when it does that. For me, I don't know exactly where it comes from."

"Music seduced me before I made any career choices," Weir explained, and Garcia quickly concurred, confiding how he sought to imitate admired artists, such as the Everly Brothers—"for the sound—their 'whole' sound."

When the Warlocks-turned–Grateful Dead took up residence in a Victorian house at 710 Ashbury St. in 1966, the unkempt rock combo that sat stoned on the front steps of their gingerbread abode scarcely seemed built to last.

Yet the Dead and their stubbornly nonaggressive commercial philosophies abided, lending a tender sense of scruples and familial warmth to a marketplace stilted by icy sales imperatives. Though best known as a touring act after their 1970 Warner apex with *Workingman's Dead* and *American Beauty*, the Dead boasted an often-richer crop of studio performances on such underrated Arista albums as *Terrapin Station* (1977), the Lowell George–produced *Shakedown Street* (1978), *Go to Heaven* (1980), *In the Dark*, and *Built to Last*.

"They've all been kinda fun," Garcia enthused of the Arista releases. "They've all had their moments."

Jerome John Garcia was born August 1, 1942, and he says his ancestors came to California circa 1914 from the Galicia province of La Coruña in northwestern Spain. The wild, rocky region has been known since antiquity for its devil-may-care *tunos*, or vagabond minstrels, and Jerry Garcia saw to it that his restless heritage helped shape the modern temperament of popular music.

Late in the afternoon during the 1989 visit, Garcia suddenly asserted of the Dead that "whenever we all write songs, they kinda come at you funny, you know? Sometimes the parts you normally consider the most important come at the end."

As a prized example, Garcia offered the wistful "Standing on the Moon," the parting epistle of someone staring at Earth from a celestial distance, Jerry adding, "I'm so happy with the way it came out—it's a lyric I think is really beautiful":

"Standing on the moon, where talk is cheap and vision true/Standing on the moon, but I would rather be with you/Somewhere in San Francisco, on a back porch in July/Just looking up at heaven, at this crescent in the sky/Standing on the moon with nothing left to do/A lovely view of heaven, but I'd rather be with you."

Such a pensive song, full of clarity and discipline, spiritual and yet practical. But why did Jerry Garcia treasure it so much?

"There's a purity there that I wanted to preserve," he counseled softly. "That's part of what makes it beautiful. It's a love song, is what it is."

DID STONES SELL THEIR MUSIC SHORT?

WHETHER ITS NEW COMPUTER SOFTWARE IS PURCHASED BY a country parson or a cyberpunk hedonist, Microsoft apparently considers the product to be exciting enough to "make a dead man come." One can only assume that the company intends for this unchaste message to underlie its ad campaign for the Windows '95 program, since that phrase is the central point and climactic assertion of "Start Me Up," the 1981 Rolling Stones song the company has licensed as theme music for its sales pitch.

The biggest Stones hit of the last seventeen years, "Start Me Up" lingered in the Hot 100's number-two spot for three weeks on the lascivious strength of Jagger/Richards's lyrical tribute to a woman so goading in her coital charms that her male "riders" actually "cry" as their "eyes dilate" and their "lips go green." Scanning the operating instructions on the back of the Windows '95 package, buyers may logically conclude that such parlance as "plug and play," "push the button on the taskbar," and "an open door

The Rolling Stones

to doing more" mirrors the debauched double-entendres the Stones included in "Start Me Up's" rammish ode to "a mean, mean" female "machine."

If one aims to appropriate the eighties credibility of the Rolling Stones, one must accept their unequivocal artistry as originally conveyed. "What I do is sexual," Keith Richards said as early as 1966, adding to this writer in 1989, "I'm a Sagittarius—half-man, half-horse—with a license to shit in the street." Thus, the rock community welcomes Bill Gates and his disk/file patrons to a universal inbox of uniquely earthy dimensions.

And what do the Rolling Stones get out of this transaction? Money-wise, Microsoft says, the permissions fee for the deal (which is commencing at the close of a 1994–95 Rolling Stones world tour that grossed some $315 million) is confidential, and the company asserts that press reports of $12 million are "grossly exaggerated." As for the professional esteem and artistic enhancement gained from such a move, those consequences are murky.

Apologists might say that Microsoft merely acquired thirty- to sixty-second edits of the guitar-and-vocal hook from "Start Me Up," although it's exactly that musical trademark—which helped make the song a hit in the first place—that triggers one's memory of the full work and renders its presence in the promotional realm potentially meaningful.

Other defenders of the Stones could cite the ample precedents for such classic rock-meets-commerce payoffs, noting that a performer of the stature of Bob Dylan allowed the accounting firm of Coopers and Lybrand to exploit a hymn of moral reawakening, "The Times They Are A-Changin'," for its own rather humble marketing purposes.

However, if the Stones or Dylan were so smitten with the notion of using their music to sell another's wares, perhaps they should have accepted assignments to contrive singular jingles for the occasion, as young Billy Joel once did for Bachman Pretzels, or they might simply have sung time-honored slogans, such as those proffered to Ray Charles or Whitney Houston by soft drink or coffee firms. If the artist actually appreciates and uses the product, then such ringing musical endorsements are concordant with the desired perceptions of impressionable consumers.

And then there are the extenuating circumstances wherein an act's song catalog is owned/controlled by a third party, with licensing done despite the composers' objections (as in the case of Michael Jackson and the Beatles' output) or with the agreement of the songwriter's representatives (as in the case of Paul McCartney's administration of Buddy Holly's body of work).

But of all these contracts, the most fragile is the social/cultural bond of trust between the artist and his or her audience. The traditional, generationally renewed understanding between rock'n'roll performers and their devotees is that rock's value is based on the degree to which it inhabits a candid sphere beyond the bounds of show business proprieties or entertainment industry artifice. By this criteria, the best rock'n'roll is made only by those artists who have not compromised their primary expressions—with all exceptions to the rule relegated to lesser status.

At its highest end, creativity is an honorable calling, protective of its purity of purpose. We are touched that Picasso found the courage to paint *Guernica* in condemnation of war and fascism, and we feel proud that he did not later allow that masterpiece to become a prop to peddle Pepto-Bismol.

At its finest, a song in the multigenre rock'n'roll canon is a public pronouncement of a personal truth. Its author makes a living by sharing that truth; and the truth cannot serve two masters. For the opportunist to state that such a song is no longer about the truth from which it sprang, implying that it is no longer useful as an emblem of honest insight and self-revelation, is to say that one is now done with the truth. And any culture that believes it is ever done with the truth has ceased to function as an engine of human ideals.

Many in the media were quick to claim last week that there was "hardly a whimper" (*Newsweek*) from Stones fans, or that they "sneered" (the *Wall Street Journal*) when news surfaced of the Microsoft pact. More accurately, reactions are still finding form in the hearts of those who take the Stones' legacy seriously.

Over at Atlantic Records, the label where the band built its modern reputation, emerging groups experiencing their own initial hits are reevaluating the Stones as role models; they realize "Start Me Up" is the Stones' property, to dispose of as they please, and their comments aren't punitive, just perplexed or deeply disappointed.

"We were offered a huge sum of money from a fast-food company to either write a new song or let them use 'Hold My Hand,' " explains singer-songwriter Darius Rucker of Hootie & the Blowfish. "I would never, ever let any of our songs be used to sell some product. These things are just a matter of money, and you're selling yourself and your music short when you do it. I'm not knocking anybody, and I'm not saying what we do is art, but whatever artistic integrity we have we plan to keep intact."

"A computer company offered *us* a million dollars to use 'Shine,' " says Ed Roland of Collective Soul, "but the song wasn't written for or about a computer, so that was out of the question. To write something from within yourself and then allow it to be used to sell some product seems hypocritical to me.

"I saw the Stones' commercial for the computer [software] on TV the other night," Roland adds. " 'Start Me Up' was the first time I ever heard the Stones, and that song was very personal to me. It doesn't make me want to buy that computer program; it just makes me feel that what's happening with the song itself is very false."

SOMETHING IN THE
WAY SHE GRIEVES

MANHATTAN IS THE ETERNAL METROPOLIS OF THE IMPATIENT
heart, where young artists, poets, and seekers come first to reimagine
themselves. Occasionally, the expectant rovers return to reflect on the
mature results. As the city embraces another autumn, a single woman
named Madonna looks down from her Upper West Side aerie and contemplates the equinoxes of the spirit as captured on *Something to
Remember* (Maverick/Sire/Warner Bros., due November 7), a fourteen-
track treatise of her best old and new balladry.

"Listening to this record took me on my own journey," says Madonna
with a sad smile, shifting on the
couch in her apartment overlooking Central Park. "Each song
is like a map of my life."

Dressed almost austerely in
a snug, black skirt and pink
sweater, her blond hair pulled
back in a crisply tucked bun
as she drinks hot tea, the performer shows the tensile grace
of someone who takes excellent
care of her physical form. The
broad, rounded features of
the careless, young diva who
cut "Holiday" in 1983 have
vanished, however, replaced

Madonna

by a narrower, subtler countenance that harsh experience has made handsome.

"I don't really listen to my records once I've done them," she says. "I'm onto the next thing. And I think most of the time when my records come out, people are so distracted by so much fanfare and controversy that nobody pays attention to the music. But this is, for the most part, a retrospective, and I just wanted to put it out in a very simple way. The songs, they choke me up," she adds with a nervous chuckle, "and *I* wrote them. Isn't that weird? I can't tell you how painful the idea of singing 'Like a Virgin' or 'Material Girl' is to me now. I didn't write either of those songs and wasn't digging deep then. I also feel more connected emotionally to the music I'm writing now, so it's more of a pleasure to do it."

Madonna has included three new songs on the collection: a moody cover (in funky and orchestral versions) of Marvin Gaye's 1976 hit "I Want You," which was suggested and subsequently produced by Nellee Hooper and features Massive Attack, and two bittersweet serenades ("You'll See" and "One More Chance"), cocreated with David Foster during the third weekend of September in a whirlwind writing/recording session. Shortly after this talk, she was to leave for London to start recording the music for the film version of *Evita,* the musical that was the toast of Broadway in 1979—the year Madonna wrote her first song in the basement of a dormant Queens, New York, synagogue.

"I remember calling up my father back in Detroit and making him hear it on the tape recorder over the phone," she confides, blushing. "He said, 'Oh, that's very nice.' I felt proud. The song was called 'Tell the Truth.' "

Thus, *Something to Remember* is a stock-taking exercise, as well as a farewell to Madonna's first fifteen years as a singer-songwriter, the record's pensive material delivering on the candid impulse that launched her remarkable career. Born August 16, 1958, in Bay City, Michigan, Madonna is the eldest daughter of six children born to defense engineer Sylvio Anthony Ciccone and the former Madonna Louise Fortin. A self-assessed "roller-coaster Catholic," she grew up sharing the middle bunk in a three-tier bed with two of her sisters. "I didn't have any free time as a child," she says. "My mother died of breast cancer when I was seven, and then my father remarried when I was ten. I had a lot of responsibility, taking care of my younger brothers and sisters."

Like her siblings, Madonna was obliged to study music, specifically piano. "But I couldn't sit still, and I begged my father to let me take dance lessons," which served as a means of escape from the family's cramped home in a black/Hispanic neighborhood in Pontiac, Michigan. Madonna was in the church choir and acted in school musicals, while sharing her mother's mantralike habit of idly intoning her favorite tunes. "As a teenager, I loved Aretha Franklin's 'A Natural Woman,' and in high school I worshipped Joni Mitchell and sang everything from *Court and Spark*, my coming-of-age record."

But her pivotal developmental trial was the death of her mother, and as Madonna passes this fall afternoon discussing the themes behind her often acutely wistful ballads, she ultimately says, "My mother is part of a *lot* of my music."

Although love songs, such as "Live to Tell," "One More Chance," and "I'll Remember," also invoke the early fever of a failed marriage to Sean Penn, tensions with a stepmother who could not replace her lost parent, or later relationships that fell short, a larger phantom overshadows each mourning of life's missed linkages.

"I think about my mother and a certain emptiness—a longing—in my songs," Madonna explains. "There are tragic, traumatic moments where I think, 'I wish that I could call my mother.' And there isn't anybody that can make me feel better. It's this primal thing that has been a springboard for the work I do."

How did she learn her mother was gone?

"I was at my grandmother's house. The phone rang, and it was my father, and he told my grandmother that my mother had died. I'd just seen her in the hospital. The rest of that day I blocked out—I probably went outside and played. I was majorly into denial and didn't really understand."

Poised on the edge of the couch, Madonna pauses and gulps, growing glassy-eyed. "And it unfortunately wasn't something that my father ever really prepared us for or discussed afterward. I suddenly developed a strange throwing-up disease, where every time I would leave the house, I would throw up. If I was away from my father, I threw up. It was a nervous condition."

In recent years, when Madonna was under attack for her frank *Erotica* album and *Sex* book, the artist says she drew strength from her late parent's nonjudgmental "fervor" for fulfilling one's personal vision: "She had an unbelievable level of tolerance and forgiveness. She was tremendously religious in a really passionate—almost sexual—way, like she was in love with God. If you read the letters she wrote, even when she was

sick and dying, she was completely happy about everything. It was frightening, but there was just that faith of hers. My mother loved to take care
of people. My older brothers and I were sometimes brutal to her, and she
never complained."

It sounds like the materfamilias had an essential serenity. "Exactly,"
says her daughter. "And I could probably use more of it in my life."

A brisk September breeze catches the leafy scent rising from the
freshly mowed lawns of Central Park, the tangy end-of-season smell
betokening the coming solstice. Madonna shivers slightly as she sips the
last of her tea.

"I think my mother made people angry, because they couldn't shake
her beliefs," she concludes in a near whisper. "And she was just thirty-
two when she died—just a baby. Madonna Louise. So, basically, I'm here
to take her place."

PRETENDERS' HYNDE APPRECIATES THE *VIEW*

SOME PEOPLE ALWAYS FEEL AT HOME, NO MATTER HOW FAR they wander. And the luckiest can even find new routes for savoring the distance covered.

"The way rock affected me when I was younger, growing up in Akron, Ohio, was that it was a form of escapism," mused Chrissie Hynde in March 1987, playing with her two toddler daughters in her Manhattan dressing room just prior to a sold-out Pretenders' concert at Radio City Music Hall. "When I was in bed at night, I could hear a train whistle in the distance, and it was that great feeling of imagining that *you* were going somewhere. There was that sense of adventure, a sense of discovering something new, just a sense of getting away from the mundane. Having to deal with the mundane is some-thing we all have to learn to do," she counseled, brushing back her eyebrow-level auburn bangs as she rolled lemons across the carpet into empty teacups to amuse her squealing offspring. "But how not to *become* mundane, that's something else."

Pretenders

Roughly two years later, Hynde was back in Akron on a visit, listening to Baltimore & Ohio rail cars rolling below her window at the converted grain silos of the Quaker Hilton as she wrote "Criminal," a song about the guilty malaise of lonely lovesickness—and a self-exposing peak of the Pretenders' quietly impassioned new fifteen-track live acoustic suite, *The Isle of View* (Warner Bros., due October 24).

"In a way, that song reminds me of the two odors that pervaded Akron when I was a kid," says Hynde, chatting as she unwinds in her home in the pristine countryside of England, the singer-bandleader's adopted base since 1973. "There was the putrid scent of burning rubber from the Goodyear factories and the fantastic aroma of the raw oatmeal coming from the Quaker Oats mills in town. You felt basic, just like those smells.

"Maybe it's because I've never been in drug rehab or a weight-loss clinic, but I really haven't changed much from the day I started playing music at seventeen. I've adapted along the way, but philosophically, I'm the same vegetarian hippie musician I was when I left home for London with everything I owned in one suitcase, or when we spoke in New York in 1987. Except now I'm more comfortable with everything.

"I just came from Akron, where I go about twice a year with my children to see relatives," she says, "and now I can appreciate the resemblance of the lush Ohio hills to rural England. Or I borrow my mother's car to drive through every old Akron neighborhood where a house of ours once stood, before they put the interstate through. But that's my perspective as a resident of the isle England, which is where the name of the new record comes from. It's also the title of the unlisted final melody on the record, which I wrote before I put the Pretenders together, and, when spoken, it sounds like 'I love you.' "

Arriving on the tail wind of the Pretenders' 1994 album, *Last of the Independents*, a merrily lurid and impertinent work that tendered some of the testiest rock of the last twelve months, the *Isle* sessions might be mistaken at first blush for a demure back step. But these unclad versions of Pretenders hits and cherished relics from Hynde's two-decade songbook (taped at London's Jacob Street Studios in May with the group's current lineup, plus the Duke Quartet) each divulge the deeper emotions grinding beneath their rock'n'roll release mechanisms. Like an automobile with its bodywork torn away, this lean, defenseless music makes it possible to see why the tires squealed whenever Hynde raced her engine.

" 'The Phone Call' is another song that feels so natural on the new album," says Hynde, referring to the 1977 demo that occasioned the Pretenders' U.K. deal with Real Records. "Our new performance is so ethereal, but so close to the bone. Rock'n'roll should always reflect the setting in which it's made."

Chrissie Ellen Hynde was born September 7, 1951, in Akron, the second child (she has an older brother, Terry) of telephone company employee Melville "Bud" Hynde and his wife, Dolores, who had a local beauty salon. "My dad's father worked for a rubber company, and my mom's father was a cop," says Chrissie. To prevent familial occupations from repeating themselves, she studied art at Kent State and then departed for London, where she toiled in boutiques and wrote rock criticism for *New Musical Express* until her own music career drew raves in 1978–79 with the newly formed Pretenders' cover version of the Kinks' "Stop Your Sobbing." A subsequent three-year relationship with Kinks' founder Ray Davies yielded a child, Natalie, and a later five-year marriage to singer Jim Kerr of Simple Minds produced her second daughter, Yasmin. Much of Hynde's songwriting since the 1990 *packed!* album, which contained "Criminal," has addressed with dry-eyed clarity the role of single mothers in a world starved for lasting attachments.

"There's been a return to more adolescent impulses in our culture," she suggests, "where the emphasis is on youth, cosmetic things, female and male sexism, and a spectating attitude on society that's similar to sports. Back in eighty-seven, I said I wouldn't let my songs be used for product-endorsement deals, and I still won't—even though that attitude now makes most consumer-minded Americans quizzical. Rock'n'roll gives us the sense of community we lack, but the commercial importance we sometimes place on it shows how vapid people have become spiritually.

"And yet, when it's put in its proper place and makes a contribution towards a greater good, music has the elevating spirit we all need to help us deal with our responsibilities. I mean, I can still put on a favorite record, like Phyllis Nelson's eighties [U.K.] hit 'Move Closer,' stand in the middle of the room, and swoon from her awesome delivery."

How does Chrissie Hynde respond to her own output?

"Well, I've been a witness to what Charles Mingus wrote in his book *Beneath the Underdog* about musicians dwelling on a 'colorless' island beyond the racial divide we currently suffer from. Back before my band had settled on a name, this biker in a white supremacy–type cycle club took me into his room one day, bolted the door, and said he didn't want his friends to hear the song that meant the most to him—and he played me the Sam Cooke version of the Platters' 'The Great Pretender.'

"The way that moment affected me, giving our band a name and something to aim for, is the same kind of consciousness I hope comes out in our stuff on *The Isle of View*. Artists always play the role of leaders, in a cultural sense, but the best thing they can do is *publicly* share their soulfulness. No matter how much my biker friend or the rest of us try to resist it, music is a vision of our salvation."

ACTUAL MILES: HENLEY WON'T GO QUIETLY

IN OUR APPARENT PREFERENCE FOR LEGALITY OVER MORALITY, our culture increasingly perceives no imperative but winning in the moment. Thus, we gamble against eternity while bending fundamental terms and beliefs to suit short-term aims.

As author Andrew Delbanco points out in his absorbing new book, *The Death of Satan: How Americans Have Lost the Sense of Evil* (Farrar, Straus and Giroux), the Hebrew word *Satan* in the Old Testament originally meant obstructor or adversary, but was translated during the third century by the Greeks into *diabolos* (from *dia-bollein*, to tear apart). In the Greek rendering of the New Testament, the devil became not a tempter but *satanas*, an enemy of God. Post-Renaissance English translations made him a paradoxical creature and then an ugly pest. "By 1900," writes Delbanco, "it was impossible to reattach the word 'sin' to its original sense (transgression, violation, trespass), because the target of the violation—God—was gone."

"But in the end," reckons singer-songwriter Don Henley, "we all must answer for our own behavior. If our reply is with a code of conve-

Don Henley

nience, that means the concept 'we're all in this together' has gone to hell."

Henley's sentiment neatly abridges the satanic, no-exit scenario of "The Garden of Allah," the seven-minute suite that's one of three new songs (the others are the blues-rocker "You Don't Know Me at All" and Henley's recent cover of Leonard Cohen's "Everybody Knows") on his forthcoming anthology album, *Actual Miles: Henley's Greatest Hits* (Geffen), due November 21.

" 'The Garden of Allah' is a solo sequel to 'Hotel California,' " notes Henley. "To give you an overview of the lyrics, the devil appears to a young man—a writer, agent, whatever—who is tooling in his BMW through the San Fernando Valley [California]. Satan is frustrated because things have gotten so bad that even he is confounded. The weather, for instance, is so hot that it reminds him of his own dwelling place below, and he's sweating through his fine seersucker suit. He realizes that the entire culture has lost its moral compass and that there is no longer any distinction between good and evil. Therefore, the devil's job has become obsolete. He waxes nostalgic about the good ol' days hanging out in Hollywood with F. Scott Fitzgerald and Aldous Huxley, alluding to the historic Garden of Allah."

A three-and-a-half-acre hotel complex of Spanish-style bungalows that once stood at 8150 Sunset Boulevard, the Garden of Allah was built on the former estate of Russian silent film actress–producer Alla Nazimova, a concert violinist who abandoned music for the stage and screen. Known for her bizarre, highly stylized movie roles, Nazimova created a sanctuary along similar lines for her celebrity visitors, who included Errol Flynn, Gloria Swanson, Greta Garbo, Tallulah Bankhead, Robert Benchley, Dorothy Parker, and Leopold Stokowski. Nazimova was financially ruined in the Great Depression and died a year after her last movie, *Since You Went Away* (1944); following her death, a local bank assumed control of her retreat and, in the fifties, demolished it to build offices. But during its three-decade heyday, the Garden of Allah was the site of robberies, orgies, drunken rages, tense honeymoons, bloody brawls, divorces, suicides, and murder.

Henley's ode to the unseemly spa is a churning rock drama built around Danny Kortchmar's forewarning guitar figures, Sheryl Crow's ill-boding backing vocals, and Vinnie Colaiuta's violent drums. Henley's voice is electronically reprocessed during two spoken-word intervals in which he offers Beelzebub's lament, the fallen angel explaining his role as an expert witness in a recent court appearance. The problem is, Lucifer is too honest ("I'm a gun for hire, I'm a saint, I'm a liar . . . I can get you any result you like"), and what use is a devil who fails to deceive?

"I knew I had tapped into the *Zeitgeist,*" says Henley, laughing, "when I picked up the *Los Angeles Times* on the day we finished mixing the song and it had a big review of Delbanco's new book."

What's fascinating is how well such disturbing themes fit within the highlights of Henley's solo work. Few songwriters since the seventies have made more adventurous use of modern studio hardware in expanding the topical/interpretative spectrum of popular music, yet Henley began as a small-town Texas country-rock drummer-singer who took up songwriting after reading Ralph Waldo Emerson's *Self-Reliance* and Henry David Thoreau's *Walden.*

"It's likely," Henley admits, "that there's a running thread in all the songs on the album." These include "Dirty Laundry," "The Boys of Summer," "All She Wants to Do Is Dance," "Not Enough Love in the World," "Sunset Grill," "The End of the Innocence," "The Last Worthless Evening," "New York Minute," "I Will Not Go Quietly," and "The Heart of the Matter." "I suppose," he says, "that all the songs touch on modern society's nonacceptance of any essential principles or beauty. Mr. Thoreau saw those things in the world around him, but where I part company a little bit with him is in his belief in rugged individualism, which I think we've all embraced at the sacrifice of a sense of community."

Henley nonetheless confesses his relief at being a "free agent" in the music community for the first time in his adult life, since "Actual Miles" fulfills his Geffen solo contract. Apart from lingering overseas tour commitments with the Eagles, he has no current obligations whatsoever. And the witty cover art for *Actual Miles,* in which Henley portrays a polyester-clad auto salesman, is intended to underscore the "commodity mentality" he sees as rife in music.

"It's a commentary," he says, "on how all the mergers and market-share obsessions in our business make artists feel like pork bellies, soybean futures, or used cars."

Newly married and resettled in Dallas, with a baby on the way, Henley reaffirms his interest in a possible "joint record and documentary film on Texas root music."

Meanwhile, he thinks that "You Don't Know Me at All" best expresses his ambivalence toward the rock industry to which he devoted "the first half of my life."

"The song is in the guise of a guy-girl breakup," he explains, "but it's really about our snap judgments of our neighbors. For instance, I didn't know I could write a song as heartfelt as 'The Heart of the Matter,' so I'm touched when people send notes saying they got as much out of the experience as I did—'cause I really learned from it. I want my child to grow up in a world that believes there's real evil out there, but also some good things yet to be discovered within each of us."

ANNUAL SEARCH
FOR PEACE ON
EARTH

THE HOLIDAY SEASON, NINETIES STYLE, HAS BECOME THAT
regular speed bump in our popular routine when we rear up and exercise
impartial prejudice, applying political pressure to banish cultural influences that threaten our capacity for tolerance.

It seems that no one in a free country should be able to parade a pagan
rite like Halloween before unsympathetic fellow members of an open,
inclusive nation. Thanksgiving is just as vexing; its visions of seventeenth-
century race-mixing at frontier suppers all but coerce an enlightened
response from citizens, who deserve to be shielded from the banal details of
democracy in action.

Christmas, however, is the ultimate ordeal for all who endure self-
rule, since its onerous altruistic traditions appear to reach back to post-
Constitutional antiquity.

Jill Sobule, Juliana Hatfield, and Jane Siberry

"Christmas isn't my favorite time of year, even though my parents were secular Jews who traded it for Hanukkah," jests sweetly sarcastic singer Jill Sobule, who contributes a definitive rendition of Robert Earl Keen's withering "Merry Christmas from the Family" to "You Sleigh Me!," one of two anthologies of Christmas songs (the other is "Winter, Fire & Snow") just issued as a charitable gesture by Atlantic Records. "Growing up, you could see that an occasion commemorating the birth of the son of God couldn't compete too well with the miracle of some oil in ancient Israel burning for eight straight days—I mean, big deal, you know?

"It's just that Christmas is such a family thing, and since my parents got divorced fifteen years ago, and then my dad died eight years ago, I've had a hard time keeping up. When I was recording my last album [her self-titled Atlantic debut], I wanted to finally be brave and do a Christmas carol. We were recording at the same Nashville studio where my engineer, Brad Jones, had worked on Robert Earl Keen's perfect white-trash trailer-park Christmas song, which has lines like 'Send somebody to the Stop'n Go/We need some celery and a can of fake snow/A bag of lemons and some Diet Sprite/A box of tampons and some Salem Lights.' "

Sung in Sobule's best deadpan nasal chirp, the ballad soars beyond Keen's shit-kicker instincts and strikes more universal chords in a consumerist society that barely has the patience to wait for Santa Claus, let alone the Messiah. "And now that my brother has married a non-Jew," adds Sobule, "one of his little boys is into Jesus, while the other prefers Hanukkah, so I have to be a good Jewish aunt and do the dreidel games, while following through on the electric guitar and amp I told the other boy I'd get from Santa."

Trouble is, Santa Claus has never been the simple Anglo-Christian figure we make him out to be. The original St. Nicholas was a fourth-century Turk from the town of Lycia who was tortured for his faith by Roman emperor Gaius Diocletianus and later adopted by the Greeks (who have never gotten along with the Turks) as their patron saint. During the Protestant Reformation, the Yuletide image of St. Nick was banned from most of Europe, and it was the Dutch who brought him to America as a religious protector-of-sailors icon carved onto the prow of the first Dutch ship that docked here.

Once ashore, Santa Claus evolved from a Yankee vagabond to a yeoman German farmer to a woman referred to as "the queen of handsome girls" in an 1815 New York newspaper account. Five years later, he was described as a kindly Jewish peddler. By 1827, as noted in Leigh Eric

Schmidt's new book *Consumer Rites: The Buying and Selling of American Holidays* (Princeton University Press), Kris Kringle was being portrayed as "a little old negro, who descends the chimney at night and distributes a variety of rewards with impartial justice."

Regardless of Father Christmas's race, creed, or mythic origins, alternative rocker Juliana Hatfield recalls "leaving out milk and cookies for him every Christmas Eve," but admits that as an adult she "no longer observes any Christmas rituals," finding the holiday so "draining that I sometimes wish it didn't happen."

It's exactly this emotional frostbite that makes Hatfield's heartfelt hymn "Make It Home" on *You Sleigh Me!* so marvelously warming. "I wrote the song in 1994 for the Christmas episode of the *My So-Called Life* TV series," she says. "I was asked to play the part of this homeless girl-angel on the show, and the song is intended for Ricky, the gay character who gets kicked out of his house by his parents, who can't deal with him, so he walks the streets at Christmastime.

"The song starts off with the melody of 'Silent Night,' and the bridge has the melody of 'O Come All Ye Faithful.' I was really moved by the experience of writing it. I guess it's trying to comfort Ricky and all the other lost souls at Christmas."

As we struggle each year to wrest real meaning from the inherited symbols of the past, it's important to understand how unending that process has always been. The concept of Christmas gift giving didn't emerge until the 1820s, before which New Year's Day was the preferred festive celebration, commemorating themes as diverse as homage to the Roman god Janus, the aging of Father Time, and the Biblical visitation of the Wise Men to a certain stable in Bethlehem.

In an 1880 editorial, the *New York Times* lamented, "Very few Americans have the moral courage to be economical or even sensible at this season of the year." And attempts to curb the sense of cultural alienation moved sociologist Maulana Karenga in 1966 to create the African-American holiday of Kwanzaa as a way, in Al Sharpton's words, of "de-whitizing" the racially chilly winter carnival. In 1993, the *New York Times* wondered, "Will Success Spoil Kwanzaa?" as a Kwanzaa Holiday Expo at a New York convention center was bursting with merchandise and corporate sponsors. At the time, an African-American entrepreneur advised, "Black people need not be embarrassed about making money. That is what pays the rent and that is what makes America tick."

Meanwhile, Canadian singer-songwriter Jane Siberry offers a lovely canticle on *Winter, Fire & Snow* titled "Are You Burning, Little Candle?" which can be heard as a Christmas, Kwanzaa, pagan, Hanukkah, or non-secular ode.

"Even if you don't believe an infant savior was born in a manger," says Siberry, "every culture's tales of candle lights, starry nights, innocent babes, hope and charity, and new beginnings should at least inspire us to believe each year in a world of fresh possibilities."

ENYA: *MEMORY, MYTH, AND MELODY*

THE DRUIDS OF CELTIC HISTORY ARE NAMED FOR *DRU-VID* (or derw-ydd), Welsh for "oak-knowledge," since the people of this ancient culture worshiped the woodlands as the eternal source of earthly wisdom. And like Merlin of Arthurian legend, Druid priests made wands of branches from the sacred yew, hazel, and rowan timber to orient this botanical sapience for supernatural purposes.

So when cozily uncanny Irish singer-songwriter Enya decided to call her new album *The Memory of Trees* (Reprise, due December 5), it was not an ecological homage to a plant form that could die out, but rather out of regard for what the foliage may one day recall about *our* fleeting activities.

"I love the ambiguity of the idea," says Enya, laughing, who poured her impressions into the record's opening instrumental title track, "but it's got more to do with what the trees have been through and their awareness of us, instead of our awareness of them. That's why the Druids placed great importance on trees and their spiritual power."

Enya

This belief led to the earliest form of Irish writing, called Ogham or "the tree alphabet," its characters composing a secret script with both ordinary and otherworldly meanings. According to legend, the system was devised by Ogma, god of eloquence and literature. Enya herself perceives great importance in legend, its relationship to Irish heritage, and its modern impact on its people.

"I get inspiration from the countryside," she says. "I live in northwest Donegal on the Atlantic coast, and it's quite wild, with mostly mountains, moors, and brown bogs filled with rushes. There's something terribly breathtaking about it, and it moves me to write melodies that can be uplifting, but which I personally find can be very emotional and draining.

"I'm a *verr-y* private person," adds the publicity-shy, seldom-interviewed artist, her halting English laced with the curled Donegal articulation of her childhood Gaelic. "I have to go so deep into myself to compose, so the place where I perform is not in public but in the studio." Since 1982, her collaborators in this cloistered process have been producer Nicky Ryan and his lyricist wife, Roma, who met Enya in 1979 when Ryan was managing Clannad, an Irish group in which Enya became a junior component.

"It was Nicky who asked me to join Clannad," says Enya, "even though it was a true family group [*Clannad* is Gaelic for family], with two of my brothers, Pol and Ciaran; a sister, Maire; and two uncles, Noel and Padraig. So I did keyboards and backing vocals." She participated, uncredited, on Clannad's fifth album, *Crann Ull*, in 1980 and was made a full member for the followup in 1982, *Fuaim*.

"All the while," Enya continues, "I loved Nicky's wonderful concepts of the layering of vocals, and Roma had wonderful stories from Irish mythology, so late in 1982 we decided to leave Clannad to see what we three could evolve together. Our first project was the theme music for David Puttnam's film *The Frog Prince,* and then we did the soundtrack for a six-part BBC television history of the Irish called *The Celts.*"

The BBC was sufficiently excited by the results to issue it in 1986 as the singer's solo debut, *Enya*, its innovative ambient Irish folk milieu attracting a U.S. licensing deal with Atlantic Records.

But it was not until October 1988 that the elusive, nonconcertizing Enya became a superstar with the British release of "Orinoco Flow [Sail Away]," the single from her then impending WEA/Geffen album, *Watermark.* The song seized the Irish airwaves the week U2 was to unveil its

Rattle and Hum opus, and this writer was in a Dublin cab en route to the local premiere of U2's companion film when RTE broadcast what was soon to be the number-one record in the United Kingdom. U2 was forced to share its country's collective pop consciousness that fall with Enya because, as Dublin's citizens openly confessed, they'd never heard anything quite like "Orinoco Flow (Sail Away)."

Recalling the explosion of interest in the song, with its multifarious abstractions concerning Venezuela's Orinoco River, the shores of Tripoli, and Avalon, the fabled Celtic paradise known as "The Summer Land," Enya chuckles about the irony of her accomplishments. "Back then, I actually thought I was still more likely to end up teaching music than making it," she says. "And what's funny, too, is that unlike Clannad, whose background was in traditional Irish songs, my background was in classical music. Yet Nicky's influences were totally different! He was a fan of Phil Spector and the Beach Boys. And Roma was a serious poet studying Irish folklore. None of us really knew what was around the next corner"—specifically, cumulative world sales of eighteen million units for *Watermark*, 1991's *Shepherd Moons*, and *The Celts*, which Reprise reissued in 1992.

As with much of Enya's music, the melody for "Anywhere Is," the addictive pop adagio from *The Memory of Trees*, was the impetus for Roma Ryan's stanzas about the search for the temporal heaven all cultures call "home."

"That's a subject I understand the best," says Enya, "because I can't compose unless I'm home . . . in the Gaeltacht area of Donegal."

Enya was born Eithne Ní Bhraonaín on May 17, 1961, the daughter of musician-bandleader Leo Bhraonaín and the former Maira Duggan, a music teacher at Gweedore Comprehensive School in County Donegal. From age eleven to seventeen, Enya (she adopted the phonetic spelling in the early eighties) attended a convent college in Millford run by the Loretto order, studying music and art (she excelled in watercolor landscapes), before immersing herself in the sounds reverberating from Leo's Tavern, a pub her father ran in rural Meenaleck that became Clannad's proving ground.

"I was brought up Catholic," says Enya, "but as you grow older, rather than attending Mass out of habit, you decide for yourself what you want from religion. I'm the same with music, in that I can go for months without playing a radio or a CD, but when I do, it's usually to hear something like Rachmaninov's *Piano Sonata No. 2* or his *Rhapsody on a Theme of Paganini.*

"My taste in music is like my choices of where I want to spend my time: climbing a hill overlooking the ocean or visiting Spain to see flamenco dancing because of my mother's Spanish roots, dating back to when ships of the Spanish Armada were wrecked off Ireland [in 1588] and her ancestors settled on Tory Island.

"The Druids understood the meaning of remembrance and that the purpose of art is to bind people around a belief in continuity. This music is the sound of something being passed on."

TRACY BONHAM'S
FEAST OF *BURDENS*

MUCH GETS SAID ABOUT THE BUSINESS OF SELLING MODERN
rock—a calling as seemingly prevalent in the collapsed social and economic order of the nineties as sharecropping was after the Civil War—but
precious little gets sung about the daily chore of envisioning, composing,
and performing such music.

Several decades after rock'n'roll gained acceptance as a valid blue-
collar profession for the average guy, the average girl appears just as likely
to be the leader of the band. And, hey, when she comes home from work,
she needs to unburden herself with family, lovers, and friends.

Take, for example, twenty-eight-year-old vocalist-guitarist-fiddler
Tracy Bonham, whose emotionally
volcanic debut album, *The Burdens
of Being Upright* (Island, due March
12), is the keen accrual of a lifetime
of musical seasoning and six years
of occupational struggle.

"I've been playing music every
day since I was nine," she reflects
softly, "and I've been making money
as a musician since I was twenty-
two, but I'm afraid it's getting to be
more of a job all the time, especially
after my record deal brought new
pressures.

Tracy Bonham

"So many people my age earn their living these days from music," she adds, "and since I want to write about what goes on in my head, I just thought anything that's such a big part of me personally and professionally could be shared."

With the job market undependable, the minimum wage certain to stay minimal, and social assistance programs scuttled with mounting intensity, many young work seekers are forced to confront nineties fables of the reconstruction and admit that they've been largely abandoned to their own rock'n'roll resources. Like no album released since rock or a hard place became prime alternatives for a generation of option-deprived postgraduates, *The Burdens of Being Upright* conveys the pangs of subsistence in a scavenger age.

As Bonham declaims during a dutiful phone call depicted on "Mother Mother," the record's fast-detonating first single: "When you sent me off to see the world/Were you scared that I might get hurt/Would I try a little tobacco/Would I keep on hiking up my skirt . . . Yeah, I'm working, making money, I'm just starting to build a name/I can feel it around the corner/I could make it any day."

Satisfied that she has been sincere, the quaking singer swallows hard and concludes with a seismic, plasma-curdling coda: "I'm hungry, I'm dirty, I'm losing my mind!/I'm freezing, I'm starving, I'm bleeding to death!!/Everything's *fine.*"

There is humor here. Tenderness, too. And high-octane indignation. But mostly just the logical end-of-the-millennium chagrin of earning an income by serenading a public torn between episodes of *Friends* and the Republican Party's Contract with America.

"Actually, I originally wrote 'Mother Mother' when I was twenty-four," says Bonham with a chuckle. "But it felt more and more appropriate as time went on. I left the song off a six-song indie EP I did for the CherryDisc label [*The Liverpool Sessions, 1995*], although it was on an eight-song demo that got me signed to Island.

"I avoided playing the song for my mother until I rerecorded it for Island," Tracy confides. "I didn't want to hurt her. But when she saw tapes labeled 'Mother Mother' in my bedroom during a trip home, she got scared, so I had to let her hear it. She was relieved it was really about me and not her."

Not that the rest of *Burdens* is free of fulminations capable of upsetting an anxious parent. The grandeur of the Boston-based Bonham's songwriting lies in her plucky ability to wring richly sardonic parables from the effects of everyday degradation. With the brashly ballistic "The One" and "Navy Bean" (both fortified by poetic guitar from Ed Ackerson of Polara) Bonham dispels shadows of old relationships in which she was misused, notably "two years spent with a terrible, manipulative guy who wanted to show me off in a way that brought to mind the odd image of a woman in a G-string no more concealing than"—nervous snigger—"a navy bean."

On the mordant "One Hit Wonder," Bonham deflects the faint praise bestowed by parochial rock critics who believe she and her compatriots could never excel beyond local awards and regional radio polls, wryly vowing to outgrow their provincial gauges for fulfillment: "I own the world/I bought the whole damn world/From the man who sold the world."

Touchingly, the disc closes on a humble note with "Every Breath," the cautionary "30 Seconds," and "The Real." Bonham explains, "I started recording *Burdens* last July, just as my boyfriend moved from Boston to Syracuse, New York, for family reasons. 'Every Breath' shows how isolated I felt, but we got through it because to keep things 'real,' you must figure out your life rather than your career."

Tracy Kristin Bonham was born in Eugene, Oregon, on March 16, 1967, the daughter of Donald Lewis Bonham, city editor of the *Eugene Register Guard,* and the former Lee Anne Leach, a music teacher whom Donald met while she was attending the University of Oregon. Tracy's dad died when she was two, and her mom remarried five years later to mortgage loan officer Edward Robert Robertson; Tracy was reared with her eight half- and step-siblings.

Trained as a classical musician, at sixteen she attended the prestigious Interlochen Arts Camp in Michigan. ("But I was kicked out when I got caught smoking—cigarettes, not reefer—in the dorms.") Bonham graduated from South Eugene High School with a scholarship in violin to the University of Southern California in Los Angeles, where she practiced four hours a day and composed pieces in the style of Debussy. "Then I got burnt out and took up singing, which always came easier to me."

She transferred in 1987 to Boston's Berklee School of Music, explored the jazz of vocalist Betty Carter and violinist Stephane Grappelli, and held recitals of classics such as Benny Goodman and Charlie Christian's "Air Mail Special." By day, Tracy waitressed at the Atlantic Fish Company on Boylston Street, worked at the Allston Cassette Copy duplication service, and cut jingles for Pontiac and Toyota car dealerships.

"Gradually," she says, "my tastes changed to the Pixies and the Buzz-cocks. I took up rock'n'roll around 'ninety-two and was inspired by woman singers like Sam Phillips and Jennifer Trynin. I got in touch with my feelings in a way I never could have with classical music, where you can bury things for the sake of discipline. I doubt I could've dealt with the issues in 'Navy Bean' outside rock.

"Basically," she finishes, "*The Burdens of Being Upright* expresses the choices I've made from 'ninety-two until now. The beauty of rock-'n'roll is that it's a common language that tells us—no matter what we do for a living—that we're still linked together."

ANGÉLIQUE KIDJO FÊTES FREEDOM IN *FIFA*

SINGER ANGÉLIQUE KIDJO PERCEIVES THE FREEDOM SHE experienced during her idyllic childhood in the West African country of Benin as "what I'd wish for anyone: complete independence of movement, yet everybody, whether family or strangers, watches out for you."

This concept of liberation via reciprocal caring is the essence of *fifa*—the word for "cool, calm, and peaceful" in the southern Beninoise dialect of Fon, as well as the title of Kidjo's vigorously spiritual fourth album (and her first partially in English) for Mango Records, due March 19. As Kidjo sees it, we are initially implanted, however temporarily, with this impression of fifa. And it is only through the lifelong struggle to regain it that we grasp its deeper meaning—and responsibilities.

"For me, everything comes with a bit more difficulty," says Kidjo with a crisp chortle, "and that just means that these things I want to accomplish are important in my evolution. All of the songs on *fifa* are stories that reflect what I've been through emotionally. For instance, the first song [a caroming welter of percussive and choral cries called "Sound of the

Angélique Kidjo

Drums"] is an answer to a question I was asking myself since a trip back to Benin in 1994: 'I've been away for so long that I wonder/If the sound of the drums still has its power.'

"The second song [and first single] from the record, 'Wombo Lombo,' is about how dance describes and affects our lives, the dance in this case being the one when you're possessed by the gods in a voodoo ceremony.

"Like most people from Benin," Kidjo explains, "I am an animist [one who believes in the worship of the spirit in all things, the central tenet of voodoo]. I practice voodoo in addition to my other religion, which is Catholicism, and my great-uncle Daagbo Hounon is a well-known voodoo chief.

"Respect for ancestors is very big in my life," adds Kidjo, one of three daughters and six sons of postal worker, photographer, and part-time banjo player Franck Kidjo and his choreographer wife, Yvonne. "After I was born [on July 14, 1960, in the coastal city of Cotonou]," says Kidjo, "my baptism ceremony took place in Ouidah, the town of my ancestors.

"When a mother has a baby girl, she shaves all the hair from her head and the baby's head, too. This my mother did, and, as a baby, I stayed with her for seven days in a special place called the Room of the Assins in Ouidah that's filled with all these ancient pictures, relics, and fetishes of my relatives. During the ceremony, the voodoo chiefs call the spirits of these ancestors and ask, 'What spirit will guide this baby all her days?'

"I was the only girl in my family for centuries who got a male spirit to guide her, and his name is Linhounhinto. He died nearly a hundred years ago, and he was known as a very honest man, very mad with anyone who lies to him, and very strict. In fact, my mother tried at first to chase his spirit away during the ceremony because she knew from his reputation that he would be very tough on me. But it was too late; our spirits became linked."

So Linhounhinto is a guardian angel?

"Exactly! And when he's angry with me, I can *feel* it. He tests me and tests my surroundings, too, the people who are closest to me." Not the least of which are Kidjo's husband, noted bassist-arranger Jean Hébrail, whom she wed in Paris in August 1987, and their three-year-old daughter, Naîma. "None of my family could believe I was a wife until they met my white French husband," the feisty Kidjo says, laughing, "because I was such a tomboy as a child, being the goalie for my brothers' soccer games and swearing I'd never marry or be a slave to a man!"

Hébrail produced the sensational new record, which mingles the rhythmic and rhetorical might of modern gospel, rap, and Afro-pop with the earthy drive of Kidjo's trumpetlike vocal vim (a Paris-trained jazz shout rippling with bluesy *zilin* forms descended from the folklore-steeped Fon village of Abomey). All attempts at creating a hit-bound universal ascension of world beat, hip-hop, and top-forty urban pop will have to form a flight path behind *fifa*, which swoops around listeners on wings of sonic fire.

There are sobering issues enmeshed in this achievement, however, and they concern the voodoo-borne interconnections of guardian angels, ghosts of bygone slaves, and children raised to heed both spirits' admonishments. As reflected in the newly republished *The Interesting Narrative* (Penguin Classics, 1995) by Olaudah Equiano, a Benin native from the 1700s who was sold into slavery at the age of ten by his own people, the legacy of Kidjo's homeland is a complex one facing contemporary reexamination. In the memoir, penned after he bought his freedom and became a successful journalist-businessman, Equiano writes, "When a trader wants slaves, he applies to a chief for them. Accordingly, [the chief] falls on his neighbors, and a desperate battle ensues. If he prevails and takes prisoners, he gratifies his avarice by selling them."

"These stories are true," says Kidjo sadly, "and after many years under communism, the first thing done by the new democratic government [Benin's President Nicéphore Soglo was elected in 1991] was to resume a festival called the Route of the Slaves, where we retrace the itineraries in Ouidah that slaves had to follow to board slave ships. We must overcome the bitterness created by those who gave up our culture by selling each other's family members.

"As you mention, regarding that *Narrative* book," Kidjo continues, "many of those Benin slaves went to America or the Caribbean, then got free and came back home, bringing African-American musical influences, like gospel, with them! I realized this in December 1994, when I canceled a local tour in order to tape field recordings of music in central and northern Benin—where I'd never traveled before."

That ambitious project was the resolution of a moral crisis Kidjo confronted when planning her most extensive West African concert trek since her refusal to play procommunist music forced her to move to France in 1980. "It's not possible, expenses-wise, to tour in West Africa without the sponsorship of cigarettes or alcohol," she notes. "I rejected my Philip Morris sponsors to fight against the double-nicotine cigarettes I believe they sell to my people."

Instead, Kidjo and her husband journeyed from Benin's capital of Porto Novo to hamlets like Korontiere to tape flutes, cow horns, and bamboo percussion, saying, "Let's spread Benin's true culture." And when they entered the Muslim town of Manigri, smiling women hugged them and sang "welcome home" in gospel harmony.

All these field recordings and more are woven into *fifa* in a loving manner that would make Equiano and his lineage proud.

"The lesson in life, which any child feels, is that we're supposed to take care of each other. But how much longer," Angélique Kidjo wonders, "until we all learn this?"

CRANBERRIES' HYMNS *TO THE* *FAITHFUL*

PEOPLE ARE DESTINED TO OVERLOOK THE POETRY IN THEIR lives until the day they can recognize its absence. By appreciating the merest building blocks of each momentous occurrence, the Cranberries have created music that is more mythic and consequential than many of the intentional big statements rock'n'roll has attempted in the nineties.

"It's strange how we all find reasons for not dealing with things that are in our faces," says Dolores O'Riordan, the fervent lead singer–lyricist of the Limerick, Ireland–based rock quartet, which also includes brothers Noel (lead guitar) and Mike Hogan (bassist) and Fergal Lawler (drummer). "And yet when we write these simple songs about family, growing up, love, and death, most people generally enjoy the discussions they bring about." She shrugs with a shy grin. "So if it's uncool to write about these matters, I guess we don't care to be cool."

"Sometimes there's so much emphasis on image, but we were always under the impression that the music would say who and what we are," adds the soft-spoken Noel Hogan, as if describing his tender cloudbursts-of-chords guitar style and the defenseless sensibilities of *To the Faithful Departed* (Island,

Cranberries

due April 30), the Cranberries' third album. If the band members seem reticent offstage, they are strikingly unwary in their music, examining postadolescent apprehensions in such early hits as "Linger" and "Dreams" from 1993's *Everybody Else Is Doing It, So Why Can't We?*, and then shielding their hearths against the sectarian violence that is Europe's spreading affliction on "Zombie" and "Ode to My Family" from 1994's *No Need to Argue.*

To the Faithful Departed—whose title is derived from a Catholic homily for the deceased—continues in the same vulnerable vein as the group's previous work, offering a benevolent yet unblinking look at the fragility of life and the preciousness of its passing pleasures. Pairing pretty music with tangible dismay ("Hollywood," "When You're Gone"), triumphant riffs with terrible tragedy ("Warchild," "I Just Shot John Lennon," "Bosnia"), and anthems of derring-do with prayers of grateful relief ("Free to Decide," "Electric Blue"), the Cranberries have arranged a thirteen-track psychic circuit of our social wilderness that is as sincere as it is absorbingly ceremonial.

Ireland is a place where fact and fable coexist with equal force. The procession of somber tests, surprise setbacks, and uncertain final judgments on *To the Faithful Departed* carries hints of the Stations of the Cross, as well as flashes of Ireland's sardonic classical storytelling à la Yeats, Sean O'Casey, and Flann O'Brien. But most of all, the stirring compassion of the material recalls "The Children of Lir," one of the saddest tales in Irish folklore, in which a stepmother, driven mad with envy by husband King Lir's love for his four children, transforms them into white swans for nine hundred years. Stricken with guilt, the stepmother relents somewhat and gives them the gift of song.

The sense of being stranded or victimized in a disaffected world permeates the drug-besotted households portrayed on "Salvation," the new album's first single. "It's looking at a dark subject in a lighthearted way," Dolores explains. "Kids go straight for the things they grew up being told not to do, and then parents, because they love them and they're upset, begin behaving *awfully* toward them.

"I was writing that from the aspect of me becoming a woman, thinking that I'm going to be a mother in the next five to ten years—yet it seems it was only five to ten years ago that I was a defiant child, thinking my mother was a pain in my butt."

Dolores Mary Eileen O'Riordan was born September 6, 1971, and grew up outside of Limerick in the village of Ballybricken, the youngest of seven children by Terence O'Riordan and the former Eileen Green-smith. "My dad's mother came from a family of tailors who made clothes for the Irish army," says O'Riordan. Dolores's mum embarked on a catering business after her husband was injured in a serious motorcycle accident.

Domestic distress intensified when O'Riordan's older sister accidentally burned down the family home, but music was a mood-lightening mainstay as kindly neighbors helped the industrious clan relocate. When young Dolores wasn't assisting her mum or helping her older brothers with their mobile food concessions, she was playing piano, the tin whistle, and bodhrán; learning the button accordion from her dad; and entering the annual Slogadh music and folk dancing competitions.

By her teens, O'Riordan was writing verse, singing with some local cover bands, and dividing the rest of her time between Laurel Hill public school, for which her mother scrimped to send her, and part-time employment at Cassidy's clothing shop and the Dunnes Stores chain. Meeting the Hogans and Lawler (whose combo then went by the pun Cranberry Saw Us) through a local girlfriend, she auditioned in 1990, took tapes of Noel's chord changes home, and constructed a forlorn song around them called "Linger."

For his part, Noel Hogan (born December 25, 1971, to the former Anne Ryan and baker Noel Hogan), his sibling Mike, and the rest of the four-child brood are descended from noted Irish poet Michael Hogan (1832–99), the Bard of Thomond, whose "Lays and Legends of Thomond" is compared to Robert Burns. None of these ancestral credits helped Noel to endure "hated" stints repairing cash registers and tending bar at the Rhine Hotel, when Dolores and company (now called the Cranberries) cut a 1991 EP for tiny Xerica Records. A rash of major-label interest plus fickle British press boosterism led to the signing with Island, and worldwide sales of more than twenty million records.

The quiet realm the band left behind is recalled in "The Rebels," in which Dolores contemplates "the two-liter containers of [hard] cider that we'd take down to drink by the River Shannon, because there were never any police there." She says that "I Just Shot John Lennon" is a song about "someone my age being deprived of seeing him in the flesh. I also made sure I didn't mention the name of the man who took his life, because he's as irrelevant as John Lennon is extraordinary." She also wrote "Joe," a requiem for her late grandfather Joe Greensmith, a supportive "second dad."

Once chided as rustic curiosities, the Cranberries have coalesced into a hardy, close-knit unit, happy in their private lives, protective of one another. "I married two years ago," says O'Riordan, "and Noel and Fergie are getting married, too. We've been through so much together as a band; I think everybody's decided to keep their heads together and follow their hearts."

Which returns us to the tale of the "Children of Lir," who regained human form after their ordeal but were so debilitated that they expired shortly after a long-postponed baptism, finding salvation in the after-world Celts call "The Land of Eternal Youth." This may be why King Lir decreed that no swans in Ireland should ever again be mistreated or killed. The edict remains in effect to this day.

"A lot of what we sing about on *To the Faithful Departed* is done, and we can never go back to it or regain it," O'Riordan says. " 'The Rebels' reflects that, and my grandfather Joe, I guess his song is part of my acceptance that he's gone—and so is my childhood."

LIST OF ILLUSTRATIONS

22. Judie Tzuke (Peter Mountain/Courtesy Essential Records)
23. Rage Against The Machine (Lisa Johnson/Courtesy Epic Records)
24. Belly (Deborah Feingold/Courtesy Sire/Reprise Records)
25. Lord Kitchener, 1962 (Timothy White Collection)
26. Sting (Andrew Cooper/Courtesy A&M Records)
27. Ray Charles (Mark Hanauer/Courtesy Warner Bros. Records)
28. Aimee Mann (Anton Corbijn/Courtesy Imago Records)
29. Donald Fagen (Cesar Vega/Courtesy Giant Records)
30. Bruce Hornsby (Greg Gorman/Courtesy RCA Records)
31. Wynonna Judd (Randee St. Nicholas/Courtesy Curb/MCA Nashville Records)
32. Robert Plant (Kevin Westenberg/Courtesy Esparanza/Atlantic Records)
33. Liz Phair (Stephen Apicella-Hitchcock/Courtesy Matador/Atlantic Records)
34. Billy Joel (Courtesy Billy Joel Collection)
35. The Story (Dan Nelkin/Courtesy Elektra Records)
36. Umar Bin Hassan (Thi-Linh Le/Courtesy Axiom/Island Records)
37. James Taylor (Andrew Brucker/Courtesy Columbia Records)
38. Terrance Simien (Brian Ashley White/Courtesy Restless Records)
39. Cab Calloway (Courtesy Columbia Legacy Records)
40. Rickie Lee Jones (Annalisa/Courtesy Geffen Records)
41. Mariah Carey (Daniela Federici/Courtesy Columbia Records)
42. Cocteau Twins (Kevin Davies/Courtesy Capitol Records)
43. Wailing Souls (Dennis Keeley/Courtesy Chaos Records)
44. Trisha Yearwood (McGuire/Courtesy MCA Nashville Records)
45. Michael Nyman (Matt Anker/Courtesy Venture Records)
46. Blinky & The Roadmasters (Kevin Burke/Courtesy Rounder Records)
47. David Bowie (Courtesy Arista U.K./BMG International Records)
48. Sarah McLachlan (Courtesy Arista/Nettwerk Records)
49. Sam Phillips (Melodie McDaniel/Courtesy Virgin Records)
50. Elvis Costello (Paul Spencer/Courtesy Warner Bros. Records)
51. Latin Playboys (Ken Schles/Courtesy Slash/Warner Bros. Records)
52. Afro-Plane (Courtesy RCA Records)
53. The Auteurs (Courtesy Hut Recordings)
54. O'Yaba (Frans Dely/Courtesy Shanachie Records)
55. David Byrne (Jean Baptiste-Mondino/Courtesy Luaka Bob/Sire/Warner Bros. Records)
56. Jack Logan (Jay Smiley/Courtesy Medium Cool Records)
57. Paula Cole (Michael Halsband/Courtesy Imago Records)

INDEX